OECD ECONOMIC SURVEYS

1996-1997

AUSTRIA

ORGANISATION FOR ECONOMIC CO-OPERATION AND DEVELOPMENT

ORGANISATION FOR ECONOMIC CO-OPERATION AND DEVELOPMENT

Pursuant to Article 1 of the Convention signed in Paris on 14th December 1960, and which came into force on 30th September 1961, the Organisation for Economic Co-operation and Development (OECD) shall promote policies designed:

- to achieve the highest sustainable economic growth and employment and a rising standard of living in Member countries, while maintaining financial stability, and thus to contribute to the development of the world economy;
- to contribute to sound economic expansion in Member as well as non-member countries in the process of economic development; and
- to contribute to the expansion of world trade on a multilateral, non-discriminatory basis in accordance with international obligations.

The original Member countries of the OECD are Austria, Belgium, Canada, Denmark, France, Germany, Greece, Iceland, Ireland, Italy, Luxembourg, the Netherlands, Norway, Portugal, Spain, Sweden, Switzerland, Turkey, the United Kingdom and the United States. The following countries became Members subsequently through accession at the dates indicated hereafter: Japan (28th April 1964), Finland (28th January 1969), Australia (7th June 1971), New Zealand (29th May 1973), Mexico (18th May 1994), the Czech Republic (21st December 1995), Hungary (7th May 1996), Poland (22nd November 1996) and the Republic of Korea (12th December 1996). The Commission of the European Communities takes part in the work of the OECD (Article 13 of the OECD Convention).

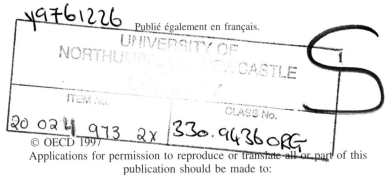

© OECD 1997
Applications for permission to reproduce or translate all or part of this publication should be made to:
Head of Publications Service, OECD
2, rue André-Pascal, 75775 PARIS CEDEX 16, France.

Table of contents

Boxes

Tables

OECD and CCET *Economic Surveys* 1997
Electronic Books

The OECD *Economic Surveys*, both for the Member countries and for countries of Central and Eastern Europe covered by the Organisation's Centre for Co-operation with Economies in Transition, are also published as electronic books – incorporating the text, tables and figures of the printed version. The information will appear on screen in an identical format, including the use of colour in graphs.

The electronic book, which retains the quality and readability of the printed version throughout, will enable readers to take advantage of the new tools that the ACROBAT software (included with the diskette) provides by offering the following benefits:

❑ User-friendly and intuitive interface
❑ Comprehensive index for rapid text retrieval, including a table of contents, as well as a list of numbered tables and figures
❑ Rapid browse and search facilities
❑ Zoom facility for magnifying graphics or for increasing page size for easy readability
❑ Cut and paste capabilities
❑ Printing facility
❑ Reduced volume for easy filing/portability

Working environment: DOS, Windows or Macintosh

Subscription 97: FF 1 800   US$317   £230   DM 550

Complete 1995 series on CD-ROM:
FF 2 000   US$365   £255   DM 600

Complete 1996 series on CD-ROM (to be issued early 1997):
FF 2 000   US$365   £255   DM 600

Please send your order to OECD Publications 2, rue André-Pascal 75775 PARIS CEDEX 16 France or, preferably, to the Centre or bookshop with whom you placed your initial order for this Economic Survey.

Figures

BASIC STATISTICS OF AUSTRIA

THE LAND

Area, (thousand sq. km)	84	Major cities, 1991 census (thousand inhabitants)	
Agricultural area (thousand sq. km), 1994	35	Vienna	1 540
Exploited forest area (thousand sq. km), 1994	32	Graz	238
		Linz	203
		Salzburg	144
		Innsbruck	118

THE PEOPLE

Population, 1995 thousands	8 047	Net migration, 1994, thousands	14
Number of inhabitants per sq. km	96	Total employment,[1] monthly average 1995, thousands	3 068
Net natural increase, 1995 thousands	7	*of which:* Primary sector	26
Net natural increase per 1 000 inhabitants, 1995	0.9	Secondary sector	945
		Tertiary sector	2 001

PRODUCTION

Gross domestic product in 1995 (Sch billion)	2 352	Industrial origin of GDP at market prices,	
GDP per head, US$	29 003	1994 (per cent)	
Gross fixed capital formation in 1995	582	Agriculture	2
Per cent of GDP	25	Industry	24
Per head US$	7 175	Construction	8
		Other	66

THE GOVERNMENT

Per cent of GDP in 1995		Composition of Federal Parliament:	Seats
Public consumption	18.9	Socialist Party	71
General government current revenue	46.7	Austrian People's Party	52
Federal government debt, end 1994	53.7	Freedom Union	42
		Liberal Forum	9
		Greens	9
		Last general election: December 1995	

FOREIGN TRADE

Exports of goods and services,		Imports of goods and services	
as a per cent of GDP, 1994	36.9	as a per cent of GDP, 1994	37.2
Main exports in 1994 (per cent of merchandise exports):		Main imports in 1994 (per cent of merchandise imports):	
Food, beverages, tobacco	3.5	Food, beverages, tobacco	4.9
Raw materials and energy	5.5	Raw materials and energy	8.7
Semi-finished goods	15.3	Semi-finished goods	13.7
Finished goods	75.6	Finished goods	72.7
of which: Machinery and transport equipment	39.0	*of which:* Machinery and transport equipment	38.0

THE CURRENCY

Monetary unit: Schilling		Currency units per US$, average of daily figures:	
		Year 1996	10.58
		December 1996	10.92

1. Wage and salary earners.
Note: An international comparison of certain basic statistics is given in an Annex table.

This Survey is based on the Secretariat's study prepared for the annual review of Austria by the Economic and Development Review Committee on 28 November 1996.

•

After revisions in the light of discussions during the review, final approval of the Survey for publication was given by the Committee on 31 December 1996.

•

The previous Survey of Austria was issued in May 1995.

Assessment and recommendations

Overview of current policy issues

The Committee last examined the Austrian economy in February 1995, at a time when a rather robust economic recovery appeared to be under way and growth of some 2½ to 3 per cent a year was in prospect. In the event, developments in the following twelve months were less propitious, with political uncertainty exacerbating the problem of a budgetary overshoot during 1995 and the downturn in Europe making for much weaker growth of output. 1996 has been characterised by a return to political consensus and budgetary retrenchment, and there are recent signs of resumed growth. But the experience of the economy in the past few years underlines the need for issues of budgetary control and employment creation to be framed in the context of the structural improvements needed to achieve better longer-run balance, in an economy which is having to adapt rapidly to the more competitive environment provided by EU membership and developments in Eastern Europe. Against this background, the principal focus of the structural analysis of the *Survey* is on issues of public sector efficiency, as they affect the health sector in particular, and on the labour and product-market requirements for faster employment creation, following the *OECD Jobs Strategy*.

Indications of renewed expansion

The current expansion, which began in the first half of 1993 after a relatively mild recession, was initially more robust than its predecessors. Following the typical characteristics of an Austrian upswing, the economy continued to register

1

fairly solid growth in the first half of 1995, with export growth leading rapidly to increased investment. However, there was a rapid slowdown in activity in the second half of 1995, led by a deceleration of export demand, due both to the strength of the schilling and weak growth in export markets, especially in Germany; and once exports started to slow, investment plans were quickly revised downward. Inventories reached levels requiring further adjustment by enterprises, and real GDP declined by around 1 per cent in the second half, this weakness continuing into the first quarter of 1996. Offsetting these contractionary influences, household saving declined from historically high levels, but domestic factors have nonetheless also played an important role in the slowdown: construction activity has been particularly weak – the adverse winter contributed to a further dampening of the economy during early 1996 – while the tourism sector is only gradually responding to changing patterns of demand. There are now indications of a resumption in growth after the weakness of the winter months. The economy seems to have rebounded during the spring, business expectations have been steadily improving as enterprises report increasing export orders, and a stock-building cycle characteristic of the early stages of an expansion appears to be getting under way.

... but growth is likely to be slow, with inflation steady and unemployment rising

Growth is likely to be slow in 1996 and 1997, relying principally on rising exports and the associated boost to investment in plant and machinery. To the extent that the expansion will be supported by consumption, this would necessitate a fall in the household savings rate, since tax increases will make for negative real income growth in 1997. Government consumption is projected to remain relatively stable in volume terms throughout the projection period. With the output gap widening initially, inflation should remain low and stable, but unemployment is projected to increase until 1998. Pessimism about the labour market constitutes one of the main sources of potential uncertainty, insofar as household savings have declined since 1995 and employment insecurity could reverse this tendency, causing private consumption to remain a brake on activity. Since the projected growth depends on exports, any weakening in major European countries also represents an important risk. It should be noted, though, that the assessment of trade performance and of economic conditions is surrounded by more than the usual degree of uncertainty, because of the statistical difficulties experienced in recent years. Accession to the European Union required the conversion of production statistics to European standards and the collection of trade statistics directly from firms rather than from border controls. Trade data for 1995 became available only in August 1996 but are considered unreliable, while industrial production data are still not available. Transitional difficulties have also been experienced in the refocusing of statistical collection efforts on basic economic indicators, though the government's decision to reallocate resources within the statistical office is welcome from a longer-term perspective.

Monetary policy remains a supportive influence

The value of a credible monetary and exchange rate policy, built up since the early 1980s, was underlined during the period of political and budgetary uncertainty in late 1995 and 1996. The monetary authorities were successful in maintaining the close link to the Deutschemark, within the formal framework of the ERM as from January 1995, without significant pressure on either interest rates or international reserves. At the time of the elections in December 1995 long-term interest rate differentials with the Deutschemark did widen to about 40 basis points, but capital inflows were well maintained and yields quickly moved back to within historical ranges in the months following the election. Moreover, the authorities were able to match the decrease in policy-controlled interest rates by the

3

Bundesbank during 1995 and into 1996. Domestic liquidity has remained ample and the Austrian national bank was able to restructure successfully the instruments of monetary policy toward greater emphasis on repurchase operations (i.e. toward a supply-oriented monetary policy), as part of the process of harmonising monetary policy instruments in preparation for the EMU. More fundamentally, Austria already fulfils the inflation, exchange rate and interest-rate criteria necessary to join the European Monetary Union in 1999. As a corollary, monetary conditions in general remain favourable, with room for further cuts in policy-controlled rates if German interest rates were to move in this direction.

... while after a surge the budget deficit is being brought back under control

Fiscal consolidation is now in line with monetary policy objectives of exchange-rate and price stability, following a period when the two arms of policy seemed to be in longer-term conflict. Allowing for the costs of EU membership, the intention of the government was to stabilise the general government deficit at 4½ per cent of GDP in 1995, but it surged to 5.9 per cent. The sharp slowdown in activity was only one factor contributing to this situation, other elements being more structural in nature. The tax reform of 1994 and earlier increases in social benefits both had a lagged effect on the budget, decreasing tax revenues and raising social benefits respectively. More importantly, following a longer-run underlying budget trend, social expenditures continued to grow strongly, with pension and health expenditures being particularly acute sources of spending pressure. In the absence of corrective measures the general government deficit threatened to deteriorate further in 1996, to around 8 per cent of GDP. Against this background, the 1996 and 1997 budgets, passed simultaneously by Parliament, with widespread public support, set out to bring the deficit below 3 per cent of GDP in 1997, the largest consolidation programme in Austrian history. Intended fiscal tightening amounts to around 2 percentage points of GDP in 1996, compared with 1995, and a further percentage point in 1997. Though the contractionary effects on demand could be offset to some extent by more generous investment incentives and higher capital spending by the railways, who are now free to borrow on the capital market, consolidation is likely to have a negative short-term effect on household demand, as reflected in the projections. Successful implementation of the fiscal consolidation programme should, however, quite rapidly lead to a general improvement in confidence which would have a beneficial offsetting impact on activity.

Despite the progress made towards budgetary stability, more remains to be done

The consolidation effort has relied to an important extent on measures which address the structural nature of the deficit: entitlement programmes have been restricted, the incentives for early retirement reduced and limits placed on manning levels in the public sector. Nevertheless, a significant part of the combined budget savings of some Sch 100 billion are due to possibly transitory measures, such as an abnormally low public sector wage round and changes in the timing of tax receipts. Unless the restrictive stance of policy is maintained, the deficit could increase again in 1998 according to OECD projections. Since the budget package also incorporates a number of items whose savings effects will become effective only after 1997, the Ministry of Finance's assessment is that significant slippage should not occur after 1997. However, irrespective of the exact value of the likely outcome for 1998, it is evident that the level of fiscal ambition should not be confined to lowering the deficit to the Maastricht ceiling, nor to ensuring that slippage does not occur, but should more fundamentally be to pursue a strategy which would bring the budget nearer to balance through the cycle. The government's medium-term programme targets a 2 per cent deficit in the year 2000, which is a step in this direction.

Meanwhile, the debt-to-GDP ratio is likely to continue growing, reaching 74 per cent of GDP in 1998 in the absence of major privatisation receipts.

... particularly to deal with the longer-run problem of pensions

The need for greater consolidation is reinforced by the fact that the share of pension expenditures has steadily risen since the mid-1950s and in 1995 amounted to more than 15 per cent of GDP. Since employment, and thus the number of contributors, will increase only slightly during the 1990s, while the number of retirees is scheduled to undergo a simultaneous rise, the pressures on the working population caused by this trend can only increase. Surpluses in the government accounts would help to meet future liabilities, but funding the system in this way would be impractical without an overhaul of its structure and generosity. Adverse demographic developments are reinforced by a very low average retirement age: since 1970 the average retirement age has gradually declined from about 62 to 58 years, without any changes in the statutory retirement age. Early retirement has been one of the instruments to alleviate structural and cyclical problems in the labour market by allowing older employees to receive pension benefits earlier instead of facing unemployment. The heterogeneity of public pension insurance, which results in many different insurance agencies (*e.g.* for employees, civil servants, self-employed, farmers, miners) responsible for their own clientele and many different rates of contribution aggravates the future financing of pension benefits as each group is intent on preserving its own benefit system. This complexity makes compromises hard to reach. Revisions to replacement rates have only just begun to come in for discussion, current prospects being for only minor alterations in the medium term. While the government has recently taken steps to induce people to stay in the workforce longer, requiring longer contribution periods and making early retirement financially less attractive, it is apparent that further policy changes are necessary if the system is to be sustainable in the long run.

Controls over public spending in general need to be improved

The need for further, medium-term, retrenchment is acknowledged in the four-year fiscal programme, but the present role of this is mainly to provide fiscal guidance and it does not yet contain all the individual legal measures necessary at the level of individual ministries to reach the required medium-term goals. The guidelines so far set down emphasise the need to contain public expenditures by freezing personnel and operating costs, social expenditures and subsidies to firms in nominal terms until 2000. This should help to provide a binding cap on these expenditures. However, as an essential counterpart, the consolidation process needs to be backed by initiatives to improve expenditure control, including further steps to increase efficiency and accountability within the federal fiscal structure. Recent moves in this direction include:

– The Länder's responsibility for spending decisions whose financial consequences are largely borne by the federal government has created an upward bias in spending for public services. The first steps have now been taken towards closer co-ordination of the fiscal decisions of the territorial authorities, which are committed to applying the savings measures of the federal government concerning personnel in 1996 and 1997; for the Länder this implies agreement to cut personnel in the state-run education system, where spending has been buoyant;

– The territorial authorities also agreed to establish a system of consultations and surveillance which will serve to avoid the involuntary transfer of costs between the three layers of the government. To this end it is envisaged that the immediate and follow-up costs of legislative initiatives of all levels of government will be systematically analysed. At present negotiations are under way in order to establish the legal base for this common surveillance

7

and budgeting mechanism and a constitutional change would seem to be required to introduce legally binding burden sharing mechanisms between the different levels of government;

– Earmarking has now been lessened by fixing yearly grants for housing promotion and to the Catastrophe Fund and the Water Supply and Waste Water Fund.

In general, these reforms of the public services are to be welcomed and will need to be continued, since adjustment pressure needs to be shared more equally with the Länder. The measures should contribute to an increase in the efficiency of public sector spending. But they are still only the first steps towards better budgetary control. In particular, new mechanisms should be found to enable earmarked transfers from the federal government to the states to be replaced by own taxes in order to increase their financial responsibilities.

... and the policy of privatisation continued

The government's privatisation policy plans would seem to be an essential adjunct of the above reforms, as are proposals to increase the number of public services for which fees will be introduced. The Post, which since May 1996 has been a stock company whose shares are held by the government, will go public within three years; participation of the Federal government in the two largest commercial banks is set to be terminated; the Post Savings Bank is planned to be transformed into a stock company and will be placed on the stock exchange. Other public companies are also considered candidates for privatisation. Also, the Finance Minister has drawn up a list of some seventy public entities which should be removed from federal budgetary control because they have a commercial objective. Applying to such entities as the Motorway and Transit Road Financing Agency, the new institutional set-up should ensure greater public efficiency to the extent that they are relieved from the restrictive practices inherent in bureaucratic control. The same should be envisaged for communal services such as water, gas, sewage, garbage collection, etc. One rationale for such reforms is that they help to meet the Maastricht debt criterion, but they are worth pursuing in themselves. Moves which expose public sector entities to competition with the private sector, and which set up corresponding management structures, can only help to underpin the process of fiscal consolidation.

The expansion in health spending is a major budgetary problem

Health expenditures and health costs have been the most rapidly growing sector of public spending, pressure being particularly marked in the hospital sector. The *Survey* identifies a number of serious shortcomings in the control of health spending. Several of these, such as the difficulties of reconciling universal – and virtually open-ended – access to health care with the practicalities of public budget constraints are general to OECD economies. Rising incomes, an ageing population and increasingly sophisticated treatments all make for a rising demand for medical services. However, the Austrian health care problem is exacerbated by defects in the system of control. In the first place, the health-care system is a hybrid, financed in major part by contributions, but with substantial ultimate recourse to general taxation. This weakens the link between contributions and benefits. Second, under the Austrian federalist fiscal system, revenue-raising powers are centralised while spending powers are to a much greater degree decentralised: popular spending decisions are taken at the lower levels of government close to the electorate but unpopular taxing decisions are taken at the more distant central level. Because hospitals are often owned by lower levels of government, budgetary tensions emerge there in the first instance, but over the longer term fiscal pressure is exposed at the federal level via generous fiscal equalisation arrangements. Moreover, until recently, generous revenue-sharing with the states has meant that their budgets have normally remained in balance despite rising expenditures. Taken together, the illusion has been created among local politicians and populations that government services are practically "free" and this weakens accountability. A third structural problem, arising from the division of responsibilities is that the health funds, while exercising quite tight control over ambulatory care, have an incentive to encourage in-patient hospital care, creating a severe allocative inefficiency. Finally, these inefficiencies may be exacerbated by supply restrictions on medical practices and regulatory restraints which give Austria some of the highest medicine prices in Europe. To a significant extent, therefore, the imbalances in the Austrian health system derive from behavioural responses which are shaped by institutions.

... and the government is introducing wide-ranging health reforms.

Based on the assessment that problems in the hospital sector require institutional changes, the government has introduced wide-ranging reforms to take effect in 1997. The programme was supported by the social partners. The main features of the reform include:

- Unifying financing of hospitals in nine Länder funds in which the states will have a majority vote and will not have to take decisions by consensus.
- A federal commission to establish a broad plan for the development and construction of hospitals and major investments, and on which the federal government will have a majority vote together with the power to take decisions.
- Financial incentives for the states to follow the federal hospital plan.
- The introduction of diagnostic-based remuneration for hospitals rather than fee-for-service.
- A number of measures which lead to increased patient co-payments.

10

*But measures
taken so far
should be
regarded as a
first step*

The government's reform measures constitute a major effort to introduce economic rationality into a health system which provides a high standard of service, but may not adequately exploit the potential for reducing costs. The emphasis remains on command-and-control techniques which, while introducing a more effective means of remunerating hospitals, do not provide the individual hospitals with adequate incentives to strive for greater longer-term efficiency. Also, the health system remains divided into hospital and ambulatory services and it is with respect to the allocation of resources between these two areas that major deficiencies are apparent. An essential element of any reform aimed at improving allocative efficiency in the health service without jeopardising the aim of universality would be to introduce an active purchaser for all types of health services. This could be achieved for example by integrating the Länder health funds with the normal health funds, requiring them to purchase rather than simply finance health – and in particular hospital – expenditures. This would introduce an element of managed competition into the system and increase the effectiveness of the new diagnostic payments system as hospitals compete for contracts.

*Unemployment is
relatively low, but
so is labour
utilisation*

Unemployment in Austria, including youth and long-term unemployment, remains low in comparison with other OECD countries and this represents a major achievement of the society's institutions; aggregate real wage flexibility is high and labour flows indicate a rather fluid labour market. Overall employment growth has been slightly higher than the European average, although output growth in the Austrian economy has been associated with a relatively low employment intensity. Early retirement and rising public sector employment have contributed significantly to these developments. Early retirement has created a major burden on current workers through the pay-as-you-go pensions system and this will become worse in the future, while expanding public sector employment has created budgetary strains as well as microeconomic distortions. Moreover, as in other countries, the level of long-term unemployment has been rising as has unemployment among older workers, both developments reflecting a tendency for unemployment to persist once it has occurred. Entry into the EU, the rising competitive challenge from central and eastern Europe, and increased globalisation suggest that if these characteristics persist, the Austrian labour market will face increased tensions in the future.

... so that a wide-ranging policy response is necessary

Improving the job-generating capacity of the economy and increasing labour utilisation should thus be one of the main priorities of economic policy, requiring wide-ranging measures embodying short and long-term effects relating to the labour market proper and to competitive conditions in the enterprise sector. Applied to the Austrian case, the *OECD Jobs Strategy* would call, in particular, for: *i)* while preserving the existing high degree of aggregate wage flexibility, introducing greater sensitivity of wage developments to circumstances at the enterprise level, to ensure that wages align more effectively with productivity differentials; *ii)* reform to the tax and transfer system to encourage job search and work effort; *iii)* a rebalancing of arrangements relating to employment protection to reduce insider/outsider mechanisms, and more work-time flexibility; *iv)* a redirection of resources towards active labour market policies targeted to lower long-term joblessness by focusing on groups at risk; *v)* a reappraisal of the effectiveness of the education and training systems; and *vi)* an enhancement of competition, particularly in the service sector. Fundamental to achieving these objectives is the nurturing of an entrepreneurial climate which favours enterprise creation and technology diffusion. Most immediately, the objectives require reforms in tax and transfer systems, in employment security and wage-bargaining arrangements, in active labour market and educational policies, and in the regulatory system to promote competition. A start has been made with the 1996/1997 budget, which has reduced the incentives for early retirement and restructured some benefits, but more is required.

Greater room for manoeuvre needs to be created at sector and enterprise level

Although there is a significant degree of aggregate real wage flexibility in Austria, the process of setting a basic standard for wages over broad sectors of the economy and then allowing only an upward adjustment at the enterprise level – an approach designed to promote the longer-term growth of productivity – tends to create problems for an economy facing the need for more rapid structural change. The same observation is also valid for work-time regulations. As a result, it appears that an increasing number of enterprises are reaching *de facto* agreements with their employees in the direction of greater flexibility. Alternatively, they are creating a dualistic labour market by using possibilities such as those offered by work contracts (*Werkverträge)* to create flexibility at the enterprise level. The government should consider facilitating arrangements for more flexibility at the enterprise level while reforming the laws on work time also in this direction. Job protection provisions also need to be liberalised, dismissal regulations which protect older workers from becoming unemployed constituting an inadvertent barrier to re-employment. While the provisions regarding works contracts have recently been amended so as to prevent these from being used as a means of avoiding social security contributions, it is important that reforms should not inhibit labour market flexibility.

13

| **Work incentives for the unemployed need to be improved** | Net replacement rates provided by the unemployment benefits system (taking account of its interaction with the tax system) are not high by international standards, but the structure nevertheless could adversely affect work incentives for higher-paid, older workers. Moreover, the combination of existing replacement rates and low thresholds at which earnings can be subtracted from benefits can make it uneconomical to look for part-time jobs, or to accept lower-paid full-time jobs. This is an example where the search for budgetary savings might be in conflict with microeconomic incentives and where some rebalancing is necessary. Controls on the willingness to work have not been effectively enforced for seasonal workers, temporary layoffs and for some older workers. Policy initiatives are called for in these areas. First, the government should launch a detailed investigation into the incidence of poverty and unemployment traps in the system. If these prove to be significant, the government should consider the introduction of a wider range of in-work benefits, thereby encouraging those affected to accept lower reservation wages. Second, work incentives need to be strengthened, to allow the older unemployed, in particular, to price themselves back into a job. In this respect a gradual reduction in the base wage for calculating benefits might be considered as the duration of unemployment increases. |

| **Active labour market schemes should receive greater emphasis** | Though some of the past programmes have proved successful, active labour market measures remain modest in Austria. With the development of a decentralised labour office, the time now seems appropriate to extend these programmes, which should remain focused on those groups at risk of entering long term unemployment. Increased retraining programmes might prove necessary but in this case additional efforts to stimulate a more contestable market in the provision of training would be useful. |

And the focus of the education and innovation system needs changing

Although Austria has been successful in equipping the population with high standards of vocational education, this investment has not reaped the technological benefits necessary to sustain a high wage economy. Several deficiencies need to be dealt with to correct this situation. The compartmentalisation between branches of the education system need to be reduced and the new polytechnic system (*Fachhochschule*) expanded. Apprenticeships are too narrow in scope and need to be broadened, and their cost to employers could be reduced by selectively liberalising conditions of employment. Taxing employers who do not offer training positions would be only a second-best solution and should be avoided. The need for reform is, however, greatest in the university system which needs to be placed under greater competitive pressure from both polytechnics and specialised research institutes. Links between universities and industry need to be developed so as to increase the transfer of knowledge between the academic and business sectors. But to be able to respond to the challenge, greater powers would have to be devolved to the universities themselves.

But above all the competitive and entrepreneurial environment needs to be sharpened

A notable feature of the Austrian economy is the low rate of business start-ups. This is due in part to the general absence of a risk-taking entrepreneurial behaviour, but it is also due to a restrictive legal and regulatory framework. Two related areas are particularly notable: restrictions on entry into trades (*Gewerbeordnung*) and the requirements for setting up an enterprise, which may take around one year to eighteen months to be approved. The former have been partially liberalised, but regulations remain extensive and demarcation lines are often restrictive. Current members of the profession can, in some cases, exercise *de facto* insider power to influence the number of new entrants, which reduces competition. A great deal thus remains to be done in this area by reducing the number of registered

trades, defining them more widely, and in drastically simplifying the requirements to establish a new firm. At the
same time, more business opportunities also have to be
created. In particular, competition via the entry of new
enterprises is also held back by the widespread provision of
services by local governments and the Länder, who need to
be encouraged to extend market testing. But for this to be
successful, all firms need to be treated equally regardless of
ownership and ownership structure (*e.g.* co-operative or
non-profit as opposed to normal enterprises).

In other regulatory areas there has been some progress
toward making the system more competitive, but the persistent inflation differential between the service- and goods-
producing sectors still points to competitive anomalies.
With membership of the EU, competition in the retail/
wholesale sector has increased, as has foreign ownership;
however, shop opening hours are rather short and wage
agreements specify large premia for overtime. With accession to the EU, the rules of competition policy in Austria
have become more transparent and the number of cartels
has declined drastically, but the time might be appropriate
to create an independent competition authority. In the area
of network industries, such as telecommunications, electricity and gas, where European competition policy rules are
crucial, a minimalist strategy should be avoided in favour
of establishing an effective and transparent regulatory
authority as well as in specifying terms of entry (including
connection fees) for competitors.

Summing up   Austria has responded to the economic challenges that it
has faced over the past few years by implementing the
largest fiscal stabilisation programme in its history. This
has been achieved within the framework of public consensus which characterises Austria. Fiscal retrenchment will
make for slow growth in the short term, but building on the

success of the stability-oriented monetary and exchange-rate policy, and on closer integration into the European economy resulting from EU accession, it should provide a firm base for economic growth in the longer run. In addition, the first stage of a far reaching health reform has been implemented which, with improved mechanisms of budgetary control, should ensure a better balanced development of the public finances than has been evident so far in the 1990s. However, looking ahead, Austria faces challenges: to strengthen the low employment-generating capacity of the economy will require decisions as to structural reform and considerable additional institutional flexibility on the part of the social partners. Provided these issues are effectively addressed, there is every reason to believe that Austria will be able to benefit from greater integration into the European and global economies, while at the same time making progress towards fuller employment.

I. Recent developments and prospects

Overview

The strong momentum from export growth which underpinned the early stages of the recovery faded during the second half of 1995. For the year as a whole GDP growth slowed to 1.8 per cent, from 3 per cent in 1994 (Figure 1, Table 1), the deceleration being aggravated by a severe winter which brought construction to a halt. Activity continued to be weak in the first part of 1996, but the economy seems to have begun to rebound in the spring and business expectations have been steadily improving as enterprises report increasing export orders. Moreover, a stock-building cycle characteristic of the early stages of an expansion appears to be getting under way. However, growth is projected to be dependent on exports, with only modest support from private consumption, associated with a further decline in the savings rate. Prospects are thus for only moderate growth in 1997, followed by an acceleration in 1998 as domestic demand strengthens. Unemployment will remain high by Austrian standards but, as expected, inflation has declined in the wake of EU accession and is now once more below the EU average.

Developments in 1995 and 1996

Nature of the slowdown

The rapid deceleration in economic activity from an annualised rate of 3 per cent in the first half of 1995 to a decline of 1 per cent in the second was closely related to the slowing in exports to European markets: export growth (national accounts basis) dropped from 7 per cent in the first half to virtually zero in the second half. This primarily reflected the general European slowdown rather than losses in market share. Although the effective real appreciation of the currency in

Figure 1. **MACROECONOMIC PERFORMANCE**

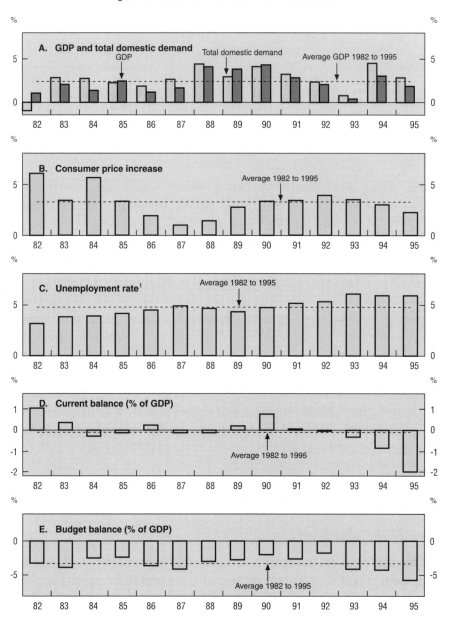

1. Registered unemployment as percentage of total labour force, including self-employment.
Source: OECD.

Table 1. **Demand and output**

Percentage change from previous year, constant 1983 prices

	1982-91 average	1992	1993	1994	1995[1]
Private consumption	2.7	2.8	0.7	2.5	1.9
Government consumption	1.4	2.2	3.1	2.2	2.1
Gross fixed investment	2.9	1.7	–1.6	6.8	2.3
Construction	2.5	5.7	2.9	5.5	–0.1
Machinery and equipment	3.5	–3.4	–7.9	8.7	5.9
Change in stocks[2]	0.1	–0.1	0.3	1.0	0.8
Total domestic demand	**2.6**	**2.3**	**0.7**	**4.5**	**2.8**
Exports of goods and services	5.2	1.2	–1.6	4.5	5.4
of which: Goods	6.9	3.5	–2.7	11.4	6.9
Imports of goods and services	5.4	1.8	–0.7	8.2	7.3
of which: Goods	6.4	3.1	–1.1	12.9	6.4
Foreign balance[2]	0.1	–0.3	–0.4	–1.5	–1.1
Gross domestic product	**2.5**	**2.0**	**0.4**	**3.0**	**1.8**
Memorandum items:					
GDP price deflator	3.7	4.1	3.4	3.4	2.1
Private consumption deflator	3.2	3.9	3.4	3.0	2.3
Unemployment rate					
Registered[3]	4.3	5.3	6.1	5.9	5.9
Eurostat				3.7	4.3

1. Estimates.
2. Change as a per cent of GDP in the previous period.
3. As a per cent of the total labour force including self-employment.
Source: WIFO; OECD.

early 1995 may have contributed to export weakness, wage developments remained more moderate than in Germany, so that the profit situation of enterprises was less of an aggravating factor on export performance. The slowdown was foreshadowed by a decline in foreign and domestic orders from a peak in the first quarter of 1995. Production and investment plans were correspondingly revised downwards and with stocks building up, inventories were increasingly judged to be excessive (Figure 2, Panels A and B). Reflecting these developments, by the third quarter of 1995 industrial production levelled off and in the fourth quarter it declined by 4 per cent (Figure 2, Panel C).

After growing by 7.5 per cent, in the first half, gross fixed investment declined at an annualised rate of 5 per cent in the second half of 1995, as business investment plans were revised downwards and public investment was curbed.

Figure 2. **THE CLIMATE IN THE BUSINESS SECTOR**

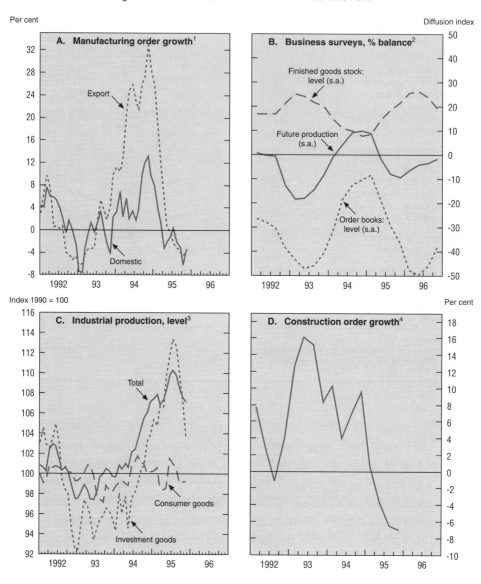

Per cent

A. Manufacturing order growth[1]

Export

Domestic

Diffusion index

B. Business surveys, % balance[2]

Finished goods stock: level (s.a.)

Future production (s.a.)

Order books: level (s.a.)

Index 1990 = 100

C. Industrial production, level[3]

Total

Consumer goods

Investment goods

Per cent

D. Construction order growth[4]

1. New orders inflows, percentage change from year ago, 3-month moving average.
2. Balance of positive – negative replies.
3. 3-month moving average.
4. Stock of orders, percentage changes from year ago.
Source: Austrian Institute for Economic Research (WIFO) and OECD, *Main Economic Indicators.*

Construction began to weaken in the first half, and with orders starting to fall in the first months of the year building activity slowed rapidly in the second even before the onset of winter (Figure 2, Panel D). Private consumption also became weaker, responding to reduced growth in disposable income due to worsening economic conditions and more restrictive public transfers. However, the effect was dampened by a fall in the household savings ratio.

Recent improvement

Due to delays in the transition to the EU statistical system, timely and precise statistics on production and trade are not generally available. However, business expectations have steadily improved during 1996. Enterprises report rising export orders, particularly in the basic goods industries, where the prevailing business optimism could indicate that a stock-building cycle characteristic of the early stages of an expansion is beginning. Most of the appreciation of the currency in the first half of 1995 has been reversed (Figure 3) and economic conditions in the EU markets appear to have stabilised. Export growth has thus

Figure 3. **INDICATORS OF COMPETITIVENESS**

Index 1991 = 100

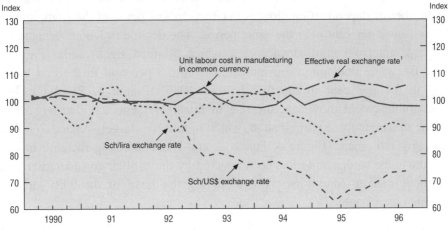

1. Deflated by the CPI.
Source: OECD.

23

picked up. Although production plans are still at a low level, on balance they are being revised upwards, as are business investment plans. According to the WIFO investment survey of May 1996, the manufacturing sector plans to increase investment outlays by $27^{1}/_{2}$ per cent in 1996: up by nine percentage points in comparison with the previous survey conducted in autumn of 1995. Construction remains weak, however, and currently there are no growth impulses from government spending. Private consumption continues to provide a significant impulse despite restrained income growth, expanding by some 2 per cent in the first half of 1996 while the household savings ratio has declined still further. The unexpected strength of household consumption is based on a strong demand for durables, probably partly in anticipation of tax changes in the middle of the year. Some weakening of household demand seems to have followed in the third quarter.

Unemployment increases and wage growth slows

The increase in employment that took place during 1994 came to a halt at the beginning of 1995 as activity slowed, and turned into a decline during the course of the year (Figure 4, Panel A). Contrary to previous down-turns, the fall in private sector employment was not compensated by high growth of employment in the public sector. Hence, between the fourth quarters of 1994 and 1995 the number of dependent employees declined by 0.7 per cent. Self-employment also fell by 2 per cent over the same period. The decline in labour demand was also apparent from unfilled vacancies, which dropped significantly (Figure 4, Panel B), while unemployment increased from 5.8 per cent in the first half of 1995 to 6.1 per cent in the first half of 1996[1] (Figure 4, Panel C). To a considerable extent, however, the rise in unemployment was dampened by a decline in labour-force participation, which in turn was largely related to inflows into early retirement (Figure 4, Panels A and D). The strong increase in early retirement due to disability has been fostered by the explicit consideration given to labour market conditions when assessing the level of disability of older workers (see Chapter IV).

The wage round for 1995 was finalised before the slowdown was evident, so that compensation per employee for the whole economy accelerated somewhat in comparison with 1994 (Table 2). The pick-up was more pronounced in the

Figure 4. **EMPLOYMENT, UNEMPLOYMENT AND THE LABOUR FORCE**

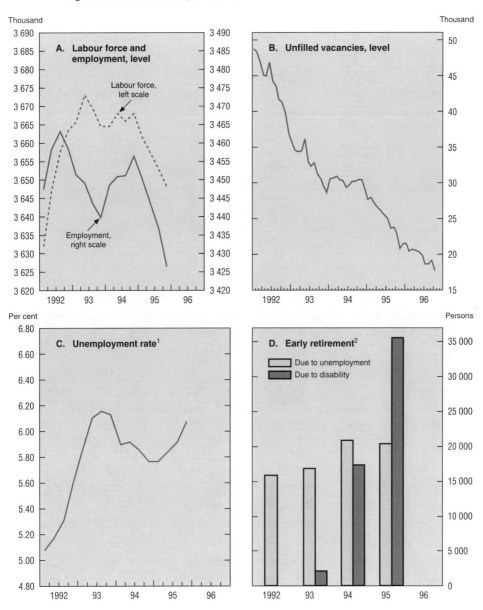

1. Registered unemployment as a per cent of total labour force, including self-employment.
2. Yearly growth rate.
Source: WIFO; Government submission; OECD, *Main Economic Indicators.*

Table 2. **Wages and prices**

Annual growth, per cent

	1982-1991 average	1992	1993	1994	1995[1]
Productivity per employee, total economy	2.1	0.6	0.7	2.9	2.2
Compensation per employee, total economy	5.7	6.6	4.2	3.6	3.8
Unit labour costs, total economy	3.2	4.5	3.8	0.5	1.9
Compensation per employee, business sector	5.3	4.4	4.4	3.4	4.1
Unit labour costs, business sector	2.7	3.6	3.1	−0.3	1.5
Hourly earnings, manufacturing	5.1	5.8	4.9	3.8	4.4
Unit labour costs, manufacturing	0.7	2.9	1.3	−5.0	−1.1
GDP deflator	3.7	4.1	3.4	3.4	2.1
Private consumption deflator	3.2	3.9	3.4	3.0	2.3

1. 1995 partly estimated.
Source: WIFO; OECD.

manufacturing sector, where hourly earnings increased by 4.4 per cent compared with 3.8 per cent in 1994. Reflecting the slow adjustment of employment to output, productivity growth slowed in the business sector as a whole and unit labour costs increased. However, in the more open manufacturing sector where firms continued to shed labour and to modernise the capital stock, productivity growth remained quite robust and unit labour costs continued to decline, although at a slower pace than in 1994.

The 1996 wage round, conducted in autumn 1995, took place against the background of the deceleration of economic activity. The wage round for metal workers and white-collar workers in manufacturing brought an increase in tariff wages of 3.8 per cent and a lump-sum payment of Sch 2 500, which gives a rise in average effective wages in these sectors of 3.6 per cent, about half a percentage point less than in 1995. With wage rates in the distribution sector rising by under 3 per cent and public sector pay under tight control, overall wage settlements appear to be more modest than in 1995. Although year-on-year productivity growth may be somewhat weaker in 1996 than 1995, the rise in unit labour costs in the business sector may also have slowed. Measured in a common currency, unit labour costs in manufacturing increased during most of 1995 but declined in the first three quarters of 1996 (Figure 3).

Trade balance improves while current account deteriorates

Trade and tourism

According to provisional balance of payments data, merchandise exports grew more strongly than Austrian export markets in 1995, and significantly faster than imports. The merchandise trade deficit thus fell by almost a third compared with 1994, to Sch 81.7 billion. Exports to EU countries increased by 14 per cent, pointing to an increasing Austrian share of intra-EU trade, while exports to non-EU countries grew by 11 per cent. Exports to Central and Eastern Europe, as well as to Switzerland and the USA, were particularly strong.

Despite the improvement in the trade balance, the deficit in the current account more than doubled to some Sch 47 billion (2 per cent of GDP). Two factors underlay the sharp increase in the current account deficit: an increase in net official transfers abroad by Sch 11½ billion, attributable to Austria's EU accession, and a narrowing in the surplus of the balance for travel services by some Sch 13 billion. Of this, Sch 10 billion was due to higher spending of Austrians abroad as the remaining border controls were removed and air travel prices continued to fall, and Sch 3 billion to reduced expenditures of foreigners in Austria (Table 3). The decline in earnings from tourism occurred against an estimated growth in European tourism by some 4 per cent in real terms. For over five years Austria has experienced a steady decline in the export surplus for tourism, which fell by 60 per cent between 1991 and 1995. The deterioration has been particularly pronounced in the last two years. While this development to a great extent reflects increasing travel and purchases of Austrians abroad, it is also the result of a trend decline in the foreign demand for Austrian tourism services, which was amplified by the appreciation of the schilling against other major currencies in 1995 and adverse income effects due to the recent slack in economic activity, in particular in Germany.

The most recent evidence confirms that the tourism industry has been subject to shifting patterns of demand. Whereas overnight stays in hotels of the lower quality range and in private accommodation dropped by more than 10 per cent, hotels in the upper quality range (four- and five-star hotels) performed quite well with a slight increase of 1 per cent in overnight stays in 1995. Over 20 years the top categories' share of bed-nights has increased from 10 to 25 per cent and the share held by private lodgings has declined from 40 to 21 per cent. Also, the

27

Table 3. **Current account of the balance of payments**

Billion schillings

	1990	1991	1992	1993	1994	1995
Goods and services	13.7	1.0	10.0	4.5	−12.4	−25.4
Merchandise payments [1]	−52.3	−69.8	−68.0	−74.4	−78.9	−72.9
Exports	583.3	611.8	622.9	615.9	669.7	732.8
Imports	635.6	681.6	690.9	690.4	748.6	805.7
Travel	64.7	74.8	67.4	61.4	42.8	29.7
Exports	152.4	161.2	159.6	157.5	150.2	147.1
Imports	87.8	86.3	92.2	96.1	107.4	117.5
Investment income	−11.0	−17.6	−13.1	−11.5	−10.8	−10.0
Other items	12.3	13.6	23.7	29.0	34.5	27.9
Transfers	0.0	−0.2	−11.6	−12.7	−8.3	−21.6
Official	−2.1	−2.3	−5.4	−6.8	−7.2	−18.7
Private	2.1	2.1	−6.2	−5.9	−1.1	−2.9
Current account	13.6	0.8	−1.6	−8.2	−20.6	−47.0

1. Due to Austria's integration into the EU, a new collection method for obtaining data on merchandise trade within the EU was introduced at the beginning of 1995. This change leads to substantial delays in the compilation and publication of foreign trade statistics. The Austrian national bank therefore publishes Austria's balance of payments without separately identifying foreign trade. Instead, the payments for merchandise deliveries including gross transit trade are shown in the balance of payments until verified foreign trade data will be available on a regular basis. The quality and accuracy of the current account position itself as well as items like goods and services or transfers are, however, not affected.

Source: Österreichische Nationalbank.

decline in city tourism was very small, with tourism to Vienna even expanding slightly. Though the structure of tourist accommodation has changed in response to the shift in tastes, it appears that further adjustment is necessary. In its 1996 *Economic Report* the government has reinforced its commitment to aid the restructuring of the tourism sector with the purpose of achieving a greater dispersion in supply and a diversification of markets towards new faster-growing areas, as well as adapting to changing tastes via greater innovation.

The capital account

Austria has become an increasingly important destination of foreign direct investment as a result of its membership first of the EEA and now of the EU. Austrian investment abroad has also continued to grow strongly, though somewhat below the peak rate recorded in 1994 (Table 4). 1995 saw a reduction in inward foreign direct investment, but it was again buoyant in the first half of 1996, exceeding the annual level of foreign direct investment in 1994 as a whole,

Table 4. **Capital account of the balance of payments**

Billion schillings

	1991	1992	1993	1994	1995[1]	January-September 1996[1]
Direct investment	−10.9	−10.2	−5.6	1.3	−4.2	12.1
Austrian abroad	15.0	20.6	17.1	13.7	10.6	7.6
Foreign in Austria	4.2	10.3	11.4	15.0	6.4	19.7
Portfolio investment in shares and investment certificates	0.9	1.0	7.5	6.1	7.6	13.6
Austrian abroad	1.5	1.5	6.3	9.1	5.0	8.9
Foreign in Austria	2.4	2.5	13.8	15.2	12.6	22.4
Portfolio investment in fixed-interest securities	12.2	37.7	92.0	−3.8	94.7	−9.6
To foreigners	18.4	27.7	14.0	39.0	24.5	50.2
To residents	30.6	65.4	106.0	35.2	119.2	40.7
Loans	−30.7	−13.5	1.4	−1.0	−6.2	−10.2
To foreigners	31.6	13.1	2.0	8.8	24.7	18.5
To residents	0.9	−0.4	3.4	7.8	18.5	8.3
Long-term capital	−24.4	7.9	75.3	9.3	79.3	4.0
Short-term capital	24.8	13.2	−34.9	24.4	−21.6	28.7

1. Provisional.
Source: Österreichische Nationalbank.

which at that time marked a record high. Inward portfolio investment has also been strong, even during the period of political uncertainty in late 1995, when a small widening of the interest rate differential to Germany was sufficient to promote a surge of foreign investment in Austrian securities. Preliminary data for 1996 indicate that after the election and with the new consolidation programme being adopted this shift has been reversed as the interest rate differential to Germany declined.

Issues in the present business cycle

Underlying the cyclical developments during 1995/1996 are several factors which will continue to exercise an important influence over the next few years: household savings, conflicting tendencies with respect to investment, and the effects of accession to the EU.

Declining household savings

Declining public and private sector employment, together with moderate wage settlements, higher taxes and reductions in social transfers can be expected to have a dampening influence on private consumption during 1996 and 1997. The degree to which private consumption will be adversely affected by these negative influences on income, and the increased uncertainty about income and employment prospects, depends crucially on how the household savings ratio responds. It is characteristic of Austrian business cycles that private households have tended to adapt their savings ratios to cushion cyclical fluctuations in disposable income, reducing the savings ratio during an economic downswing and increasing it when the economy recovers (Figure 5). This appears to reflect the desire to smooth consumption over time when income fluctuations are considered transitory. Such a pattern seems to have emerged during the current episode of slack in economic activity: in the second half of 1995, when GDP growth slowed, the savings ratio fell by almost 0.8 percentage points, and in the first half of 1996 it declined by a further 0.7 percentage points.

Figure 5. **THE SAVINGS RATIO AND THE BUSINESS CYCLE**
Per cent

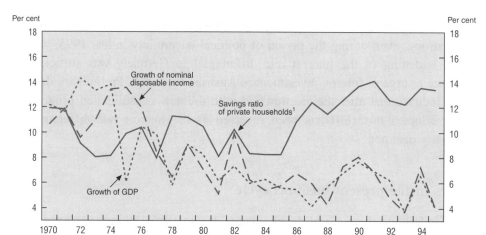

1.   As percentage of disposable income.
Source: WIFO.

The decline in the household savings ratio in 1995 and 1996 occurred against a longer run trend which saw it rise from an average of about 9 per cent of disposable income in the mid-1980s to around 13 per cent in the 1990s (Figure 5). There is, therefore, a question as to whether the long-term trend rise in the savings rate will reassert itself as the economy picks up. The rise in the savings ratio prior to 1995 coincided with a phase of above-average real interest rates, which was also associated with a marked shift in income distribution toward property income. A further rise in the savings ratio related to interest rates may be unlikely. On the other hand, the drop in the savings ratio in 1995 and in the first half of 1996 appears to have been partly influenced by new consumption opportunities following the EU accession. Although partly temporary in nature, this behavioural response points to the possibility that the present counter-cyclical decline in saving could be reinforced by a structural fall in the propensity to save, as consumer choice widens with Austria's greater integration into the EU and relative consumer prices fall.

Conflicting tendencies in the development of investment

Although the decline in gross fixed investment in the second half of 1995 reflected a fall in both investment in machinery and equipment and in construction, the underlying forces affecting the two components differ significantly (Figure 6). The downturn in business investment in machinery and equipment that occurred in the second half of 1995 reflected a correction after the rapid expansion of the capital stock that accompanied the recovery after the 1993 slowdown. In the first half of 1995 investment in machinery and equipment grew at an abnormally high rate of 17.7 per cent, which was probably influenced by a temporary increase in the investment allowance from 15 to 30 per cent. The lack of agreement among the coalition partners about the means of achieving fiscal consolidation may also have contributed negatively to the investment climate prior to the election. During the first half of 1996, as noted, an upward revision to investment plans by manufacturing firms suggests that the drop in activity was only transitory.

The need for restructuring implied by more intense competition following the EU accession and the economic development of the central and eastern European countries, with their geographical proximity to Austria, remains intense. Indeed, the recent increase in bankruptcies, only in part due to the slow-

Figure 6. **INVESTMENT ACTIVITY**
Percentage changes (1983 prices)

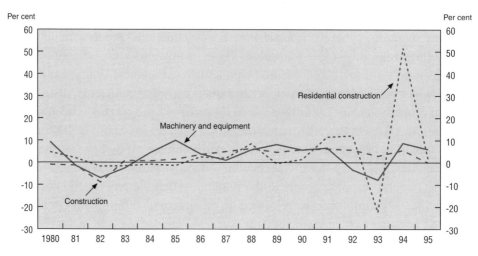

Source: WIFO.

down in economic activity, points to increased restructuring activity, as does anecdotal evidence suggesting that the dispersion of profits across firms may have recently increased. Overall, the profitability of enterprises appears to be sound enough to support increased investment, although estimates differ with the method employed. While estimates based on the national accounts show an increase in profitability in 1995, estimates by the Austrian national bank indicate that there may have been a decline in the rate of return on capital for industrial enterprises.

In the construction sector, by contrast, the slowdown began in the first half in 1995, leading the general downturn in economic activity, and marking the end of a nine-year long phase of expansion. From 1986 to 1994, annual real growth rates in the construction sector averaged around 5 per cent, supported by robust public sector investment. The slowdown is importantly affected by public poli-cies, reflecting the completion of large-scale public sector projects and a reduc-tion in public sector investment in civil engineering as a result of the consolida-tion programme. In particular, infrastructure investment of the municipalities, which accounts for about one-third of public sector investment, has been significantly reduced. At the same time, federal transfers to the Länder used for the subsidisation of residential construction, which saw a trend increase from the end of the 1980s through 1995, were frozen in spring 1996, with the result that in 1996 residential construction is not likely to increase from the 1995 pace. A fast turn-around in construction is not to be expected, but a major government infrastructure programme is likely to help maintain construction output in 1997.

Initial effects of EU accession

Accession to the EU was expected to generate a significant reduction in the price level due to increased competition and the adoption of the Common Agricultural Policy. Though it is difficult to disentangle the impact of EU accession from other factors, such as the dampening effect of the rapid schilling appreciation in the first half of 1995, the cost of the new recycling system for packaging material, or the increase in the mineral oil tax in May 1995, available evidence suggests that accession to the EU has contributed to the marked decrease in inflation that occurred over the review period. While the food price index declined from the first half of 1995, inflation rates for other products were slower to decline. The price index for consumer durables fell from the third quarter of 1995 onwards and the index for manufactured goods started to fall in the first quarter of 1996. The differential in consumer price inflation relative to Germany narrowed in the autumn 1995 and into the first half of 1996, before widening again in the summer 1996 in response to the June increase in the energy tax and the rise in prescription fees in August.

Based on a comparison of inflation developments in Austria and in Germany, the Austrian Institute of Economic Research estimates that joining the EU has been instrumental in lowering inflation by $^1/_2$ to $^3/_4$ percentage points in 1995 (Figure 7). To a considerable degree, this is attributable to lower prices for non-food items, induced by EU membership and acceleration of cross-border shopping as Austrians have taken advantage of lower priced goods in other EU countries, mainly in Italy and Germany. Cross-border purchases of consumer goods by Austrians increased by 19 per cent in 1995, with an estimated further rise of $5^1/_2$ per cent in the first half of 1996. Overall, the price-dampening effects of EU membership have been less pronounced than had been expected by some analysts prior to accession. Inflation in the service sector remained at 3.4 per cent

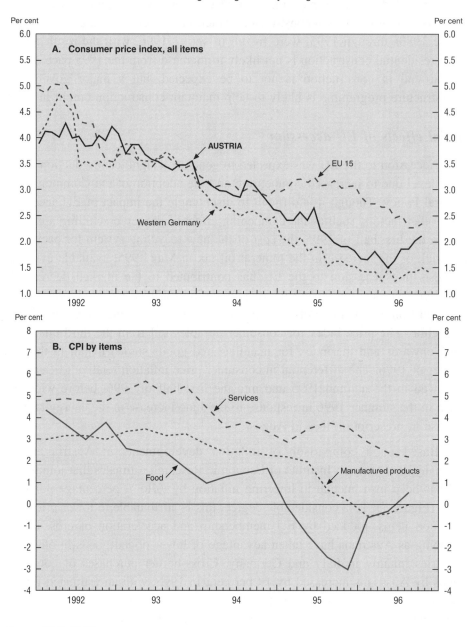

Figure 7. **DISINFLATION IN THE CONSUMER PRICE INDEX**

Percentage changes from year ago

Source: WIFO; OECD.

in 1995 and appears to have been largely unaffected. Indeed, while membership of the EU is leading to greater product-market competition in the exposed sectors, in part through the increasing engagement of foreign businesses in Austria, the apparent lack of adjustment in services points to persistent structural rigidities, perhaps attributable to monopolistic competition or excessive regulation, in large segments of the sheltered economy (see *OECD Economic Survey of Austria* (1995) for a detailed discussion).

The short-term outlook

During 1997 and 1998 growth will be supported by rising exports and the associated boost to investment in plant and machinery, but is likely to be slow in the face of the restraints facing domestic demand. It is assumed that Austrian exports of goods broadly follow market growth, which should increase from about 5 per cent in 1995 to some 7 per cent in 1998. Underlying this projection are rising import growth rates of Austria's main trading partners in the EU and the Central and Eastern European countries. Export growth in services is assumed to be weaker, reflecting the structural problems in tourism. Construction is also projected to remain weak in 1997, with a recovery occurring in 1998 when government investment is expected to pick up.

Growth during 1997 will need to be sustained to some extent by a fall in the household savings rate, as higher tax revenues will result in a fall in real household disposable income. But, even so the growth rate of private consumption is expected to be only around 0.5 per cent. By 1998 disposable income should be growing more strongly, and private consumption is projected to accelerate. Government consumption is expected to remain stagnant in 1997, although a rebound in public sector wages could occur in 1998, leading to a nominal acceleration. With the output gap closing only in 1998, unemployment is not projected to decrease until then, with inflation remaining low and stable (Table 5).

The principal uncertainty attaches to the effects of fiscal consolidation. While the immediate impact will be deflationary, the projections are potentially subject to the confidence and interest rate effects of meeting the Maastricht deficit ceiling, which could lead to higher investment and growth than expected. Household saving may also be subject to confidence effects, but in this case greater

Table 5. **Economic projections to 1998**

Percentage change from previous year, constant 1983 prices

	1995	1996[1]	1997[2]	1998[2]
Private consumption	1.9	1.4	0.5	1.7
Government consumption	2.1	0.3	0.1	0.4
Gross fixed investment	2.3	0.9	1.9	3.2
Construction	−0.1	−1.0	0.0	2.1
Machinery and equipment	5.9	3.5	4.5	4.6
Change in stocks[3]	0.8	−0.3	0.0	0.0
Total domestic demand	2.8	0.7	0.8	1.8
Exports of goods and services	5.4	4.0	5.3	6.1
Imports of goods and services	7.3	3.1	3.8	5.0
Foreign balance[3]	−1.1	0.3	0.6	0.4
Gross domestic product	1.8	1.1	1.4	2.3
Memorandum items:				
Private consumption deflator	2.3	1.9	1.8	1.7
GDP price deflator	2.1	1.6	1.5	1.5
Total employment	−0.4	−0.7	−0.2	0.3
Unemployment rate, level[4]	5.9	6.2	6.5	6.4
Household saving rate ratio, level	13.4	12.2	11.4	11.7
Export market growth[5]	8.5	5.1	6.0	7.2
Short-term interest rate	4.3	3.1	2.9	3.5
Long-term interest rate	6.5	5.4	5.2	5.3
General government budget balance, per cent of GDP	−5.9	−4.3	−3.0	−3.4
Current balance, per cent of GDP	−2.0	−1.8	−1.4	−1.1

1. Estimates as of October 1996.
2. OECD projections updated to October 1996.
3. Change as a percentage of GDP in the previous period.
4. Registered unemployed, as a percentage of the total labour force including self-employed.
5. Manufactured goods.
Source: WIFO; OECD.

employment insecurity could act as a brake on private consumption. Since the projected growth depends heavily on exports, the course of activity in the major European countries also represent an important source of uncertainty.

II. Macroeconomic policies

Having emerged from a period when budgetary policy appeared to be on an unsustainable path, Austria is now in a position from which it should fulfil the criteria for European Monetary Union. Inflation has fallen by almost one percentage point since Austria's accession to the EU and is now around 2 per cent per annum; interest rates are low, with virtually no differential *vis-à-vis* German rates, and the exchange rate has been stable against the Deutschemark for more than twenty years. On the fiscal policy side, the substantial deviation from medium-term plans which opened up between 1993 and 1995 is in the process of being corrected by the consolidation programme enacted in the spring of 1996, which covers the years 1996 and 1997. This is the largest such programme in recent Austrian history, and has been backed by general political acceptance of the need for retrenchment. It aims to reduce government expenditures and broaden the tax base by more than 4 per cent of GDP (more than Sch 100 billion) in the course of only one and a half years. Fully implemented, this would enable Austria to achieve the required 3 per cent target deficit rate by 1997. For government debt to fall significantly, additional measures (privatisations, financial measures, moving self-financing sectors off budget, etc.) will need to be taken. Also, while attention has focused on 1997, continued budget stringency will be required to meet deficit goals in 1998 and beyond.

Monetary and exchange rate policies

The downward trend in interest rates and ERM membership

With the entry into the European Monetary System on 1 January 1995 and its participation in the Exchange Rate Mechanism from 9 January 1995, the schilling became part of a formal monetary system for the first time since the breakdown of the Bretton Woods system. However, *de facto,* the schilling has been tied to the Deutschemark since the early 1980s, a stable exchange rate providing the anchor of Austrian monetary policy. The credibility of this strategy has become so well established that the entry of Austria into the ERM, to be followed by membership of the European Monetary Union in 1999, can be seen as an extension of a stability-oriented monetary policy which has already been internationally accepted. Indeed, the economies of Germany and Austria being now so closely interlinked structurally and cyclically, pressures for a differentiated monetary stance from cyclical desynchronisation rarely, if ever, occur. Differentials between Austrian and German interest rates are thus very small.

Given the exchange rate target, monetary policy measures have shadowed the developments in the European stable currency area and have been characterised by a downward tendency of interest rates since the beginning of 1995. The Austrian discount rate is currently at 2.5 per cent, having been progressively reduced from 4.5 per cent at the beginning of 1995 (Figure 8, Panel A). The Österreichische Nationalbank acted with other central banks to make cuts in the rate in March, August and December 1995, followed by a further cut in April 1996. In practical terms, the discount rate has always been equal to that of the Deutsche Bundesbank since May 1994. The rate for short-term open market transactions (GOMEX) now stands at 3.4 per cent, down from 4.7 per cent in early 1995 (Box 1). The average interest rate charged by banks for commercial credits contracted by 1.15 percentage points to 7.13 per cent during the same period, so that changes in policy and market interest rates can be seen to have fed through to rates charged by banks to business customers. However, in view of the continuing high level of insolvencies, banks have been increasing their loan loss provisions. The estimated risk provisions of banks for the year as a whole are Sch 18.3 billion, down from Sch 24.8 billion in 1995, when banks increased their provisions in the face of a peak in insolvencies. An improved earnings position is facilitating this move. Given the evolving improvement of the economic situation and the increased loan loss reserves, Austrian banks should be sufficiently provisioned against potential loan losses.

Following the run-up in yields during 1994, ten-year Federal government bonds fell by 124 basis points during 1995, to end the year at 6.46 per cent. By the end of November 1996 they had fallen by about 50 basis points, to below 6 per cent, the average monthly differential relative to Germany declining from

Figure 8. **INTEREST RATE DEVELOPMENTS**

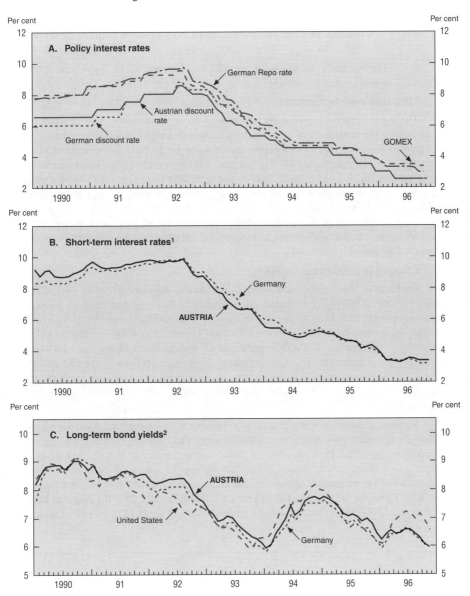

1. Austria: 3-month VIBOR; Germany: 3-month FIBOR.
2. Austria: 10-year benchmark bond; Germany: yields on listed federal securities with residual maturities of 9 to 10 years; United States: US Government bonds (composite over 10 years).
Source: Österreichische Nationalbank; Deutsche Bundesbank; OECD, *Main Economic Indicators.*

Box 1. Changes in refinancing facilities and reserve requirements

Following Austria's accession to the EU the Österreichische Nationalbank has revised its monetary policy instruments.

Minimum reserve measures

The legal framework governing *minimum reserve requirements* has changed. To comply with the provisions of the Treaty on European Union, in July 1995 short-term government paper (*Bundeschatzscheine*) ceased to be creditable against required minimum reserves. To compensate for this restraint, minimum reserve rates were simultaneously lowered for all types of bank deposits and short term securities. Following the trend in other European countries to ease reserve requirements, minimum reserve rates were further lowered in September 1995, and the eligibility of banks' cash holdings for offsetting against minimum reserve requirements was revoked in a move to streamline the instrument. On average, minimum reserve rates fall short of their mid-1995 levels by 2 percentage points.

Changes in refinancing facilities

Furthermore, the central bank revised its standard refinancing system with effect from 1 October 1995. Prior to that date, standard refinancing had been exclusively demand-oriented, utilisation of standing refinancing lines with the central bank depending entirely on the initiative of the commercial banks. The banks took the initiative to utilise short-term open market (GOMEX) operations as well as discount and lombard deals (lending by the central bank against collateral). Austria's accession to the EU and the related efforts to harmonise monetary policy instruments made it necessary to review the domestic components of the central bank money supply and adapt them to the new requirements.

Standard refinancing was restructured in October 1995 by substantially reducing the share of refinancing provided by the standard facilities and limiting Lombard refinancing. In addition, the central bank introduced a supply-oriented tender system, through which it offers credit institutions additional liquidity by means of a tender procedure — based either on volume or interest rate tender. The money market being awash with liquidity, the new instrument was not used until year-end, and in January 1996 the National Bank started to invite banks to bid for volume tenders with a maturity of one week in weekly intervals.

20 basis points in 1995 to around 10 basis points. Yield differentials of this order mainly result from the fact that the Austrian bond market is comparatively less liquid than the German market. The differentials for both money market rates and

secondary market yields became highly volatile in the fall of 1995, mirroring the political situation of the time (federal elections and discussions about the consolidation programme): in November 1995, the average positive interest rate differential *vis-à-vis* Germany widened to 0.26 per cent on the money market and to 0.41 per cent on the secondary market (Figure 8, Panels B and C). But throughout the period of uncertainty interest rate differentials were wide enough to attract sizeable foreign investment in Austrian securities, investor confidence in the credibility of Austria's exchange rate target remaining as solid as ever.

Implications for monetary aggregates and liquidity

The fixed exchange rate policy necessarily implies that monetary aggregates are not treated as interim targets for Austria's monetary policy. Ample liquidity and the downtrend of interest rates have had a considerable impact on the development of money aggregates. M1 has been subject to a strong expansion (+15.1 per cent in 1995; +1.9 per cent in the first half of 1996) which can be traced to a strong increase in sight deposits, whereas the M3 aggregate overcompensated this development by a shift toward investments with higher yields (1995: +4.8 per cent; first half of 1996; –1.5 per cent). Falling interest rates and higher levies on life insurance policies, effective as of mid-1996, have recently boosted the shift of financial assets from savings deposits and sight deposits to banks' own domestic issues and/or fixed-rate papers in general, as well as to mutual funds and life insurances.

Due to the degree of liquidity on the domestic market the Federal government was in a position to limit new borrowing abroad to the amounts necessary to service existing external debt, without causing crowding-out effects on the private sector which have been evident on similar occasions in the past. Moreover, while the economic situation would seem to warrant lower real interest rates, especially on the long end of the spectrum, internal financing from cash flow continues to play an important role in Austria. Following DM rates has thus not created problems for enterprise financing.

Developments in financial markets

The legal framework regulating Austria's financial markets has already been harmonised with the respective EU regulations to a large extent. This holds true, for example, for the supervision of banks on a consolidated basis. Moreover, a separate regulation authority for securities is in the process of being set up. Austria's financial markets are characterised by a comparatively high, if diminishing, degree of involvement of all-purpose banks as intermediaries. While the integration of Austrian financial markets into the Common Market has intensified competition, this implies that the Austrian capital market in general, and the stock market in particular, have a rather limited capability of attracting funds of private nonbanks. Although banks appear to be more oriented towards increasing efficiency, the marginal decline in the number of branches that occurred in 1994 did not continue in 1995. Banks are setting new priorities in cross-border transactions by expanding their positions in South East and Central European markets.

Fiscal policy

From 1993-1995 fiscal policy was following a course which would have been unsustainable if left uncorrected. During each of these three years, the initial estimate of the Federal budget deficit was exceeded. From 1992 to 1995 the general government deficit increased from Sch 39.1 billion (1.9 per cent of GDP) to Sch 138.2 billion (5.9 per cent of GDP). The need to rein in the deficit expansion led to the introduction of a comprehensive fiscal programme during 1995, aimed at bringing down the general government deficit to a level consistent with the 3 per cent deficit ceiling set out in the Maastricht treaty, the main emphasis being on spending cuts, though increases in tax revenues also played a role. However, many of the details of the programme had still to be worked out in co-operation with the social partners, and during the course of attempting to implement the proposed budgetary consolidation, in autumn 1995, the coalition of SPÖ and ÖVP broke apart. This led to new elections in December 1995 and to a new coalition of SPÖ and ÖVP at the beginning of 1996. Thus, no action to redress the budgetary deterioration could be taken in 1995, with the consequence of additional slippage. The problem needing correcting in the 1996 budget was thus severe.

The 1995 budget outcome: substantial deterioration

Budget developments in 1995 were affected by a number of decisions taken in earlier years. The 1994 tax reform had a growing impact in 1995, leading to a shortfall in tax revenues.[2] A further significant influence on the 1995 budget came from Austria's EU accession, implying net budgetary costs of EU membership of around Sch 36.1 billion in 1995 (1.5 per cent of GDP, cash basis). Of this total Sch 7.7 billion were transitory aid to the agricultural sector to ease the adaptation to the common EU agricultural policy. The 1995 budget thus showed an initial Sch 19 billion increase in the central government budget deficit on a cash basis (but a small decline on an administrative basis, which includes a rundown in reserves). For the general government as a whole, the deficit was projected to widen from 4 to 4½ per cent of GDP. Excluding transfers to the EU budget, federal expenditure was programmed to grow more slowly than nominal GDP (some 4 per cent compared with nearly 6 per cent), while gross tax revenue was expected to grow by 1½ per cent. The restraint in expenditure growth reflected a number of new retrenchment measures, such as controls on civil service expenditures designed to reduce overtime and other pay ''extras''; higher pension contributions by civil servants; restrictions on family benefits; a curtailment of unemployment benefits, and higher pension contributions of the self-employed and farmers.

In the event, the Federal budget outcome exceeded the budget plan by Sch 15.6 billion on an administrative basis, and by Sch 6.5 billion on a cash basis excluding the effects of reserve movements and other ''double entry'' items (Table 6). On the expenditure side, certain spending categories grew moderately or even declined, reflecting the effects from the 1995 consolidation package. The wage bill for public sector employees (including teachers employed by the states) expanded only slowly, as personnel were reduced by about 3 000, and overtime pay and benefits were cut. Pensions to federal civil servants and federal contributions to pensions paid by the states dropped substantially, reflecting the reforms noted above. Family allowances also fell, reflecting the cuts in child allowances and an increase in co-payments for transport of pupils and students. Outlays for unemployment benefits remained stable, in part attributable to more rigid criteria for entitlements, but also because a high inflow into early retirement prevented unemployment rates from rising more strongly. Current spending on goods, and investment spending also grew only weakly. However, the financial relief stemming from restraint in the above spending items did not fully compensate for massive spending increases in other categories. Federal transfers to cover a potential deficit in the social security system, mainly pensions, increased by Sch 13.5 billion, nearly two-thirds of which was unanticipated (Sch 8.1 billion).

Table 6. **The Federal budget**

Cash basis, adjusted,[1] billions of schillings

	1993 Outturn	1994 Outturn	1995 Budget	1995 Outturn[2]	1996 Budget	1997 Budget
Revenue	560.5	580.0	589.3	584.3	612.2	632.3
(percentage change)	(+0.3)	(+3.5)	(+1.6)	(+0.7)	(4.7)	(+3.3)
Taxes before revenue sharing	512.8	524.5	532.1	521.2	587.8	631.6
Wage tax	139.2	134.8	150.0	150.2	160.0	183.3
Taxes on other income and profits	66.3	57.0	58.1	61.0	79.9	89.0
Value-added tax	176.0	202.6	189.0	179.9	209.0	213.0
Major excise taxes[3]	37.0	39.3	46.5	43.7	48.1	47.2
Other taxes	94.3	90.8	88.5	86.4	90.8	99.1
Minus: Tax-sharing transfers	173.7	166.1	162.6	156.5	171.4	178.4
Minus: Transfers to EU budget			28.1	18.8	29.4	30.1
Taxes after revenue sharing	339.1	358.4	341.5	345.8	386.9	423.2
Tax transfers to federal funds	19.1	19.3	19.7	19.7	19.4	18.5
Tax-like revenue[4]	72.2	79.5	84.0	82.6	85.0	87.8
Federal enterprises	78.8	63.9	65.9	65.1	25.3	2.9
Other revenue	51.3	59.0	78.2	71.1	95.6	100.0
Expenditure	663.8	679.9	708.6	710.2	708.1	701.1
(percentage change)	(+7.4)	(+2.4)	(+4.2)	(+4.5)	(−0.3)	(1.0)
Wages and salaries	155.5	136.5	140.5	140.3	137.0	135.6
Pensions	63.6	66.9	49.7	48.8	43.7	40.0
Current expenditure on goods	62.0	65.6	67.0	66.5	65.4	65.3
Gross investment	26.4	24.3	25.8	25.5	20.2	12.8
Transfer payments	259.2	282.3	312.0	320.7	326.6	330.2
Family allowances	59.3	62.1	58.5	57.5	56.1	53.8
Unemployment benefits	31.1	32.8	33.5	32.8	34.9	35.6
Transfers to the social security	68.9	73.4	78.8	86.9	89.7	86.7
Transfers to enterprises	20.7	31.5	47.4	45.3	54.4	59.8
Other transfers[5]	79.3	82.5	93.8	98.2	91.5	94.3
Interest	75.8	77.5	86.6	84.1	90.5	94.8
Other expenditure	21.3	26.9	26.9	24.4	24.7	22.4
Net balance	−103.3	−99.8	−119.4	−125.9	−95.8	−68.7
(in per cent of GDP)	(4.9)	(4.4)	(5.0)	(5.3)	(3.9)	(2.8)
Memorandum item:						
Net balance, administrative basis	−98.2	−104.8	−102.3	−117.9	−89.8	−68.0
(in per cent of GDP)	(4.7)	(4.7)	(4.3)	(5.0)	(3.7)	(2.7)

1. Adjusted for double counting.
2. Autumn 1996 estimate.
3. Mineral oil and tobacco taxes.
4. Mainly contributions to unemployment insurance and to the fund for family allowances.
5. Including agriculture.
Source: Ministry of Finance.

1995 saw a rapid increase in early retirements on account of the weakness in economic activity. Such transfers would have needed to rise further if contribution rates had not been raised in 1995 for self-employed and farmers.

Gross tax revenues, prior to tax sharing with the Länder and municipalities and the deductions of the EU transfers, fell short of estimate by Sch 10.9 and were actually Sch 3.3 billion lower than in 1994. This was mainly attributable to a Sch 22.7 billion decline in VAT proceeds of which Sch 9.1 billion were unexpected. The drop in VAT receipts was a one-time effect of the alignment to the EU system, while weaker-than-expected economic activity, cross-border shopping by Austrians and lower tax pre-payments accounted for the unexpected part of the revenues shortfall. The budget had been based on a nominal GDP

Table 7. **Net lending of the general government**

National accounts basis, billions of schillings

	1993	1994	1995	1996	1997	1998
Current receipts	**1 040.3**	**1 073.7**	**1 097.8**	**1 157.6**	**1 202.7**	**1 234.4**
Total direct taxes	312.7	299.2	326.4	351.5	371.3	376.4
Households	267.9	265.8	285.8	299.4	317.5	325.9
Business	44.8	33.4	40.6	52.1	53.8	50.4
Total indirect taxes	339.1	366.4	334.6	364.2	376.1	389.3
Social security and other current transfers received	343.0	362.1	387.4	389.8	406.3	422.5
Property and entrepreneurial income	45.5	46.1	49.4	52.1	49.0	46.2
Current disbursements	**1 037.3**	**1 078.5**	**1 133.3**	**1 155.1**	**1 173.8**	**1 214.6**
Government consumption	405.0	425.7	442.5	449.1	455.9	468.4
of which: Wages and salaries	273.8	287.8	297.9	300.9	303.9	310.7
Interest on public debt	92.0	91.8	102.0	109.9	114.0	120.3
Subsidies	68.0	57.4	60.4	54.0	54.0	56.2
Social security and other current transfers paid	472.4	503.6	528.4	542.1	549.9	569.7
Capital outlays	**91.8**	**93.7**	**102.6**	**105.6**	**103.9**	**106.4**
Gross investment	68.7	72.9	74.2	75.1	76.3	78.5
Net capital transfers paid and other capital transactions	37.5	35.9	44.1	46.7	44.2	45.1
Less: Consumption of fixed capital	14.5	15.1	15.7	16.2	16.6	17.2
Net lending	**−88.7**	**−98.5**	**−138.2**	**−103.1**	**−75.0**	**−86.6**
(as a percentage of GDP)	−4.2	−4.4	−5.9	−4.3	−3.0	−3.4
Structural budget balance						
(as a percentage of potential GDP)	−3.3	−4.2	−5.7	−3.7	−2.3	−2.8

Source: OECD.

45

Table 8.   **General government deficit by government level**

National accounts basis, billions of schillings

	1991	1992	1993	1994	1995
Federal Government	−71.9	−56.7	−100.5	−101.4	−121.5
States (excluding Vienna)	16.8	17.6	15.6	9.5	−1.1
Communities (including Vienna)	2.2	3.5	−4.1	−8.1	−15.8
Social security funds	0.1	−3.4	0.2	1.5	0.3
General government	−52.8	−39.1	−88.7	−98.5	−138.2
(as a percentage of GDP)	2.7	1.9	4.2	4.4	5.9

− = deficit; + = surplus.
Source: Ministry of Finance; OECD.

growth rate of 5.8 per cent, whereas the actual outcome was 4 per cent. Non-tax revenues were weak because the volume of privatisations fell short of expectations by Sch 7.1 billion. By contrast, there was a stronger growth in income and profit taxes, and federal contributions to the EU remained Sch 9.3 billion below the proposed value.

At the general government level, the deficit reached on a national accounts basis 5.9 per cent of GDP in 1995, from 4.4 per cent in 1994, marking a record high (Table 7). The Länder surplus had been gradually decreasing since 1992 and in 1995 it swung into a small deficit. The deficit of the communities deteriorated further from Sch 8.1 billion in 1994 to Sch 15.8 billion in 1995 (Table 8). Weaker-than-expected economic activity account for part of the deterioration in the finances of the Länder. But other factors appear to have exercised an even stronger influence, especially a change in the provision of housing subsidies to annuity payments, and a continuing rise in public outlays for health care. EU accession also contributed significantly to the budgetary slippage of the Länder in that they mostly financed the costs of EU membership by loans instead of providing for them by reductions in spending or raising revenues.

The fiscal consolidation programme for 1996 and 1997

The new fiscal strategy

In January 1996 the government projected that without fiscal action the 1997 general government deficit would reach some 8 per cent of GDP. To meet the Maastricht deficit target in 1997 a consolidation need of about Sch 100 billion was identified relative to the current baseline. In February the parties forming the new government agreed on a savings package which was then further elaborated in the draft budgets for 1996 and 1997. The package contains overall savings relative to the old baseline amounting to Sch 100 billion for the Federal government and some Sch 113 billion at the general government level. Two-thirds of the Federal government savings are to be realised by restraining spending and one third via raising revenues.

The consolidation package aims at reducing the general government deficit to not more than 3 per cent of GDP by 1997. This profile is based on the assumption that real GDP grows at a rate of 0.7 per cent in 1996 (originally assumed to be 1.6 per cent) and 1 per cent in 1997. The spending restraints of the package concern both the Federal government and the social security system. However, meeting the 3 per cent deficit target in 1997 also requires additional spending restraint by the Länder and the local authorities. An agreement was therefore made in February 1996 that in 1997 the combined share of the Länder and the local authorities in the general government deficit should not exceed 0.3 per cent of GDP and that the Federal deficit should be not higher than 2.7 per cent of GDP.

Based on the consolidation package, in March the government presented two draft budgets for 1996 and 1997. In April, the budget for 1996 was adopted by Parliament with minor modifications, mainly taking into account a downwards revision in growth projections and a revised assessment of contributions to the EU. The 1997 budget passed Parliament unchanged.

The consolidation package for 1996 and 1997

On the expenditure side, the programme is designed to generate savings relative to the 1995 baseline totalling Sch 66.7 billion by 1997 (Table 9). Broadly, savings are to be generated by restraining spending on personnel in the public sector, curbing social transfers, increasing the efficiency of the public administration, stabilising subsidies to enterprises and increasing the efficiency of funding of public sector entities (see Box 2). In the Federal budget, wages and salaries – which account for around a fifth of overall outlays by the Federal government – are set to decline by 2.4 per cent in 1996 and 1 per cent in 1997, by curbing personnel and tightly controlling wage growth in 1996 and 1997. Pensions and family allowances are set to be reduced and gross investment to decline

Table 9. **The government's consolidation package 1996-1997**

Savings 1997 in billions of schillings against the 1995 baseline

Expenditures	66.7
Personnel in the public sector	16.0
Family allowances	6.3
Long-term care	1.9
Unemployment compensation and labour market measures	5.3
Pensions	13.5
Subsidies	2.8
General administration	16.4
Earmarked provisions	4.5
Revenues	46.7
Wage tax and personal income tax	22.9
Corporate income tax	8.1
Interest tax	3.0
Energy tax	7.0
Indirect taxes (except energy tax)	3.2
Miscellaneous taxes	2.6
Total	113.4

Source: Ministry of Finance; OECD.

substantially. All of the reduction in public investment between 1995 and 1997 is due to the Post Office being moved off-budget.[3] Transfers to enterprises, on the other hand rose because the payments of pension liabilities to Post Office employees were correspondingly reclassified.

The tax measures contained in the consolidation programme are estimated to generate additional receipts of Sch 46.7 billion by 1997, of which around two-thirds accrue to the Federal government (Table 9). Taxes from income account for almost three quarters of the additional revenues, with the remainder mainly consisting of increases in indirect taxes, including a new tax on consumption of electricity and gas. Apart from raising the tax rate on interest income from 22 per cent to 25 per cent, additional income tax receipts are mainly generated by cutting tax allowances and deductions, thus widening the tax base. Certain tax measures with respect to income from entrepreneurial activity are transitory only, while others will become effective only after 1997. The rate of tax prepayments will be raised by 5 percentage points for the years 1996 to 1998, and the possibility of deducting from profits losses that have been incurred in the past and carried forwards is temporarily suspended for fiscal 1996 and 1997. Also, for

Box 2. **Expenditure restraint in the 1996-97 consolidation package**

The major elements of expenditure restraint in the consolidation package are the following:

- Outlays for personnel in the public sector, including the federal administration, the railways, the social security system and other public sector entities in the responsibility of the federal government, are to be broadly stabilised at 1995 levels. This mainly involves modest wage increases in 1996 and 1997, a reduction in the number of employees (including the Post Office) by 10 500 by the end of 1997, reductions in the remuneration for overtime, and various measures to reduce the personnel costs at schools and universities. Early retirement in the public sector will be discouraged by paying full pensions from the age of 60 onwards only.
- Family allowances are to be curbed. Measures comprise the splitting of maternity leave between parents and restricting the maximum duration for one partner to 1½ years, the abolition of lump-sum payments for new-borns; the elimination of free public transport for children who are older than 19 years; and the elimination of allowances for non-resident children of foreigners. Family allowances for students will be linked to the students' performance, and support for the purchase of school books will be capped.
- Costs for nursing care are to be cut by freezing benefits for 1996 and 1997 and restricting eligibility for benefits.
- Various measures aim at relieving the unemployment insurance system. The eligibility period for receiving unemployment benefits will be extended from 26 to 28 months and the reference period from 6 to 12 months. The level of unemployment assistance will be made dependent on the time of former employment. The funds for active labour market measures will be frozen at the 1995 level. There will be tighter controls against abuse of unemployment benefits. Financial benefits for the long-term unemployed prior to early retirement are abolished, and employment of elderly people is fostered by varying the employers' contributions to the unemployment insurance system.
- To reduce the costs of the pension insurance system the government aims at increasing the average retirement age. Eligibility for early retirement is reduced by requiring longer contribution periods to the pension scheme, and early retirement is discouraged by making it financially less attractive.
- Various other measures designed to curb spending include the introduction of co-payments for spas, more modest yearly pension adjustments, stricter requirements to deduct multiple pensions and additional labour income, and reductions in federal transfers to the pension insurance of self-employed. Revenues are raised

(continued on next page)

by introducing the obligation for commissioned employment (*Werkverträge*) to pay social security contributions.

– Subsidies to the business sector will be stabilised at the 1995 level. If no economic or labour market effect is discernible, subsidies are to be lowered by 10 per cent until 1997.

– Outlays for general administration are also to be stabilised at the 1995 level. This is to be achieved by increasing the efficiency of the administration, a stabilisation of federal transfers to the railways, and a lowering of housing subsidies. But the main savings in the sphere of general administration are expected from items which strictly are revenue-raising rather than expenditure restraining. These comprise higher licence income from the telecommunications sector which is passed to the federal government through the Post Office, and higher prepayments of corporation tax.

– Earmarked federal transfers to off-budgets are to be reduced, affecting in particular the Catastrophe Fund, and the Water Supply and Waste Water Fund.

the assessment of tax pre-payments in 1996 and 1997 the level of losses that have been carried forwards in the past will be disregarded, raising the level of the pre-payments. These transitory measures account for the bulk of additional receipts from corporate income taxes, but they also affect, to a minor degree, personal income tax receipts. Receipts from privatisations amount to Sch 8.5 billion in 1996. For 1997 no privatisations are budgeted.

The consolidation programme also contains a number of stimulatory measures which are mainly directed towards construction with the purpose of stabilising employment. The measures include the establishment of an off-budget fund for the financing of investment by the railways with a borrowing limit of Sch 60 billion over five years, an increase in subsidies for private residential construction of around Sch 2½ billion per year, incentives to spend taxation depreciation allowances for rental accommodation on new investment which could lead to increased expenditure of around Sch 3 billion until the end of 1998, an increase in spending on road construction from about Sch 1½ billion per year (1994-95) to some Sch 3 billion per year, and a temporary increase in the investment tax allowance from 9 per cent to 12 per cent. Overall, it is estimated that such measures might increase investment expenditures by some Sch 20 billion per year (some 1 per cent of GDP).

The consolidation measures imply considerable fiscal restraint for the next two years and should – if fully implemented – reduce the general government deficit to 3 per cent of GDP by 1997 as targeted. Indeed, the most recent information shows that the programme is on track. Even though a number of provisions have not yet taken effect, or have taken effect only recently, preliminary figures suggest that there is a high probability for 1996 of reaching the target of a Sch 90 billion deficit on an administrative basis for the Federal government and of Sch 103 billion on NIA basis for general government.

Though it should be interpreted with care, the path of the structural deficit, which measures the component of the overall deficit which is independent from conjunctural fluctuations, helps to summarise the stance of fiscal policy and budgetary consolidation (Table 7). In 1993 the structural deficit was estimated to amount to 3.3 per cent of GDP, and increased to 4.2 per cent in 1994 and 5.7 per cent in 1995. This deterioration can be attributed, among other factors, to lower receipts from the 1994 tax reform and the budgetary burden from the EU accession as well as a trend increase in the utilisation of social services. In the current OECD projections the structural deficit will decline to 3.7 per cent in 1996 and 2.3 per cent in 1997 indicating a significant tightening in fiscal policy.

Medium-term fiscal outlook and public debt

Though it has important structural consequences, the consolidation package is principally designed for its short-term impact. As outlined above, some tax measures lead to temporarily higher revenues in 1996 and within the following one or two years, but the bringing forward of tax payments will lead to corresponding revenue shortfalls in later years. There may thus be problems in keeping the deficit below 3 per cent in 1998. On the other hand, the budget package also incorporates a number of items whose savings effects will become effective only after 1997. This pertains mainly to the measures relating to personal and corporate income taxes. The Ministry of Finance's assessment is that these one-off effects have been relatively evenly distributed over the years 1997, 1998 and 1999 so that significant slippage should not occur after 1997. Some of the items becoming effective only after 1997 are the maternity leave reductions and the closing of tax loopholes for liability reserves and housing maintenance reserves. While it is clear that receipts from the Post Office will be smaller in the future, there should be countervailing receipts from licence fees for additional telephone

Figure 9. **THE BUDGET BALANCE AND THE GENERAL GOVERNMENT DEBT**[1]
Per cent of GDP

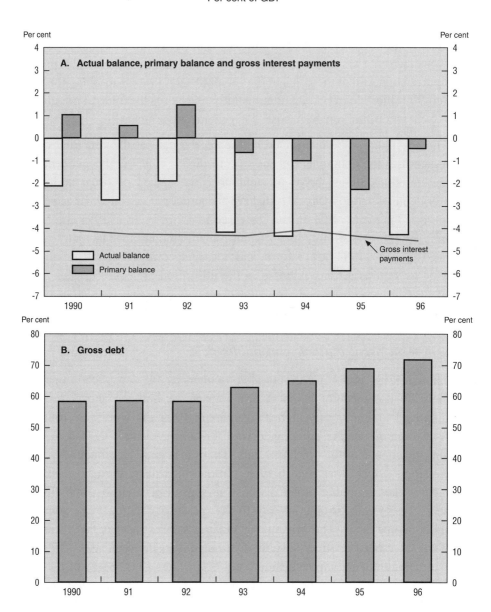

1. OECD estimates for 1996.
Source: OECD.

licences and from private radio and television. The introduction of more competition into these sectors is likely to raise sales and may bring in more VAT.

Nevertheless, in the OECD's projections, the deficit to GDP ratio increases to 3.4 per cent in 1998, and it is clear that in a medium-term context continued fiscal restraint would be required for a further deficit and debt reduction. Despite lower projected spending and higher revenues, the debt-to-GDP ratio is projected to increase further over the projection horizon, from 69 per cent of GDP in 1995 to around 75 per cent in 1998 (Figure 9). Stabilisation of the debt-to-GDP ratio would require a primary surplus of more than 2 per cent of GDP, whereas the OECD projects a primary balance of between –0.5 and +0.9 per cent in 1996 to 1998. However, a turning point for the gross debt ratio could occur earlier as a result of privatisations and restructurings in the public sector which are planned by the Government.

For the medium term, the most recent four-year budget programme, presented to Parliament in September 1996 foresees a further reduction in the Federal government deficit to 2.1 per cent of GDP by the year 2000. The Austrian Finance Minister has stated that in the medium term he intends to reduce the Austrian deficit "close to balance". At present the four-year programme has mainly a guiding function and does not yet contain all the individual legal measures necessary at the individual ministry's level to reach these goals. One guideline for the process, negotiations on which started in the second half of October, is clear, however: public expenditures on personnel and operating costs, social expenditures and subsidies to firms are to be frozen in nominal terms until 2000. This puts a binding cap on these expenditures. How these targets can be reached, will be largely left to the individual ministries and authorities involved. An increase in the number of public services for which fees will be introduced is also envisaged, as well as increased income-dependence of certain social transfers, further privatisations and further steps to increase efficiency and accountability in public sector management.

Pension insurance

The share of pension expenditures has steadily risen since the mid-fifties and in 1995 amounted to some 13½ per cent of GDP. In 1995 there was an unexpected deterioration of the finances of the pension insurance scheme by Sch 8 billion which was due to increased claims on early retirement and to the settlements of liabilities of public insurance agencies according to a ruling from the VwGH (Supreme Court for Administrative Affairs), as well as revenue losses due to the sluggish economic activity. More generally, increasing spending in the pension system is mainly due to earlier retirement of eligible persons, some considerable improvements in benefits, and the ageing of the population. In the medium term and in the long run, some major challenges to finance future pension benefits within the framework of the *"Generationenvertrag"* (the principle of the working generation paying for the old and young, which effectively relies on "pay-as-you-go") will result from this development which are briefly discussed below.

- First, according to a study by the *"Beirat für Wirtschafts- und Sozialfragen"*, the number of working people will increase only slightly during the nineties, while after 2010 a sharp decline to less than 3 million employees is projected. In conjunction with a simultaneous rise in the number of retirees, the old-age dependency ratio is projected to deteriorate from 662 (1990) to 771 (2 030) retired people per 1 000 insured persons. The ratios in the pension insurance funds for manual workers and farmers show even higher and more dramatic figures.

- Second, adverse demographic developments are reinforced by a very low average retirement age. Since 1970 the actual retirement age has been gradually declining from about 62 to 58 years, without any changes in the statutory retirement age. The actual retirement age of men and women differs only slightly despite a large gap in the legal provisions (in the social security system the difference is five years). Early retirement has been used to alleviate structural and cyclical problems in the labour market by allowing older employees to receive pension benefits earlier instead of facing unemployment. It has also given enterprises the opportunity to replace relatively expensive older employees by cheaper younger ones, thus shifting the financial burden to the public budgets.

- Third, the heterogeneity of public pension insurance which results in many different insurance agencies (*e.g.* for wage-earners, salaried employees, self-employed, farmers, miners) responsible for their own clientele, and many different kinds of benefits and – to a lesser extent – contributions, represents a very specific feature of the Austrian pension system. This aggravates the future financing of pension benefits as every group is especially intent on having its own benefit system preserved. This complexity makes compromises hard to reach.

The projections of the Beirat point to increasing financial stress in the pension insurance system. Contributions are projected to rise to more than Sch 225 billion in 2000, compared to Sch 136 billion in 1990. Nevertheless, their growth rate is assumed to fall throughout the period 1996-2000, to about 4 per cent compared with around 8 per cent at the beginning of the nineties. Furthermore, insurance contributions of farmers and self-employed are projected to exhibit a stronger upward trend than other public insurance funds whilst the growth rates of civil servants' and workers' contributions will lie much below average. Revisions to replacement rates have only begun to come in for discussion, current prospects being for only minor alterations in the medium term. The government has recently taken steps to increase the entry age into retirement by requiring longer contribution periods and making early retirement financially less attractive. It is apparent, however, that further policy changes are necessary if the system is to be sustainable in the long run (see Box 3).

Improving public sector efficiency

In general, the government's savings package aims to freeze all large expenditure categories (personnel, administration, social expenditures, subsidies and revenue sharing with regional and local entities) at their 1995 levels. However, in addition, a number or structural reforms have been introduced which should dampen public expenditures in the medium and long run and lead to quality improvements in public services.[4] The 1994 *OECD Economic Survey of Austria* described certain institutional features of the financial relations of the Federal government with the Länder and public sector funds which give rise to inefficiencies and the government's consolidation policy has implications for the treatment of these.

The Länders' responsibility for spending decisions the financial consequences of which are largely borne by the Federal government creates an upwards bias in spending for public services. The first steps have now been taken towards closer co-ordination of the fiscal decisions of the territorial authorities. In May 1995 the states and the municipalities declared that they would apply the savings measures of the Federal government concerning personnel in 1996 and 1997. For the Länder this implies agreement to cut personnel in the state-run education system, where spending has been buoyant. Also, the different levels of government agreed to establish a system of consultations and surveillance which

Box 3. **Population ageing and the sustainability of the pension system**

Although population ageing in Austria does not appear dramatic over the next few years, into the next century a sharply increasing share of the population aged above the current retirement age will place stress on the Austrian pension system. The extent of "population ageing" can be summarised by relating the number of persons aged 65 and older to the number of persons aged between 15 and 64. In Austria, this ratio was 23 per cent in 1995, and is projected to increase only slightly until the beginning of the next century. But thereafter, projections show sharp increases in the old-age ratio, which is projected to peak at 50 per cent in 2035.* It then declines with the outflow of the baby-boom generation.

The OECD has constructed illustrative scenarios to highlight the fiscal dimension of population ageing in the long run. To be operational, simplifying assumptions had to be made. The simulations are based on the assumption that pensions are indexed to wages, and the number of recipients grows proportionately to the number of elderly people above the retirement age. By the beginning of the next century, the economy is assumed to have returned to its medium term growth path and there is no cyclical unemployment. After 2000, the ratio of the employed to the working-age population is assumed to remain constant. GDP growth is determined by the growth in labour productivity, assumed to be 1½ per cent, and the projected growth in the working-age population. Wages are assumed to grow with productivity. Considered are old age, invalidity and survivors pensions in the public pension insurance schemes, covering workers, salaried employees, railways employees, miners, self-employed and farmers. Pension payments in the public administration are not considered. Three scenarios are considered:

– The baseline scenario assumes that policies remain unchanged.
– In the late retirement scenario, retirement age is gradually increased to seventy years, beginning in 2006. This proposal corresponds to suggestions to increase further the retirement age.
– The targeting scenario limits the provision of public pensions to poorer people with higher income groups relying on private pension schemes. As an illustration, the scenario assumes that from 2010 onwards the proportion of recipients gradually falls to 30 per cent of the retirees who continue to receive the average pension of the baseline scenario.

---

* The population projections are taken from the World Bank; see Bos, E., M. T. Vu, E. Massiah and R. Bulatao, *World population projections, 1994-1995,* The International Bank for Reconstruction and Development/The World Bank, Washington D.C., 1994.

(continued on next page)

(continued)

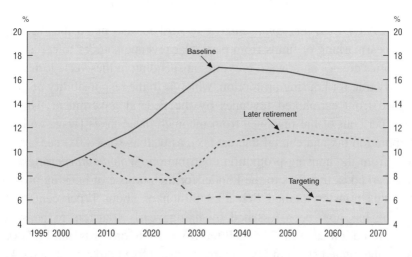

Figure B1. **PENSION EXPENDITURE SCENARIOS**
Per cent of real GDP (1995 prices)

Source: OECD.

Under the no-change-in-policy assumption, pension outlays in the public insurance scheme as a percentage of GDP would steadily increase from around nine per cent of GDP at the beginning of the next century to 17 per cent of GDP by the year 2035 (see Figure B1). Thereafter outlays are projected to decline to some 15 per cent in 2070. This path is unsustainable: under current conditions, it would produce an explosion in public debt, or, alternatively, contribution rates would have to increase sharply.

Under the late retirement option, spending would drop over a period of about twenty years. Thereafter pension outlays would rise again, peaking at a level of some 11½ per cent of GDP. Although raising the retirement age is likely to induce additional spending in the unemployment insurance system, it would have the two-fold advantage of decreasing the number of pensioners and increasing the contributions paid. Not surprisingly, the targeting scenario would lead to the most pronounced decrease in spending, but it would have to be introduced sufficiently gradually to allow people enough time to make private arrangements.

will serve to prevent costs from being passed down from one layer of the government to another. To this end it is envisaged that the immediate and follow-up costs of legislative initiatives of all levels of government will be systematically listed. At present negotiations are under way in order to establish the legal base for this common surveillance and budgeting mechanism. According to Austrian law, a constitutional amendment would be required to introduce legally binding burden sharing mechanisms between the different levels of government.

The 1994 *OECD Economic Survey of Austria* also noted the fact that the automatic earmarking of funds from particular revenue sources to certain spending categories creates an upward pressure on spending in these categories. This is particularly true for housing promotion, which is in the responsibility of the states but funded from earmarked revenues by the Federal government. Until 1995 some 9.2 per cent of the revenues from income-related taxes (wage and income tax, corporation tax and capital interest tax), as well as some 80.6 per cent of the proceeds from the housing-promotion contribution (*Wohnbauförderungsbeitrag*) were earmarked as transfers to the Länder for the purpose of housing promotion. In 1995 this transfer totalled Sch 23.3 billion or about 1 per cent of GDP. Earmarking has now been lessened by fixing yearly transfers to be spent on housing promotion at Sch 24.5 billion from 1996 onwards until 2000. The surplus of the quoted share of tax receipts over the fixed amount of Sch 24.5 billion will then be transferred to the Länder for their unrestricted disposal. The degree to which transfers are earmarked is also reduced for transfers to the catastrophe funds (*Katastrophen-Fonds*) and to the Water Supply and Waste Water Fund (*Wasserwirtschaftsfond*). These measures may contribute to increasing the efficiency of public sector spending, but are still first steps only. New mechanisms should be found to enable earmarked transfers from the federal government to the Länder to be replaced by own taxes in order to increase their financial responsibilities.

The government plans to continue its privatisation policy. The Post Office, which since May 1996 is a stock company whose shares are held by the government, will go public within three years. Participation of the Bund in Bank Austria and the Creditanstalt, Austria's largest and second largest banks, are set to be terminated. The Postal Savings Bank is to be transformed into a stock company and will be placed at the stock exchange. Other public companies are also considered candidates for privatisation. Also, the Finance Minister is drawing up a list of public entities in all sectors of government where there is a lack of the freedom necessary to conduct business, and limited access to clients outside the public sector as well as restrictions on financing and corporate control and management. These lists include mainly business units in the government, such as the Forest authority, Statistical and Accounting Units, Extra-university research institutions (National Laboratories), and a host of historically grown relatively small production and services units. The major purpose of these activities is twofold: one, to remove the status of public authority from agencies which have mainly a commercial objective and thus relieve the government of the burden of having to run these units under the rules of public service; and two, to relieve these units themselves from the restrictive practices inherent in a bureaucratic civil service. Thus efficiency within these units should be improved.

In addition, the government intends establishing public sector entities such as the Motorway and Transit Road Financing Agency (ASFINAG) as public enterprises outside the general government sector. EU rules state that operations can be redesignated ''commercial'' (off-budget) activities if 50 per cent of expenditure came from service-related fees. The same is envisaged for communal services (water, gas, sewage, garbage collection, etc.) which already now meets this criterion. Another plan is to sell off the claims which the Environment and Water Fund (UWWF) has accumulated. These measures should suffice to generate a significant drop in the level of public debt and to put its development on a downward trend. Though privatisations and the shifting of assets may leave net debt unaffected, they have a downward impact on the level of gross debt which is the relevant quantity for the Maastricht criterion. Complementing the reorganisation of these units (*Gebührenhaushalte*) the government is drawing up a blueprint statute for the establishment of financially responsible management and control structures. However, whereas privatisations are important for improving public sector efficiency thereby contributing to the consolidation of government finances, this is not automatically true for operations that move administrative units within the public sector from the general government into the sphere of public enterprises. Rather fiscal consolidation in a meaningful sense would require exposing these companies to competition with the private sector and setting up corresponding management structures.

III. Public sector reform: the health care issue

The issue of public spending control in Austria was last examined in the 1994 *Survey* and this chapter extends the analysis of public spending issues to health care. The concern two years ago was that the consolidation process had stalled as a result of control problems, largely due to the combination of unclear objectives and ambiguous incentives generated by the federal fiscal structure. At best it had shifted away from expenditure cuts to tax increases, contrary to medium-term objectives. It was recognised that efforts to contain future spending pressure needed to be intensified if the consolidation process was to be put back on track. The risks identified at the time seem now to have materialised: despite progress towards better control of public sector pay and reform of public sector pensions, 1995 saw severe public spending overruns, as described in the previous section. The budget for 1996-97 has introduced measures to correct the situation, chiefly through natural wastage, improved public sector management, further privatisations, pension and unemployment insurance reforms, trimming social spending and reducing tax loopholes. Moreover, in conjunction with the social partners, the government has agreed a plan for wide ranging reforms in the health sector which is currently in the process of being implemented. As in many other OECD countries, it is in the health sector that spending is rising most rapidly. Some of the generic institutional control deficiencies identified in the 1994 *Survey* appear to be particularly acute in the health sector, but they are exacerbated insofar as health spending has intrinsic problems of its own, making it an area of public spending pressure throughout the OECD area.

The chapter is divided into four main sections. First, recent overall trends in health spending are analysed, in the context of both overall public spending trends and the general macro-economic forces affecting health-related programmes in the OECD area. In the second section efficiency considerations are discussed in the context of the underlying institutional controls which have led to an excessive reliance on hospital care. In the third section the incentive structure and regulatory environment governing ambulatory (*i.e.* physician and out-patient care) and pharmaceutical spending is analysed. The final section assesses the institutional and policy changes needed to reshape incentives and alleviate pressures in the health care system.

Intensified pressures on public spending

Table 10 indicates where the main longer-term spending pressures have tended to arise. The central government accounts for half of all government spending, the social security funds around one-quarter, with state and local governments sharing the remaining one-quarter roughly equally. Over the last decade spending overall has been rising marginally faster at the state than at central government levels (6.8 against 6.6 per cent per annum), while revenue growth has been significantly slower in the former (5.0 compared with 6.3 per cent p.a.), resulting in the emergence of state government deficits. Communes have experienced slightly slower growth rates of spending (6.2 per cent per annum), while maintaining a better balance between spending and revenue growth, reflecting the fact that they have more revenue-raising sources of their own than do the states. The health insurance funds have maintained a balance between expenditures and receipts, as required by law, only the farmers health fund receiving direct budget support (Annex I).

As far as current spending is concerned, fully one half is accounted for by social spending, which includes the main problem areas of pensions, family benefits, and unemployment benefits. Such spending has been rising especially fast at the state level. Education and transport and communications, which respectively absorb 9 and 2½ per cent of government expenditure, have risen at slightly less than average growth rates. However, the highest rate of growth (for a non-trivial spending aggregate) has been registered in the area of health spending, both at the overall and at the individual sub-levels of government (though not at the central government level, whose direct involvement is limited) annual growth rates having averaged 8-13 per cent in nominal terms over the last decade. Moreover, this category has absorbed a rapidly increasing share of the resources of the social security funds. Health spending is also of particular concern for the future because, like pensions, it is highly sensitive to population pressures

Table 10. Government spending by function
Per cent of GDP

	Central government			State government			Local government			Social security funds			General government		
	1985	1993	Annual growth rate	1985	1993	Annual growth rate	1985	1993	Annual growth rate	1985	1993	Annual growth rate	1985	1993	Annual growth rate
Current expenditure	**25.6**	**27.8**	**6.9**	**6.4**	**6.9**	**6.9**	**6.0**	**6.2**	**6.2**	**15.5**	**16.3**	**6.5**	**46.3**	**49.1**	**6.6**
General public services	1.9	2.0	6.8	0.9	1.0	6.9	1.4	1.5	6.3	–	–	–	3.3	3.6	6.9
Defence	1.3	0.9	1.7	–	–	4.4	–	–	0.0	–	–	–	1.3	0.9	1.7
Public order and safety	0.8	0.8	5.1	–	–	5.9	–	–	4.5	–	–	–	0.9	0.9	5.0
Education	3.7	3.9	6.4	1.6	1.7	6.2	0.7	0.7	6.1	–	–	–	4.4	4.6	6.4
Health	0.4	0.7	12.8	0.7	0.9	9.7	0.6	0.7	8.0	4.1	4.8	14.3	5.0	5.7	7.5
Social security and welfare	11.7	12.7	6.9	1.9	2.2	7.8	2.0	2.1	7.0	11.3	11.3	8.0	23.2	24.4	6.5
Housing and community amenity	–	–	1.5	0.1	0.2	10.1	0.3	0.3	8.4	–	–	–	0.3	0.3	6.7
Recreational, cultural and religious affairs	0.3	0.3	7.0	0.1	0.2	–	0.3	0.3	5.9	–	–	–	0.6	0.7	8.0
Economic services	2.7	2.6	5.5	0.8	0.7	4.2	0.4	0.4	-10.3	–	0.1	5.9	0.9	1.2	9.4
of which:															
Agriculture	0.9	0.8	4.6	0.2	0.2	5.6	–	–	–	–	–	–	1.0	0.9	4.9
Mining, manufacturing and construction, excluding fuel	0.3	0.5	13.1	0.2	0.2	4.0	–	–	6.9	–	–	–	0.9	1.2	9.4
Transport and communication	1.4	1.1	3.6	0.3	0.3	3.3	–	–	-14.1	–	0.1	13.3	1.5	1.3	3.8
Other economic affairs	0.1	0.1	8.1	–	–	4.4	–	–	9.7	–	–	13.3	0.2	0.2	7.2
Other functions[1]	2.8	3.9	10.1	0.3	0.2	-0.9	0.4	0.3	-1.1	–	–	38.2	3.5	4.3	8.5
Capital expenditure	**3.2**	**2.8**	**4.2**	**1.0**	**1.1**	**6.4**	–	–	–	**0.1**	**0.1**	**1.2**	**4.9**	**5.1**	**6.3**
Total expenditure	**28.9**	**30.7**	**6.6**	**7.4**	**8.0**	**6.8**	**6.0**	**6.2**	**6.2**	**15.6**	**16.4**	**6.5**	**51.2**	**54.2**	**6.6**
Total receipts[2]	**24.5**	**25.4**	**6.3**	**8.2**	**7.7**	**5.0**	**7.4**	**7.4**	**5.8**	**15.4**	**16.3**	**6.6**	**48.4**	**48.7**	**5.9**

1. Mainly current transfers (other than compensation of employees and subsidies) and property income.
2. Excluding transfers (other than compensation of employees and subsidies) and property income.
Source: OECD, *National Accounts.*

associated with the ageing of the baby-boom generation in the first half of the next century, since health costs rise sharply with age.

Pressures on health spending

Health expenditures have been growing significantly faster than GDP for the past few decades in most OECD countries. This reflects both an increasing per capita demand as countries and individuals become richer, and cost increases well in excess of general inflation. Price statistics need to be treated with a great deal of caution, because in respect of the health sector wage bill, national-accounts output is measured by manpower inputs. But allowing for this, the

Figure 10. **REAL HEALTH SPENDING**[1]

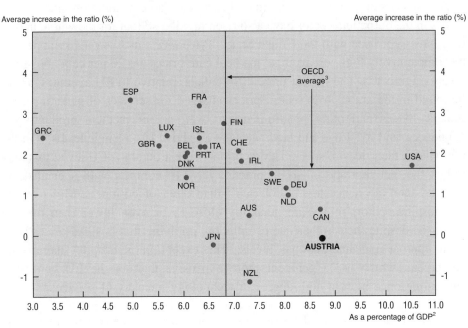

1. During 1960-1995 for Germany and Spain; 1960-1994 for Canada, France, Iceland, Switzerland and United States; 1970-1993 for Luxembourg; 1978-1993 for New Zealand; 1977-1993 for Portugal; for the remaining countries 1960-1993.
2. (Health spending/Health price index)/(GDP/GDP deflator).
3. Non weighted average.
Source: OECD Health Data 96.

63

relative level of *real* health spending (the amount of services performed in proportion to real GDP) in Austria has long been rather high: at 9 per cent of GDP over the past three and one-half decades, it has been the second highest after the United States and marginally above Canada (Figure 10). The average rate of growth in this share has been close to zero, the second lowest after New Zealand, consistent with an inverse relation between the level of spending and rate of growth observed for all countries except the United States. The main problem has thus been with the cost of providing health care.

Rising relative prices

The relative price of health care in Austria, as conventionally measured in the national accounts, has registered one of the fastest growth rates in the OECD (Figure 11). Most of this rise can in turn be traced to the hospital sector, where prices have risen two-and-a-half times faster than general inflation since 1970. Prices in the outpatient sector have also risen rapidly, so that for the whole period they have kept pace with the United States. Price *levels* in Austria also appear to be comparatively high: on average, medical care prices are 20 per cent above EU levels (Figure 12). The largest price differentials, relative to EU averages, are to be found in the ambulatory sector: prices charged for services of general practitioners, nurses and other practitioners, as well as for medical products and appliances, and for drugs and medicines are all above EU average levels.[5] On the other hand, the prices of specialist practitioners are around the EU level; this may reflect the fact that specialists in practice have to compete with specialists in hospitals and are hence less "protected" than other practitioners. Moreover, in the hospital sector, prices are generally close to or even lower than the EU averages, despite their higher rate of inflation, implying that hospital prices have been approaching international levels. The exception is hospital therapeutic equipment, which is 25 per cent more expensive than in the EU generally, suggesting once more a high degree of technology intensity of services.[6]

As a consequence of the steep rise in the relative price of health care, the *nominal* share of health spending has grown robustly, with major growth phases occurring in the 1960s and 1970s and again in the early 1990s, following a slowdown in the 1980s, in part reflecting limited reforms at that time (Table 11). Most other OECD countries experienced a progressive slowing of the nominal

Figure 11. **INTERNATIONAL TRENDS IN RELATIVE HEALTH CARE PRICES**

1970 = 100

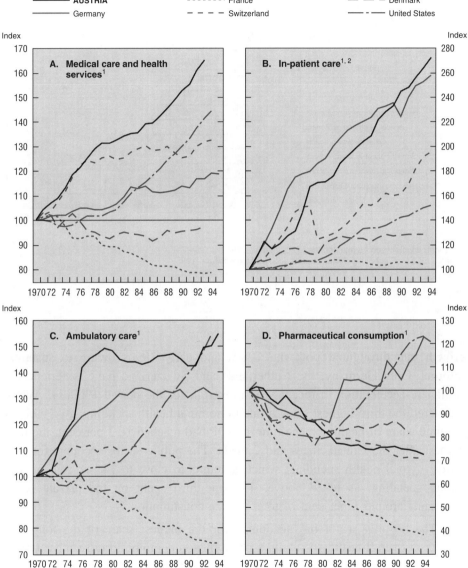

1. Deflator for health-expenditure deflator by the GDP deflator.
2. Data for Switzerland have been estimated by the OECD for the period prior to 1978.
Source: OECD Health Data 96.

Figure 12. **RELATIVE MARKET PRICE LEVELS**[1]

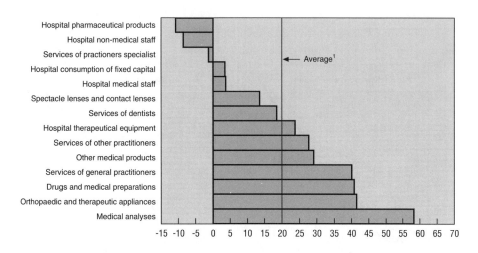

1. Difference between Austria and the EU countries in 1993.
Source: OECD, Purchasing Power Parities and Real Expenditure (1995).

growth rate throughout both the 1980s and early 1990s owing to sustained reforms. Only Germany, the Netherlands and Switzerland have experienced a similar re-acceleration in recent years. Overall, for the period 1960-94, Austria registered the third highest growth rate in nominal health spending. By 1995, the nominal share of health expenditure in GDP had reached 10.3 per cent, the third highest after the United States and Canada. The public sector accounts for two-thirds of total health spending, which amounts to close to 14 per cent of total public spending, as noted above. The one-third spent by the private sector represents around 8 per cent of total private consumption.

The hospital sector has accounted for the biggest share of the long-term growth in overall health spending, a phenomenon common to most other OECD countries (Figure 13). This has helped to boost the share of hospital care in overall current spending to almost a half, which is relatively high (Table 12). Including investment expenditures would probably make Austria's ranking even higher. As seen above, the rise in the hospital share reflects rapid price inflation

Table 11. **The growth of nominal health spending**

	Annual average growth (in excess of GDP)				As a percentage of GDP	
	1960-70	1970-80	1980-90	1990-1995[1]	1960[2]	1995[1]
Austria	**11.0**	**14.4**	**6.8**	**8.4**	**4.4**	**9.6**
United States	10.6	12.9	10.9	8.0	5.2	14.5
Japan	21.4	16.7	5.3	5.6	4.4	7.2
Germany	10.6	12.0	4.9	10.5	4.8	9.6
France	13.7	16.5	10.5	5.5	4.2	9.9
Italy	14.5	22.8	14.7	6.6	3.6	7.7
United Kingdom	8.7	18.8	9.7	7.9	3.9	6.9
Canada	11.3	13.7	10.5	4.0	5.5	9.5
Australia	10.2	17.8	11.8	5.6	4.9	8.4
New Zealand	9.2	18.7	12.5	4.5	4.3	7.5
Belgium	10.4	16.1	7.9	5.3	3.4	8.0
Denmark	17.0	13.5	7.3	4.4	3.6	6.5
Finland	15.2	16.9	12.7	1.8	3.9	8.2
Greece	14.8	19.9	22.4	20.9	2.4	5.2
Iceland	22.6	45.9	40.0	5.1	3.3	8.1
Ireland	13.7	25.3	7.7	7.1	3.8	7.9
Luxembourg	–	15.0	8.9	6.1	3.7	5.8
Netherlands	15.4	14.1	4.8	5.3	3.8	8.8
Norway	13.9	16.8	10.1	6.4	3.0	7.3
Portugal	–	31.0	22.5	14.5	2.8	7.6
Spain	24.9	24.3	15.0	9.0	1.5	7.6
Sweden	13.8	14.9	8.9	1.4	4.7	7.7
Switzerland	14.4	10.2	7.8	6.4	3.3	9.6
EU[2]	14.1	18.3	11.0	7.6	3.6	7.8
OECD[3]	14.2	18.6	11.9	7.0	3.8	8.2

1. 1994 for New Zealand, Greece, Ireland, Luxembourg, Norway, Portugal, Switzerland.
2. 1970 for Luxembourg and Portugal.
3. Unweighted average of available data.
Source: *OECD Health Data 96.*

while the above-average level reflects high volumes. By contrast, the share of out-patient care is the one of the lowest in the OECD and the share of pharmaceutical consumption is much below the European average, implying relatively low levels of real output and consumption in these sectors, as prices are well above European averages.

Macro-determinants: per capita income and population ageing

If a cross-country comparison is made of per capita health expenditures (converted at GDP purchasing power parity exchange rates), Austria's ranking

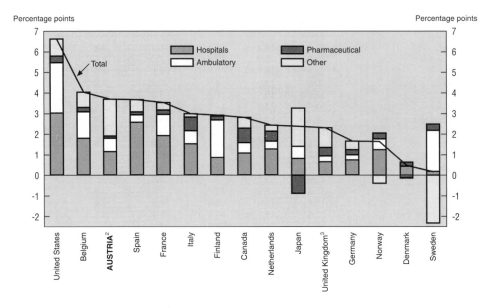

Figure 13. **DECOMPOSITION OF THE GROWTH IN HEALTH SPENDING**[1]

Change in percentage points of trend GDP over period

1. 1970-1993; current spending only. Except for Finland, United Kingdom and Sweden: 1970-1992; Japan and Spain: 1970-1991; Norway: 1970-1990.
2. Estimates of hospital costs taken from *Österreichische Ärtzekammer: Die Situation des Österreichischen Gesundheitssystems im Herbst 1995.* Revised data, based on national accounts, will be available at the end of 1996 and is expected to lead to some upward revision in hospital expenditures.
3. Hospital data for England only.
Source: OECD Health Data 96; OECD.

seems to be fully consistent with its level of GDP per capita, lying just above the fitted average correlation for the aggregate of the OECD countries (Figure 14). However, population ageing, which has not been a major factor pushing up the volume share of health spending over the last few decades, will become an important source of spending pressure for the future, as the number of elderly people increase sharply. As Figure 15 indicates, average hospital length of stay – an indication of potential cost pressures – rises markedly with age. For the OECD on average, after the age of sixty, health expenditures grow rapidly with age, and a broad rule of thumb is that persons aged over sixty together consume

Table 12. **The structure of expenditure on health**[1]

Share in total expenditure in per cent

	Latest year available	Hospital care[2]	Ambulatory care[3]	Pharmaceutical[4]
Austria	**1995**	**45.6**	**24.0**	**10.9**
United States	1994	43.3	32.4	8.3
Japan	1993	32.3	42.9	–
Germany	1993	31.3	26.9	18.9
France	1994	44.8	27.0	16.5
Italy	1995	47.7	30.1	18.1
United Kingdom	1993	42.9	–	15.3
Canada	1994	47.0	22.8	12.7
Australia	1993	43.5	27.2	11.0
Belgium	1994	36.0	36.5	17.5
Denmark	1994	60.9	21.1	11.1
Finland	1994	40.9	49.4	12.8
Greece	1992	59.2	–	23.5
Ireland	1994	56.9	–	11.5
Iceland	1995	67.6	23.6	15.8
Luxembourg	1994	32.1	52.1	15.6
Netherlands	1994	52.3	28.8	10.7
New Zealand	1993	59.1	6.9	17.0
Norway	1991	67.4	23.6	10.8
Portugal	1993	31.5	–	25.6
Spain	1993	48.7	11.4	18.2
Sweden	1993	52.8	–	12.5
Switzerland	1992	51.4	38.2	7.4
EU[5]		44.8	29.8	15.1
OECD[5]		46.6	28.5	13.3

1. Current spending only.
2. Total expenditure on in-patient care: current spending only. Public expenditure for Ireland, Portugal, and Sweden.
3. Total expenditure for all out-patient medical and paramedical services.
4. Total expenditure for the purchase of medical and paramedical services.
5. Unweighted average of available data.
Source: *OECD Health Data 96;* Österreichische Ärtzekammer, *Die Situation des österreichischen Gesundheitssystems im Herbst,* 1995.

roughly four times as much health care as those below. It has been estimated that, for the OECD as a whole, with unchanged policies and institutions, health care spending would rise by 0.4-0.7 per cent per annum between 2000 and 2020 due simply to ageing.[7] Thus an important incentive to health reform is to act early to forestall such a scenario, so that efficiency gains can help to absorb the extra burden from population ageing.

Figure 14. **HEALTH EXPENDITURE AND GDP PER CAPITA**[1]

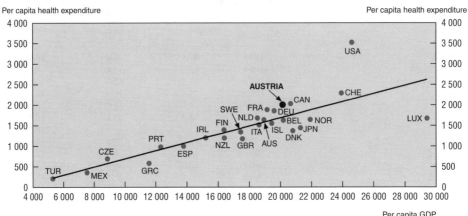

Per capita health expenditure

Figure 15. **AVERAGE IN-PATIENT DAYS BY AGE GROUP**

Social insurance data

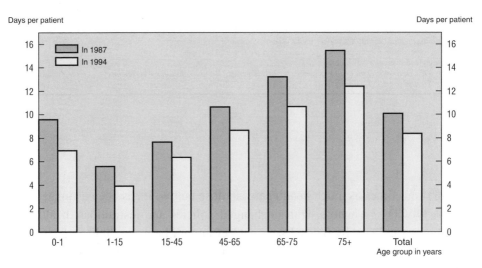

Source: Submission by Austrian authorities.

70

Efficiency aspects of the health market

High quality but at high cost

In general, the quality of health services is high in Austria and access to such services is universal. Infant mortality at 5.4 per 1 000 live births in 1995 is among the lowest in the OECD. Expectation of life at birth in 1995, though still below the OECD average, has risen to 80.1 years for women and 73.5 for men.[8] The best measure of health status, however, is normally taken to be "potential life years lost" (PLYL), which represents the shortening of life expectancy due to "avoidable" disease. Figure 16 shows that for both men and women, PLYL is significantly below the OECD average. Moreover, the improvement in PLYL for men was greater in Austria than in all other European and OECD countries during the time span 1960-1993 (Figure 17). Indicators for women also show that Austria was as successful in improving health outcomes as most other European countries. The gains in PLYL were associated with a marked increase in health costs, but these were not greatly different from other European countries where the PLYL outcome was less favourable.

Another important dimension of health care quality is that of equity. The Austrian system is, in general, highly equitable as everyone, regardless of income or employment status, has equal access to the health care system, with significant patient co-payments being required (up to a limit) only for pharmaceuticals, or for certain insured groups such as civil servants, self-employed and farmers. Contributions are geared to income (see Annex I) and since health care accounts for a far larger proportion of income of poorer households than of better-off households, the health care system performs an important redistributive function (Table 13). However, the absolute *level* of health spending per household rises with income, and in conjunction with an income ceiling on social health insurance contributions this means that the system becomes regressive beyond a certain point. Furthermore, evidence suggests that the right to choose one's treating doctor in hospital, which is made possible only by private insurance, allows for a level of personal attention often missing in public provision, even though by law the quality of care provided – which is nevertheless an ambiguous concept – should be the same. As private health insurance is heavily subsidised via the tax system but is generally only affordable by the better-off (one seventh of the population are covered, usually as an employer-provided fringe benefit), this has also added to regressivity.[9]

Figure 16. **HEALTH EXPENDITURES AND HEALTH OUTCOMES**

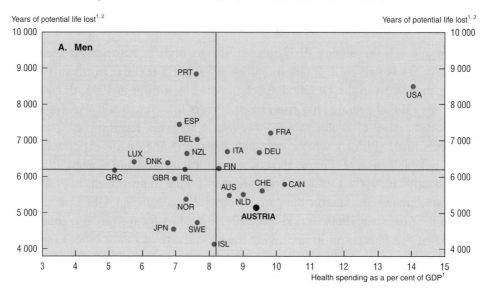

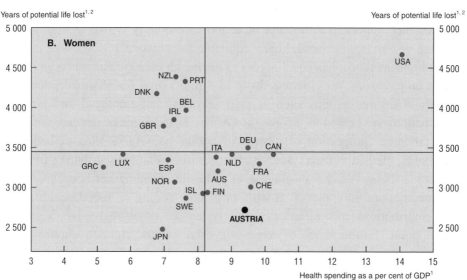

1. Latest year available in the 90s.
2. Rate per 100 000 male/female population, ages 0 to 64. These data, based on the "avoidable mortality" concept, provide a crude measure of premature mortality embracing both somatic and mental causes of death which could have been prevented if medical knowledge had been applied, if known public health principles had been in force, and if risky behavioural stances had not been so prevalent.
Source: OECD Health Data 96.

Figure 17. **CHANGES IN HEALTH EXPENDITURES AND IN HEALTH OUTCOMES**

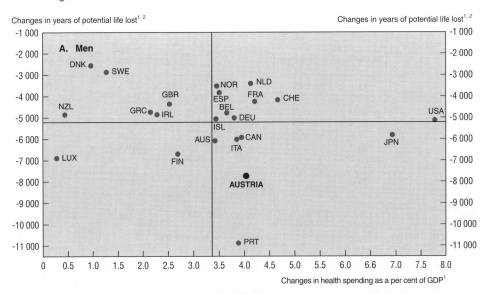

Changes in years of potential life lost[1,2]

Changes in years of potential life lost[1,2]

Changes in health spending as a per cent of GDP[1]

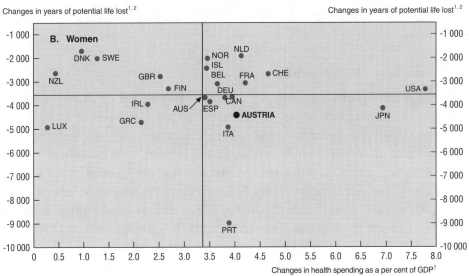

Changes in years of potential life lost[1,2]

Changes in years of potential life lost[1,2]

Changes in health spending as a per cent of GDP[1]

1. Between the end of the 60s and mid-90s.
2. Rate per 100 000 male/female population, ages 0 to 64. These data, based on the "avoidable mortality" concept, provide a crude measure of premature mortality embracing both somatic and mental causes of death which could have been prevented if medical knowledge had been applied, if known public health principles had been in force, and if risky behavioural stances had not been so prevalent.

Source: OECD Health Data 96.

Table 13. **Health spending by income level**[1]

Income deciles	Health spending levels		Spending shares		Social health insurance contributions	
	Per household (Sch thousand)	Total (Sch billion)	As per cent of total	As per cent of household income	Per head (Sch thousand)	Total (Sch billion)
1	15.5	3.9	6.4	28.9	2.5	0.9
2	18.0	4.7	7.7	13.4	4.6	1.7
3	21.0	4.8	7.9	11.0	7.1	3.1
4	23.8	5.9	9.7	9.8	8.3	4.5
5	24.5	6.2	10.0	8.3	9.8	8.3
6	26.0	6.5	10.6	7.4	10.8	6.9
7	26.7	6.6	10.8	6.3	11.9	8.3
8	27.6	6.9	11.3	3.5	12.7	9.4
9	29.6	7.3	12.0	4.6	13.8	10.9
10	33.4	8.3	13.6	3.5	15.3	13.8
Total	24.6	61.3	100.0	6.5	10.8	65.2

1.   In 1991, including pensioners and unemployed households; social insurance data.
Source: Guger, Alois, *Umverteilung durch öffentliche Haushalte in Österreich;* WIFO for the Federal Ministry of Finance, November 1995.

Incentives to over-provision

The social insurance system, which covers 84 per cent of all medical bills (the remainder being met by private insurance and patient co-payments[10]) suffers from the usual over-consumption risks of schemes where patients do not face the marginal cost of services. Moreover, in Austria patients have considerable freedom of choice, since they can change primary doctors (general practitioners) rather easily (subject to accessibility and the respective insurance scheme) and obtain from them liberal referrals to specialists and hospitals, often in other localities deemed to offer better services. Farmers, self-employed and civil servants face a co-payment of 20 per cent, but otherwise there is a general absence of patient deductibles or co-payments for the majority of treatments (Annex I). This generosity of coverage by the social health insurance system seems to exceed that of most other European countries, where the "gatekeeper" role exercised by general practitioners and stricter controls have limited access to hospital admission. Indeed, consumer choice is almost as extensive as that provided by private insurance systems of the United States and Switzerland.

The usual incentives also exist for doctors to over-provide services, since they are not bound by considerations of cost. Until January 1995, doctors were remunerated partially by a fee-for-service, which makes for "supply-induced demand": a situation where doctors maintain incomes by prescribing more services which third-party payers passively finance. Since January 1995 doctors' honoraria are increasingly based on flat per-patient fees (a quarterly lump sum based on the number of patients who have been consulted) as opposed to fee-for-

Table 14. **Practising physicians per capita**

	Average growth		Doctors per 1 000 population 1994[3]	Physician visits per capita per year 1994[3]	Proportion of specialists 1994[3]
	1970-80[1]	1980-94[2]			
Austria	**1.9**	**3.2**	**2.6**	**6.2**	**52.6**
United States	2.5	1.8	2.5	5.9	50.9
Japan	1.6	2.3	1.8	16.3	..
Germany	3.3	3.1	3.3	12.8	54.1
France	4.5	2.4	2.8	6.3	49.6
Italy	4.4	2.7	1.7	11.0	..
United Kingdom	2.6	0.9	1.5	5.8	..
Canada	2.1	1.3	2.2	6.9	40.9
Australia	3.6	2.1	2.2	10.6	34.4
Belgium	4.1	3.6	3.7	8.0	40.5
Denmark	4.5	1.8	2.9	4.8	..
Finland	6.4	2.9	2.7	4.0	57.0
Greece	4.1	3.6	4.0	5.3	55.7
Iceland	4.1	2.5	3.0	4.8	..
Ireland	1.1	1.4	2.0	6.6	..
Luxembourg	4.2	2.4	2.2	..	62.7
Netherlands	4.3	2.8	2.5	5.7	33.3
New Zealand	3.8	1.6	2.0	3.8	30.4
Norway	3.6	4.4	3.2	3.8	4.2
Portugal	7.4	2.2	2.9	3.2	58.0
Spain	5.6	3.0	4.1	6.2	..
Sweden	5.3	2.2	3.0	3.0	68.2
Switzerland	5.1	1.7	3.1	11.0	34.8
Turkey	4.6	4.2	1.1	1.2	41.9
EU[4]	4.2	2.5	2.7	6.1	52.4
OECD[4]	3.9	2.5	2.5	6.1	47.5

1. United Kingdom 1979-80; Australia 1971-80; Belgium, Ireland 1971-80.
2. United States, United Kingdom, Luxembourg, Norway, Spain 1980-93; Italy 1980-92; Australia 1980-91; Netherlands 1980-90.
3. Or nearest year available.
4. Unweighted average.
Source: OECD Health Data 96.

75

Table 15. **Pharmaceutical costs**

Social insurance data

	Spending		Number of prescriptions	Number of prescriptions per insured	Costs per insured	Costs per prescription	Memorandum item: CPI
	1 000 Sch	Index					
1975	3 571	100	81 513	17.7	776	44	100
1980	5 572	156	73 464	15.3	1 161	76	129
1985	6 966	195	72 339	14.9	1 437	96	164
1990	9 845	276	81 147	15.9	1 934	121	183
1991	10 824	303	84 497	16.3	2 086	128	189
1992	12 074	338	88 384	16.8	2 290	136	196
1993	13 260	371	90 437	17.0	2 496	147	203

Source: Association of Austrian Insurers (1994), *Gesundheitswesen in Österreich,* Summer.

service. This system serves to lower incentives for the excess provision of medical services as a whole, but may actually increase incentives to shift care into the in-patient sector by making excessive hospital referrals. The health funds have deliberately restricted the number of doctors so as to control "over-supply": in comparison with the European average, the number of medical practitioners is relatively low, indicating barriers to entry (Table 14).[11] But offsetting the benefits of a smaller number of doctors, the price of out-patient services is, as noted, correspondingly higher (Figure 12 above).

As regards medicines, Austria has also not been exempt from the phenomenon of 'supply-induced demand', insofar as the number of prescriptions per insured has tended to grow, after declining sharply over the decade of the 1970s. Costs per prescription have also grown faster than the CPI (Table 15). But again, Austrian pharmaceuticals consumption is not high in international terms (Table 12 above), since there are insurance controls over spending and tight regulatory control over drug approvals.

Hospital over-supply

The relative expansion of health care in Austria relates chiefly to hospitals, as evidenced by the fact that public health investment as a share of GDP is one of the highest in the OECD and has been on a strong upward trend since 1989 (Figure 18). Such growth results in a rising technology intensity of services, as capacity expansion has occurred in the form of both modernised buildings and

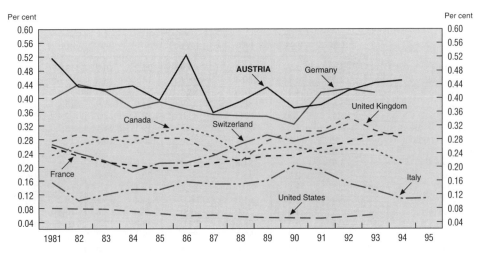

Figure 18. **PUBLIC HEALTH INVESTMENT**
As a percentage of GDP

Source: OECD Health Data 96.

the acquisition of modern medical equipment. Because the latter is so costly, it is a strong source of spending pressure not only at the point of investment but also in subsequent operating costs related to its use (indeed a way of amortising the investment).

Whereas the average length of hospital stay has been cut in half since 1970, more than in many other countries of the OECD – largely due to advances in medical knowledge as well as changed attitudes – the rate of hospital admissions has risen markedly in Austria and is now (after Iceland) the highest in the OECD by a wide margin (Table 16). Moreover, labour costs, which represent about two-thirds of hospital expenditure, have risen sharply, with an increased number of doctors per bed (Table 17). At the same time, there is indirect evidence of some unnecessary duplication of capital equipment in neighbouring hospitals, and Austria has afforded itself of machines other countries have rejected as too expensive.[12] More generally, however, weak accounting practices among both hospitals and local authorities make it difficult both to estimate and to control hospital costs in relation to the services delivered (*i.e.* cost effectiveness).

Table 16. **Hospital capacity and utilisation**

	Beds for 10 000 inhabitants		Average bed occupancy (per cent)		Average length of hospital stay[1]		Admission rate of population (per cent)	
	1970[2]	1994[2]	1970[2]	1994[2]	1970[2]	1994[2]	1970[2]	1994[2]
Austria	**3.4**	**2.7**	**86.4**	**80.0**	**22.2**	**10.3**	**15.5**	**26.5**
United States	2.3	1.1	80.3	68.7	14.9	8.8	15.5	13.0
Japan	3.0	4.1	81.6	83.1	55.3	45.4	5.4	8.9
Germany	3.6	3.2	88.5	83.9	24.9	13.9	15.4	19.9
France	3.4	2.8	83.2	83.0	18.3	11.7	7.4	22.8
Italy	3.0	1.8	77.9	72.5	19.1	11.1	15.7	16.0
United Kingdom	2.9	1.9	82.1	80.6	25.7	10.2	10.9	21.6
Canada	2.0	2.0	80.4	83.6	11.5	12.6	16.5	12.5
Australia	3.5	2.5	81.8	77.1	15.0	10.0	21.5	25.5
Belgium	2.3	2.4	85.7	83.5	20.7	12.0	9.3	19.8
Denmark	2.6	1.6	80.6	83.8	18.1	7.5	14.4	20.4
Finland	5.0	3.1	91.0	90.3	24.4	13.1	18.2	25.1
Greece	1.6	1.3	76.0	71.0	15.0	8.8	10.5	13.5
Iceland	4.6	4.7	98.3	84.0	28.3	17.8	16.4	15.4
Ireland	3.1	2.7	80.1	77.0	13.3	7.7	12.4	28.0
Luxembourg	3.6	3.3	82.6	81.4	27.0	16.5	13.4	20.5
Netherlands	3.8	3.7	90.9	88.6	38.2	32.8	10.0	11.2
New Zealand	3.0	1.6	57.3	57.3	16.1	7.7	9.3	12.5
Norway	2.8	4.6	83.1	84.5	21.0	9.1	13.2	16.5
Portugal	1.6	1.1	74.1	68.7	23.8	9.5	6.9	11.5
Spain	1.3	1.1	69.0	77.0	18.0	11.5	7.1	10.0
Sweden	4.5	1.5	83.6	82.2	27.2	8.2	16.6	19.0
Switzerland	3.4	2.8	84.6	82.6	26.0	25.2	13.1	15.0
EU[3]	3.0	2.3	82.1	80.0	22.4	12.9	12.2	18.2
OECD[3]	3.1	2.5	81.7	79.5	22.8	14.7	12.8	17.3

1. Average patient days per admission in in-patient care institutions.
2. Or nearest year available.
3. Unweighted average.
Source: OECD Health Data 96.

Table 17. **Hospital costs**
Index 1980 = 100

	1970	1990	1993	1994
Cost per in-patient day	27	241	310	320
Number of doctors per bed	65	136	164	172
Total hospital personnel per bed	65	143	169	180
Memorandum items:				
Overall economy wage index (*Tariflohnindex*)	42	162	192	198
CPI	54	141	157	162

Source: Statistical Yearbook, 1995; WIFO; OECD.

Problems with the institutional setting

The state as a residual source of financing

The above-described imbalances in the provision of health care services, both as to the matching of demand to available resources and as between in-patient and ambulatory care, to a large extent reflect behavioural responses to the incentives created by the country's institutions. Austria follows the *social insurance model,* which is, in principle, similar to the systems operating in Germany, France, the Netherlands, Japan, and Switzerland.[13] This model, described more fully in Annex I, is characterised by compulsory universal coverage, financed by employers and employees through non-profit, public sector insurance funds; with health care services being provided by a mix of public and private entities, and with principal reliance being placed on public hospitals and physicians in private practice, there is a general problem of allocating resources in the absence of price signals and effective budget constraints.[14] However, the Austrian model is distinguished from the mainstream social insurance model by virtue of the open-ended nature of its hospital financing, which tends to exacerbate the problem of budgetary discipline. Contribution rates are low by international standards,[15] and are determined by the legislature after the public health funds submit their proposed budgets. Contributions do not fully cover hospital costs so that the governments – mainly the Länder and the local governments which are the main owners of the hospitals – must assume liability for health fund deficits in the form of a guarantee. The health funds cover only a portion of health costs and until recently they have tended to run small surpluses, but in 1995 the funds incurred deficits which are projected to increase further. The structure of the system reflects a fundamental policy dilemma insofar as contributions are generally viewed as an important element in non-wage labour costs; using contributions as the marginal source of finance for what should, in principle, be insurance and contribution-based spending is thus unattractive in the short run. But the ultimate use of general taxation to cover deficits creates the danger of further distorting budgetary incentives by detaching revenue constraints from spending decisions.

Hospital financing

There are six types of hospitals – general medicine, specialist, convalescent homes, long-term care institutions, maternity homes, and sanatoriums (Table 18).

Table 18. **The distribution of hospital capacity by type and owner**[1]

	Number of hospitals	Number of beds	Number of beds, per cent
By type			
General hospitals	133	53 608	67.1
Specialist hospitals	99	18 924	23.7
Convalescent homes	10	689	0.9
Long-term care institutions	36	3 547	4.4
Maternity homes	5	52	0.1
Sanatoria	40	3 104	3.9
Total	323	79 924	100.0
By owner			
Bund	12	688	0.9
Länder	89	43 815	54.8
Communes[2]	67	12 062	15.1
Social insurance funds	42	6 222	7.9
Religious orders	52	12 486	15.6
Associations	12	1 208	1.5
Private persons	49	3 443	4.3
Total	323	79 924	100.0

1.   1992.
2.   Includes an association of all communes in Niederösterreich, Tirol and Vorarlberg (10 hospitals and 2 260 beds).
Source: Association of Austrian Insurers (1994), *Gesundheitswesen in Österreich*, Summer.

Of the 80 000 available hospital beds, the Länder supply over half and the overall public sector almost 80 per cent, while religious orders own around three-quarters of all private beds. About one-quarter of the beds in public and private non-profit hospitals are in the "special class" covered by private insurance. The availability of beds varies across regions, from 6.5 beds per 1 000 inhabitants in Burgenland to 10.9 in Styria. While the number of beds per head of population is high by international standards, so is the occupancy rate.

Investment spending

The financing of investment expenditures has been covered to a considerable extent by special investment and structural subsidies from the Hospital Co-operation Fund *Krankenanstaltenzusammenarbeitsfonds* (KRAZAF) the remainder being financed by federal, Länder and local governments. The hospital co-operation fund was established in 1978 in an attempt to harness more public funds to hospital financing while controlling hospital costs and promoting a better regional allocation of funds. The intention was also to exert control over hospital investments through a national co-ordinated plan: KRAZAF approval has been needed for all investment projects. The financial resources of the fund were provided (in decreasing order of importance) by the social insurance funds, the federal, state, and local governments, and own equity revenues. Altogether, roughly 50 per cent of its budget was used to subsidise hospital investment spending, restructuring and training. The other half went to cover hospital operating deficits (*Betriebsabgang*), *i.e.* operating and maintenance costs less normal sources of revenue (patient co-payments and insurance reimbursements).

The failure to control hospital costs – and indeed investment, another major feature of the fund's original mandate – derived from the constitution of the KRAZAF, and in particular its voting structure. The nine Länder each had one vote, the two local government associations each one vote, the federal government ten votes, and the social insurance funds only two votes, despite providing almost two-thirds of the financing (the Austrian bishops' conference also had one vote but the association of private insurers, though represented, did not have a vote). Decisions have had to be unanimous. In the event of no unanimity, a complex process had to be started which could last 2-3 years. The decision-making procedure was thus not conducive to making difficult decisions about politically sensitive investment projects. As a result, the KRAZAF was not able to carry out its mandate to achieve an appropriate regional distribution of expensive technical equipment.

Operating deficits

The system of financing hospital operating costs has been based on the principle that the maintenance and renovation of hospitals is the responsibility of the hospital owner (often ultimately a state or commune), while current costs should be mainly covered by the social and private insurers and (minor) patient co-payments. For outpatient services, the hospitals charge an ambulatory fee (*Ambulanzgebühr*), usually a flat charge fully payable by social insurance (and hence equivalent to payment to doctors in ambulatory care). For in-patient care, up until the most recent reforms (below), the system has been based on a standard daily charge (*Pflegegebühr*), regardless of the actual costs of the treatment. The daily charges of public and private non-profit hospitals are governed by the national Hospital Law (*KAG*), which requires that charges be set so as to cover only current operating costs.[16] The estimated daily charges must then be submitted by the hospital owners to the state government, which in most cases then set the hospital charges *below* this cost-covering level.[17] Moreover, the public health funds pay only part of this standard daily rate (*Pflegegebührensatz*) – currently only about 40 per cent (down from 60 per cent in the mid-1970s) – so that they may break even financially at the current contribution rate and thereby avoid increases which could ultimately rebound negatively on labour costs.

The gap between the per-day standard costs and the social insurers' coverage of these costs has been met (at least in part) by transfers from the Hospital Co-operation Fund. Such financing is limited to publicly-owned general and specialist hospitals, and non-profit private hospitals. Private insurance has also helped to subsidise a part of the hospital financing gap by routinely being billed a surcharge (*Zuschlag*) for service in the "special class" not justified by the extra amenities being offered. As a result, private insurers' expenditures have tended to grow in line with hospital deficits without any matching increase in the provision of health care. Since private insurance premia have been heavily tax-subsidised, this implied a non-transparent cross-subsidisation of hospital deficits not only by the privately insured customer but also by the general taxpayer.

Since the overall financing by the public health funds has been tied to their own contributions receipts, while the revenues of the KRAZAF were in effect tied both to VAT revenue and social security contributions,[18] the deficit of the hospital sector tended to be a growing residual (Table 19). This final *residual* hospital deficit is, in the case of public hospitals, by law the immediate responsibility of the territorial authority to which the hospital belongs and the ultimate responsibility of the appropriate state, but practices vary by state and the burden has normally been shared among legal owner, state and local government (Table 20).

The consequences of the above financing arrangements have been twofold. In the first place, public hospitals controlled at the community level have had little incentive to evaluate the costs of particular services, as only a global average has been required, making cost control all the more difficult: efficient micro management would require a knowledge of the relative costs of different treatments. Similarly, hospitals have not been required to maintain proper accounting procedures for capital charges, and in effect depreciate capital immediately upon purchase. (Private hospitals, having access only to their own funds, are in contrast to the public hospitals more committed to efficient hospital

Table 19. Revenue sources of hospitals[1]

Billion schillings

	1992	1993	1994
Social insurance funds	33.3	35.7	38.1
Per-day reimbursements	23.0	24.8	26.7
KFA	1.0	1.1	1.1
Transfers via KRAZAF	9.3	9.8	10.3
Private insurance funds	3.6	3.8	4.1
Federal government	4.6	4.9	3.9
Subsidies to teaching hospitals [1]	1.8	2.1	0.9
Transfers via KRAZAF	2.8	2.8	3.0
State and local governments	20.2	24.0	30.0
Transfers via KRAZAF	2.8	2.8	2.9
Pension payments	3.9	4.0	4.1
Transfers to cover deficits	13.6	17.2	22.9
Other	5.9	6.2	6.5
Total revenues	67.6	74.7	82.6

1.   Amounts may not equal corresponding financing entries in Tables 11, 12, and 13.
Source: Ministry of Finance.

Table 20. Deficit coverage of public hospitals by *Land*[1]

	Per cent of deficit covered by:		
	Land	*Gemeinden*	Legal owner[2]
Burgenland	80	10	10
Kärnten			
Land hospitals	30	30	40
Other public	93 [3]	..	7
Niederösterreich	40	60	..
Oberösterreich	43	40	17
Salzburg	48	32	20 [3]
Steiermark	100	..	..
Tirol [4]	25	35	40
Vorarlberg	40	40	20
Vienna	..	50	50 [5]

1.   31 December 1994.
2.   *Bund, Land, Gemeinden,* or social security institutions.
3.   Minus KRAZAF.
4.   Exceptions: LKH Innsbruck and LKH Hochzirl, covered by special rules.
5.   Except for one hospital which is owned by the social security funds, all public hospitals in Vienna are owned by the city
     of Vienna. The city and *Land* of Vienna have a single budget.
Source: Association of Austrian Insurers (1994), *Gesundheitswesen in Österreich,* Summer.

management.) And second, at the same time as the system has tended to lead to over-supply in the hospital sector, via inadequate cost control, it seems to have significantly distorted the choice between in-patient and ambulatory care. The costs of ambulatory care are borne by the health insurance funds (Annex Table A1), who thus face a payment schedule whereby the reimbursement of hospital in-patient services at the margin are far cheaper than non-hospital services. This creates an incentive to shift care from the ambulatory to the in-patient sector.

Effects of the federal fiscal structure

The federal structure of the fiscal system further weakens spending accountability at the Länder level – and also to some extent at the local government level – since it is not matched by the need to raise own revenues. The Länder are responsible for any residual hospital deficit after transfers from the hospital financing fund, but have an agreed share for several years of federal tax receipts via the tax-sharing process. In combination with their tendency in the past to run small surpluses, this has weakened incentives to cost control. Figure 19 compares the breakdown of financing with that of other federal systems, some with public health funds (Germany, Switzerland), and others relying solely on general taxation or the private sector to fund health care (United States and Canada). It can be seen that territorial authorities, mainly at the state and local levels, assume an intermediate-level financing share in Austria, while the share of the federal government is quite large in comparison with other federal countries following the social insurance model. Thus Austria has in reality a mixed system for hospitals, whereby social security contributions are augmented by general taxation in the funding of health care.

Within this framework, pressures to overspend are exacerbated by the fact that the competence for health care policy is divided between the federal and state authorities in a manner determined by the constitution. The federal government (*Bund*) is responsible for formulating the basic law (*Grundsatzgesetzgebung*), while the states (*Länder*) are charged with the execution of health policy. In addition to taking responsibility for any financial deficit generated by the hospital sector, the states' powers and responsibilities include the regulation of doctors' services and the establishment and equipment of Länder- and community-owned hospitals.

84

Figure 19. **HEALTH EXPENDITURE BY FINAL PAYER**

Per cent

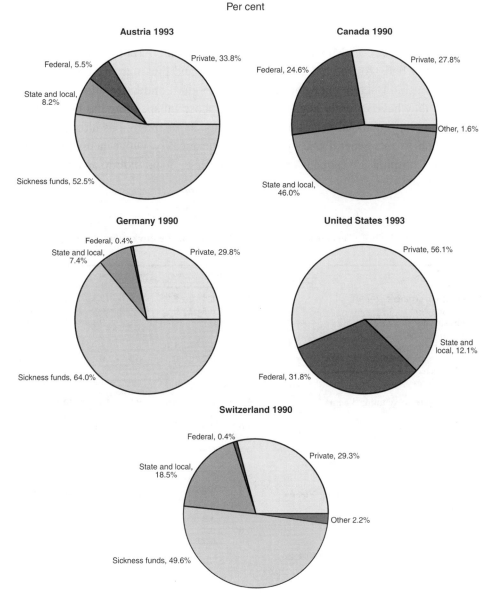

Austria 1993

Federal, 5.5%

State and local, 8.2%

Private, 33.8%

Sickness funds, 52.5%

Canada 1990

Private, 27.8%

Federal, 24.6%

Other, 1.6%

State and local, 46.0%

Germany 1990

Federal, 0.4%

State and local, 7.4%

Private, 29.8%

Sickness funds, 64.0%

United States 1993

Private, 56.1%

State and local, 12.1%

Federal, 31.8%

Switzerland 1990

Federal, 0.4%

State and local, 18.5%

Private, 29.3%

Other 2.2%

Sickness funds, 49.6%

Source: Austrian Ministry of Finance; Canadian Ministry of Health and Welfare; US Congressional Budget Office; *Statistical Yearbook* of Switzerland; *Statistisches Bundesamt*; OECD, *OECD Health Data 96*.

The Federal Ministry of Health is severely limited in its ability to exercise control over health care policy, given the devolution of executive powers to the states and its lack of a central instrument of control over the health insurance system. (The Federal Ministry of Labour and Social Affairs functions as the supervisory body for the health insurance funds and thus may have more potential influence on health care policy.) Moreover, the Länder are allowed to incur debt, as they have recently begun to do. Thus, hospital spending has been subject to few binding financial or political constraints, as financing has ultimately been passed on to the general taxpayer outside the locality which actually benefits from the hospital investment. At the same time, local politicians view such

Table 21. **Territorial authorities' financing of health expenditure**

Billion schillings

	1988	1989	1990	1991	1992	1993	1994
Federal government (*Bund*)	**7.9**	**8.4**	**8.9**	**10.0**	**10.5**	**11.7**	**12.1**
Consumption	0.8	0.8	0.9	0.6	0.6	0.7	0.9
Investments	0.1	0.1	0.1	0.1	0.1	0.1	0.1
Transfers to KRAZAF	2.3	2.4	2.5	2.7	2.8	2.9	3.0
Transfers to hospitals	4.6	4.9	5.1	6.3	6.6	7.3	7.6
Transfers to households and other	0.2	0.2	0.3	0.3	0.4	0.7	0.6
Total as percentage of overall *Bund* expenditures	1.6	1.6	1.6	1.6	1.6	..	..
States (*Länder*), excluding Vienna	**5.7**	**6.0**	**6.8**	**9.0**	**10.0**	**10.5**	**10.9**
Consumption	4.6	4.8	5.6	6.7	8.1	8.7	8.9
Investments	1.6	2.0	2.3	2.6	3.0	3.8	4.2
Transfers to KRAZAF	0.7	0.8	0.8	1.8	1.3	1.3	1.5
Transfers to households	0.4	0.4	0.4	0.4	0.5	0.5	0.6
Total as percentage of overall *Länder* expenditures	4.1	4.2	4.5	5.5	5.5	..	..
Communes (*Gemeinden*), including Vienna	**8.8**	**9.5**	**10.4**	**12.9**	**13.9**	**16.5**	**17.6**
Consumption	5.2	5.3	6.0	7.2	8.4	10.8	11.8
Investments	2.7	3.2	3.2	3.5	3.7	3.8	3.8
Transfers to KRAZAF	0.6	0.7	0.7	1.7	1.1	1.1	1.2
Transfers to households	0.3	0.4	0.5	0.5	0.7	0.7	0.8
Total as percentage of overall *Gemeinden* expenditures	5.1	5.2	5.5	6.2	6.0	..	..
Memorandum item:							
Total public sector[1]	98.3	104.4	112.3	127.5	143.5	153.7	162.9
As a percentage of overall expenditures	12.5	12.8	12.8	13.3	13.9	13.8	13.9

1. Sum of total territorial authorities and social insurance funds shown in Table 11.
Source: Ministry of Finance.

spending as being popular with the electorate, boosting the local economy and creating jobs. Health spending at the state and local levels has thus grown sharply, especially since 1990 (Table 21). Direct health spending by the federal government has also risen strongly, reflecting in part transfers to Vienna hospitals as well as special payments to university teaching hospitals, mainly for teaching staff salaries and equipment.[19]

Physicians, pharmaceuticals and the need for competition

Physicians are covered by differing arrangements depending on whether they are practising in the ambulatory or hospital sector. For those outside the hospital sector, the health funds can and do exercise cost control given more effective contract relations between themselves and practitioners. Nevertheless, for physicians in general, as well as for the supply of pharmaceuticals, there is a need for managed competition.

Regulations governing general practices

Restricted entry

Working under a contract with a health insurance fund is a necessity for most practitioners. General practitioners are more likely to have contracts than are specialists: 70 per cent in the former group but only 50 per cent in the latter. The reason for this difference is that the health insurance funds extend their contracts to doctors on the basis of a "location plan" drawn up in negotiation with the regional doctors' chambers, which specifies the number of contract doctors in each geographical location. The number of contracts given to doctors in private practice might in fact be too restricted. The highly influential doctors' chambers, which represent doctors in negotiations with the social funds over contracts and fees and influence legislation governing regulations, may also have an interest in restricting entry in order to maximise doctors' incomes. Since there is much greater competition from hospitals for specialists, the latter are usually more free to choose the location they prefer and to practise independently of an insurance contract. Thus, the distribution of practising doctors remains uneven across the regions – ranging from 1 doctor per 800 inhabitants in rural areas such as Upper Austria to 1 per 320 in Vienna,[20] with the specialist imbalance being even more severe. There has been scarcely any change in this situation in the last two decades, though the number of practising physicians has nearly tripled and the proportion of specialists has grown. One reason is that the number of additional contract posts was fixed until 1989 at only 2.2 per cent per year, and set by a decentralised annual bargaining process thereafter at around 1 per cent per annum. There has been an accompanying trend, especially among physicians practising alternative medicine, to give up their contracts in order to enter independent private practice.

The overwhelming form of delivery of practising doctors' services is individual practice. The doctors' law (*Ärztegesetz*) does not allow the sharing of personnel across individual practices, though surgery rooms and apparatus in a centralised location can be shared. Since 1991, new forms of organisation of doctors ' practices have been allowed within the context of the law on business associations (*Erwerbgesellschaftengesetz*), as it is now permissible for doctors to establish businesses, with the condition that the personal responsibility of each doctor is guaranteed and they exercise their profession in a personal and direct way. This latter condition has in effect blocked most types of group practice, with the exception of day clinics which are under the leadership of one doctor for whom other specialists work as subordinates. These restrictions, which will be lifted in 1997 as a result of a ruling by the Constitutional Court, reinforced by the opposition of both the health funds and doctors' chambers, have prevented the development of more flexible forms of delivery of ambulatory medical services that could substitute for treatments currently performed in hospitals, for instance by offering night and weekend service. There is also a strict dividing line between hospital physicians and practising physicians, as the latter are not normally able to "follow" their patients to hospitals in order to participate in the provision of care, leading to an inefficient lack of co-operation.

Roughly half of all doctors are practising physicians, of whom in turn around 60 per cent are specialists. The other half of the doctor population are exclusively salary-earners in hospitals, of which half in turn are hospital interns and the other half mostly specialists.[21] There has been a clear tendency toward more and more specialists, now comprising 45 per cent of the total doctor population, compared with 32 per cent in 1955. Since 1974 there has been a "surplus" of several hundred newly-qualified doctors each year, most wanting to go into specialist practice. This has been reflected in a lack of sufficient training places in hospitals; half of all interns are now more than 30 years old due to longer waiting periods for positions.[22]

Incentive effects of the remuneration system

Doctors in hospitals are generally paid according to the agreement reached between themselves and the owner of the hospital. For public and private non-profit hospitals, the earnings of doctor employees arise from their salaries, on the one hand, and from their share of fees from patients in the special class and for out-patient fees, on the other. Public hospitals must follow guidelines in the Länder laws which set up a system of basic pay and supplements. Doctors in public hospitals have in general the status of civil servants and thus have the same rights to job security, pensions, etc. However, fees charged for patients in the special class and in outpatient clinics are a very important means of supplementing hospital doctors' salaries, in return for the free choice of treating doctor by the patient (Annex I). This, in turn, has brought attempts to regulate such payments. The relevant Länder rules vary, with payments going either to the treating doctor, or more often to the head of department, who then may keep the fees or share them with the staff. Most heads of departments draw very large incomes in this way. In some Länder, a certain percentage of the fees also flows to the hospital owners in return for use of their facilities.

For practising physicians, the basis of honoraria for services is the general agreement (*Gesamtvertrag*) that is concluded between the *Hauptverband* of the social security institutions (Annex I) and the regional doctors' chambers. Yearly increases, in principle, follow developments in the general wage index, allowing for a measure of cost control. Individual contracts are then drawn up between individual doctors and (one or more) social insurance funds, which adhere quite closely to the conditions laid down in the general agreement. The contract doctor is paid for his services by the "health fund cheque principle" – a voucher is provided by employers to employees as a proof of entitlement and this serves as the basis for the settlement of the doctor's honorarium with the social insurance carrier. Non-contract doctors are paid by the patient directly, who in turn presents the bill (*Honorarnote*) to their insurer for reimbursement up to the contractual fee level, though this has been limited to 80 per cent of the fee since 1996. Private patients also pre-pay the doctor, and are then reimbursed by the private insurance which in turn obtains a reimbursement from the social insurance up to the contract level.

While the basic law stipulates a pure fee-for service system, on the basis of an amendment to the General Social Insurance Law (ASVG) most health insurance agencies have introduced a mixed fee-payment system according to which a flat payment per patient is combined with fees for individual services. Flat payments in turn account for roughly half of the fees of generalists and about one-third of those for specialists, although reimbursement systems vary widely among Länder (most health funds are regionally based). In some Länder, there is a declining fee-for-service scale as the number of vouchers presented by the physician per quarter rises. Though designed to discourage excessive provision of services, the high proportion of flat payments and declining remuneration of services may induce doctors to refer many cases to hospital – adding to doctors' high-risk aversion, their desire for more leisure time, and lack of co-operation between doctors and hospitals as other commonly cited reasons for excessive referrals.[23] The social insurers have done nothing to penalise such practices.

Pharmaceuticals market

A significant part of the pharmaceutical industry, in particular biotechnology, belongs to the acknowledged high-tech sectors, with productivity-enhancing spillovers into other economic sectors notably chemicals, food processing, and agriculture. While output and employment shares are relatively small (2 per cent of overall economy GDP and 1½ per cent of employment), they have doubled since 1980. Profit margins have been high – 41 per cent gross profit ratio against 31 per cent in industry overall – and this gap has grown steadily since 1980, reflecting relatively high productivity and a high investment ratio in this sector. It is also a very open sector, with exports and imports accounting for roughly 80 per cent of output and consumption respectively. However, as consumption exceeds production, imports exceed exports by about one-quarter, though down from a 40 per cent dependency ratio in 1980. At the same time, exports have become more and more specialised, as the bulk is accounted for by just *Glykosiden* (40 per cent) and antibiotics and antibiotic products (33 per cent). Around 60 firms, mostly offshoots of multinationals, supply the Austrian market.

Regulation of distribution

Unlike other components of medical spending, pharmaceutical prices are under the full authority and control of the central government: the market for pharmaceuticals is heavily regulated. Regulations (*Gewerbeordnung* and *Arzneimittelgesetz*) make the production of pharmaceuticals and drugs subject to the granting of a special allowance. Pharmaceutical companies who manufacture their products abroad and maintain only a "depot" in Austria for sales also need to acquire a licence for these depots.[24] Before a new drug can be marketed, it must be approved through a rigorous testing procedure. Generics are only approved when they have exactly the same characteristics as the parent drug. The drug must then be classified as requiring a prescription for purchase, or not. The share of medicines requiring prescriptions is high in international terms: 85 per cent, compared with 34 per cent in the United Kingdom, 45 per cent in Germany, 55 per cent in France, and 50 per cent for Switzerland (values for 1986). This share has not diminished through time (Figure 20). The medicine must then be

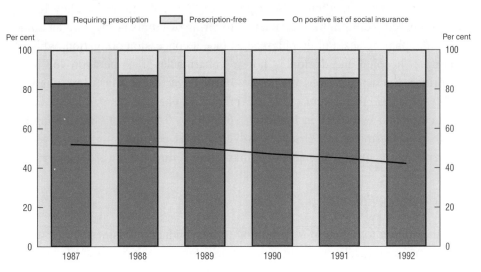

Figure 20. **THE SHARES OF REGULATED PHARMACEUTICALS**

Source: Jorg, L., K. Bayer and G. Hutschenreiter (1995).

91

put on the register of approved drugs (*Heilmittelverzeichnis*) in order to be routinely reimbursed by the social insurance funds; this necessitates a decision by the federation of health insurers (*Hauptverband*) after an application by the manufacturer or other interested party.[25] In 1992, only about 42 per cent of all registered medicines were on the positive list of the social insurance funds, compared with close to 50 per cent in 1980. Of the commercially available products, 64 per cent were on the positive list.

Wholesale trade in drugs and pharmaceuticals is a business activity requiring a licence, regulated in the context of the *Gewerbeordnung*.[26] The medicines law (*Arzneimittelgesetz*) further regulates allowable activities, granting the full range of wholesale functions (in particular, the range of products allowed in stockrooms) to only a handful of firms. Until January 1995 the so-called "Pharmig-Cartell", formed by the registered pharmacies and producers, exclusively controlled the required wholesale distribution of prescription drugs to pharmacies, as well as the permitted direct delivery of over-the-counter drugs from the factory or depot to the pharmacy.[27] Distribution of medicines to the population takes place exclusively through pharmacies, though some medicines not requiring a prescription can also be sold in licensed drug stores. In addition to the licensed public pharmacies and hospital pharmacies, physicians in some areas may keep stocks of medicines to dispense to their patients which they have in turn purchased from public pharmacies. In terms of numbers they are as numerous as the pharmacies. Public pharmacies face a concession obligation, while the running of hospital and doctors' "house" pharmacies must be approved by the authorities. Such restrictions on market entry have resulted in a low pharmacy density; in 1992, there were only 0.25 practising pharmacists per 1 000 inhabitants, compared with 0.91 in France, 0.96 in Italy, 0.58 in the United Kingdom, and 0.46 in Germany (1990 level). Advertising is permitted only for over-the-counter drugs as most pharmaceutical marketing is directed toward the physician.

Price regulations

In addition to regulations pertaining to the conduct of business, price regulations occur at all levels of pharmaceutical distribution. At the wholesale level, the price commission of the Ministry of Health allowed a maximum mark-up to the manufacturer's price of 17 per cent (wholesale price margin). The member firms of the pharmaceutical wholesale trade business, previously within the framework of their cartel, also grant volume-related price discounts: the public pharmacies receive from them discounts in the form of graduated rebates, depending on volume, of between ½ and 5 per cent (plus rebates of ½ per cent for turnover ordered electronically). At the retail level, the ''raw'' pharmacy margin varies inversely according to the level of the wholesale introductory price, ranging from 12.5 to 56 per cent.[28] The social security funds are exempt from paying the value added tax (though this will change in 1997 as the VAT system is brought into line with the EU). The health funds also obtain a volume rebate, varying from 5.7 per cent (turnover of Sch 2 million per year) to 11.9 per cent (over Sch 12 million per year). On top of this, the *Hauptverband* approves a ''fund price'' for all medicines approved for the positive list, which is about 15 per cent below the list price (Figure 21). This special price, together with the volume discounts from it, are granted not only to the sickness funds, but also to such favoured purchasers as public and non-profit private hospitals. The patient co-

Figure 21. **THE COMPONENTS OF A PHARMACEUTICAL PRICE**

In schillings for a factory gate price of 100 schillings

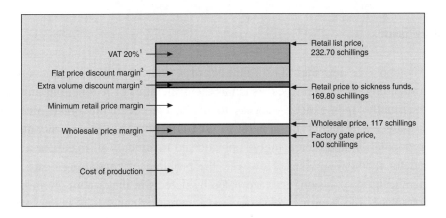

1. Sickness funds are (until 1997) exempted from paying the VAT.
2. Given to the sickness funds.
Source: Jorg, L., K. Bayer and G. Hutschenreiter (1995).

payment of Sch 42, formerly Sch 35 per prescription (on average 20 per cent), is credited by the pharmacy to the health funds. For medicines prescribed in hospitals, their cost is included in the calculation of the officially determined daily charge.

Innovation

Regulations governing market entry and pricing in the pharmaceutical market may distort the nature of innovation. Regulators may keep potentially successful drugs off the market because of overcaution in testing or protection of existing products; this may inhibit development of drugs offering important breakthroughs. On the other hand, a product which passes the testing phase faces very good chances of profitability, both because of insurance which lowers the price elasticity of demand and the protected position of being on the approved list of drugs and on the list reimbursable by the social insurance. This tends to encourage a more cautious type of innovation. As regards process innovation, regulations tend to discourage it altogether. Price and licensing regulations keep the prices of older drugs high and prohibit generics and over-the-counter drugs; together with insurance coverage of most of the cost of the drug, this gives no incentive to mix and match older with newer drug therapies to keep within budget constraints.[29]

Policy issues

The above review identifies a number of serious problems in the control of health spending. Several of these, such as the difficulties of reconciling universal – and virtually open-ended – access to health care with the practicalities of public budget constraints are general to OECD economies. Rising incomes, an ageing population and increasingly sophisticated treatments all make for a rising demand for medical services. However, the problem of containing costs in the Austrian health care system is exacerbated by defects in the system of control. In the first place, the health-care system is a hybrid, financed in major part by contributions, but with substantial recourse to general taxation. This weakens the link between contributions and benefits. Second, under the Austrian federal fiscal system, revenue-raising powers are centralised while spending powers are effectively decentralised: popular spending decisions are taken at the lower levels of government close to the electorate but unpopular taxing decisions are taken at the more distant central level. Moreover, until recently, generous revenue-sharing with the states has meant that their budgets have normally remained in balance despite rising expenditures. Taken together, the illusion has been created among local politicians and populations that government services are "free" and this weakens accountability. A third structural problem, arising from the division of responsibilities, is that the health funds have strong incentives to control ambulatory care, but much weaker ones to limit in-patient hospital care, creating a severe allocative inefficiency. Indeed, the apparent costs of in-patient relative to ambulatory care are seriously distorted both for the health funds and for medical practitioners, leading to over-use of in-patient care. Finally, these inefficiencies may be exacerbated by supply restrictions on medical practices and regulatory restraints which give Austria relatively high medicine prices. To a significant extent, therefore, the imbalances in the Austrian health system derive from behavioural responses which are shaped by institutions.

The 1996 Reform Programme

At the beginning of 1996 the social partners presented a set of proposals for reforming the health care system and in March the government reached a framework agreement with the Länder regarding a general reform to take effect in 1997. Crucial details have been under negotiation throughout the year but agreement was nearly complete at the time of writing (October 1996). The proposed reforms are summarised in Box 4. Some aspects of the reform are concerned with raising contributions and co-payments and have been incorporated in the 1996/97 Budgets. However, the reforms also make fundamental changes to the institutional background of hospital care. Austria has opted for a micro approach to control spending, centred on the switch from the present flat per-day payment to a standard per-case hospital reimbursement, with the price depending on initial diagnosis. (The alternative of having hospital budget caps to constrain health care expenditures is one of the least efficient methods of ensuring that the socially optimal amount of health care is being provided, although it may be effective for a while from the viewpoint of the budget.) It has also been decided to replace the KRAZAF by nine Länder funds, to be financed by all levels of government and which would therefore be subject the system to a global budget constraint.

Box 4. **The government's health-care reform proposals**

In addition to introducing numerous cost saving measures as part of the 1996/1997 budget, the government has agreed a wide ranging reform package for the health system and particularly for the financing and control of the hospital sector which will take effect from January 1997. The main measures are as follows:

Hospital finance reform

– A framework for a binding hospital plan and large investment plan has been agreed by the federal government and the Länder by the end of 1996. A structural commission is to be set up by the government to develop the plan and to impose sanctions for non-compliance. Unlike the KRAZAF the federal government will have a clear majority on the commission and the principle of unanimity has been dropped.

– Nine separate Länder funds are to be set up to finance hospitals, each under the control of a state structural commission. The commission in each state will be structured in such a way that the state has a clear majority vote and will oversee the introduction of a performance-oriented payment system for hospitals, based on diagnosis-related reimbursements (LKF) as well as the implementation of the hospitals investment plan. The payments scheme may be adapted to fit local conditions.

– The Länder funds will receive 1.416 per cent of VAT from the federal government annually, a flat sum of Sch 330 million and Sch 3 billion dependent on the state following the federal hospital plan. Each state will contribute 0.949 per cent of VAT receipts and the local government will also make contributions. The existing health funds will cease making payments to hospitals based on service and will instead make a flat payment of Sch 37 billion per year to the year 2000. The payment will be adjusted in line with the development of contribution revenues.

– A consultation mechanism will be set up between the health funds and their respective state in order to adjust for changes in services which will be offered by hospitals, out-patient treatment and by doctors.

Budgetary measures affecting the health system

The main measures introduced as part of the 1996/1997 budget include:

– Pensioners will pay slightly higher health care insurance contributions. (Other groups will be spared contribution increases, so as not to raise social charges on employment.)

– A patient co-payment has been introduced for spas of up to Sch 180 per day. A proposal by the Economic Chamber to introduce co-payments for hospital stays was not accepted by the government.

(continued on next page)

- All members of the health funds will have to pay Sch 50 to receive the booklet which is presented to the doctor during a first visit (*Krankenscheingebühr*).
- The patient co-payment for medicines was raised from the flat rate of Sch 35 per prescription to Sch 42, according to type of medicine.
- A patient co-payment for hospital out-patient clinics which was proposed by the social partners has not been introduced.
- The duration of sick pay (currently 60 per cent of previous pay, up to a limit) has been increased from 26 weeks to 52 weeks in response to the decision by several health funds to cut payments from 78 weeks to the legal minimum.

In addition, the social partners proposed the following cost saving measures:

- Insurance payments for eyeglasses and contact lenses should be restricted to needy cases. Expected savings: Sch 300 million.
- A small tax should be imposed on "unhealthy" consumer products, like tobacco and alcohol. Such revenues will in turn be dedicated to spending on preventive measures.
- Well-paid mothers should receive smaller payments for the mandatory confinement of eight weeks before and eight weeks after giving birth (*Wochengeld*), with income only up to the maximum for social security contributions (currently Sch 39 000) to be counted in the calculation of benefits. In addition, the mother must have been insured at least six months before becoming pregnant. Expected savings: Sch 400 million.

The interface between social and medical care

A key aspect of the current social policy on long term care is the July 1993 law (*Bundespflegegeldgesetz*), which provides benefits for the provision of care to those in need of long term care, independent of the cause of their disability but linked to its degree. It replaced all former care-linked transfers. The intention of the flat cash payment is to give persons in need of long term care the wherewithal to purchase necessary care and help and to give them greater independence and freedom to choose what they need best. A working group of government representatives (Bund, Länder, communes and social security institutions) has been set up to monitor the results obtained with the *Pflegegeld* system. Although its findings are not yet available, it appears that long-term care institutions raised their charges, in particular for formerly voluntary or largely publicly provided services, as such services were paid directly by households rather than pension insurance funds. In part due to the perceived rise in price, recipients of the *Pflegegeld* chose to retain most of the payments, or to give them to family members, rather than to spend them on care or market forms of care, but in any case 80 per cent of those in need are nursed at home. In 1994, such cash benefits accounted for 60 per cent of all social security expenditures for long-term care (Sch 23 billion); 35 per cent went for in-patient care, and 5 per cent for outpatient and home nursing care.

However, no moves have been made to improve incentives through a better market structure (deregulation) or contract relations between funders and providers which would establish managed competition.[30] Indeed, the system preserves the fundamental bureaucratic structure of decision-making, while aiming to eliminate institutional biases to over-consumption and to establish better cost control. The system would thus still seem to demand review, particularly with respect to its allocative efficiency. A synopsis of policy recommendations, building on recent reforms, is given in Box 5.

Demand-side cost sharing

It has been seen (Annex I) that patient cost sharing is absent, apart from the special cases of co-payments for pharmaceuticals and medical appliances, ambulatory co-payments for certain groups such as civil servants, and token hospital co-payments. Thus, for the most part, the price of health care faced by the consumer is close to nil. This means that even with a small price elasticity of demand, the impact of a significant rise in price through cost-sharing could be significant.[31] For this reason, some participants in the Austrian health reform debate – including the plan of the social partners presented to the government at the start of 1996 – have found the idea of greater demand side cost sharing, through generalised patient co-payments or high deductibles attractive.[32] But a generally acknowledged problem with this approach is that it may collide with the fundamental objective of equity. For example, it is a widely established fact that health status and hence health care need is negatively correlated with income.[33] This means that user charges risk transferring income from the sick and poor to the healthy and better-off. In turn, this necessitates that patient cost-sharing be carefully targeted to exclude the poor and chronically sick, which, on the other hand, tends to raise administrative costs and fraud.[34] A further concern, shown in experiments run in the United States, is that people are likely to forego necessary visits to the doctor, which in the long run could raise health care costs.

Despite these concerns, patient cost sharing at least at the margins of a basic guaranteed health care package may still be appropriate in the Austrian context, in order to curtail some obvious excesses. For example, expensive procedures with highly uncertain benefits, some procedures not related to illness or prevention, or treatments inviting obvious abuses such as spa cures should require

Box 5. **Recommendations for the further reform of the Austrian health care system**

Based on the analysis presented in the chapter, policy initiatives are needed to *i)* control the virtually open-ended access to health care; *ii)* link spending decisions more closely to local revenue resources; *iii)* prevent the federal government being the residuary source of finance via the sharing of general taxation, while improving the operational environment of the health funds, and *iv)* reduce costs in the ambulatory care and pharmaceutical areas. From this perspective the government's reform measures, which enter into force in 1997, need to be seen as a necessary step in the right direction. The chapter identifies the need to move ahead in the following areas:

Demand-side cost sharing

– *Control demand for some health services by increasing co-payments.* While maintaining the principle of open access, an extension of patient cost-sharing measures could be considered to control frivolous demand.

Hospital reform and local accountability

– *Place hospitals under tighter financial discipline.* New methods of charging such as diagnostic-based hospital remuneration are being introduced in 1997, but need to be reinforced by giving greater incentives to hospitals to increase cost control. The best solution would be to introduce a limited degree of competition within the context of active public purchasing.
– *Incentives are needed for more rational decision-making with respect to hospital investment.* The voting structure of the new Länder funds and the structural commission has been correctly oriented toward majority decisions and away from consensus. However, bureaucratic decisions are still open to political pressure, and the financial incentives for the Länder to follow the federal hospital plan might be too small.
– *The budget constraint facing the Länder needs to be tightened by reducing fiscal transfers, while local government should only receive limited budgetary support from the respective state.* Residual public hospital financing should be based more on revenues raised within the Länder.
– *Control access to hospital treatment by implementing the newly-established process of monitoring of doctor referrals.*

Resource allocation within the health service

Efforts to contain overall budgetary pressures will not result in greater allocational efficiency unless accompanied by more fundamental reforms:

(continued on next page)

(continued)

- *Extend the financial obligations of health funds to cover hospitals.* Because health funds cover only a part of hospital costs they have an incentive to pass the burden of health care onto hospitals. The costs of health care need to be internalised under one category of institution which would thereby improve decisions concerning all forms of competing health care. The role of the purchaser, to act on behalf of the consumer and to place pressure on the suppliers of health services – in particular hospitals – to lower costs, should ultimately be put in the hands of the public health funds.
- *Establish a nation-wide database on best practice.* High costs are currently generated by treatment uncertainty and trial and error approaches. Research in other countries shows that this is the single most effective step government can take in the field of health care.
- *The provision of long-term nursing care needs to be reformed.* The population is ageing, increasing the demand for nursing care which is at present largely provided by relatively expensive hospitals, or cash benefits to encourage home nursing. The promotion of specialised institutions needs to be continued.

Medical practice

- *Deregulate the barriers to group medical practice.* One reason for the uneconomical load on hospitals is the underdeveloped ambulatory sector which provides only limited access to a full range of services in the one location. Most forms of group practice were considered illegal until recently.
- *Improve incentives to doctors to provide a wider range of services.* One reason for hospital admissions is the lack of weekend services and home visits. Careful balancing of capitation and fee-for-service is required while permitting larger numbers of doctors to establish individual and group practices would help alleviate the problem.
- *Improve co-operation of doctors with hospitals.* Doctors in the ambulatory sector currently are not permitted to follow their patients to hospital and participate in their treatment, leading to duplicate tests and inefficient provision of care. Nor are they allowed to use hospital facilities for minor surgery.

Pharmacies and pharmaceuticals

- *Deregulate pharmacies and the pricing of medicines.* Austria has relatively high pharmaceutical prices which are highly regulated. Pharmacy density is low due to extensive restrictions on entry.

substantial patient cost-sharing components or should not be covered by the social insurance at all. Given also the widespread abuse of hospital emergency room facilities, a penalty might be imposed for their use in non-emergencies.

Further, a positive health bonus incentive might be introduced into the social schemes, modelled on the private insurance "health banking accounts" (Annex I), to encourage better preventive care and give a financial incentive to avoid getting sick in the first place.

Proposals developed by the Social Partners partially summarised in Box 4 featured a variety of patient cost sharing measures, which were on the whole fair and these were adopted in part by the government. Modest increases in contribution rates were also considered during the year in response to a sharp deterioration in the prospective budgets for the health funds in 1997. Out of concern to avoid any increase in non-wage labour costs, the request was rejected by the government in favour of *ad hoc* reallocation of social responsibilities (*i.e.* such as some free transport) away from the health funds to other budgetary funds.

Supply-side cost sharing and hospital reform

Austria's system of passive financing of hospital deficits, in the first instance by the KRAZAF, and in the second by different levels of government – together with the system of federal/state financial transfers which has maintained Länder budgets close to balance until recently – has ensured that all risks and marginal costs eventually fall on the taxpayer – through the revenue-sharing process of the Federal budget – while the provider has no incentive to cost control. Rather, the incentive has been to supply as many services as possible and for lower levels of government to build and equip hospitals. Fixed hospital budgeting or physician capitation payments (flat fee per patient) would overcome these risks to the budget, as all risks of unexpected demand or costs fall on the provider (*i.e.* hospital, physician) who would bear all of the marginal costs of treatment, but at the cost of rationing. In between these two extremes is the notion of payment-by-case or the diagnostic-related group approach (DRG), whereby the funder accepts the risk of the particular case mix facing the provider, by reimbursing the average "normative" costs for each given case, but the provider accepts responsibility for any variations in treatment costs for each particular case. In the area of out-patient care, risk-sharing could take the form of capitation payments combined with partial fee for service.

The government has already adopted a "performance-oriented" reimbursement system, or "LKF" (*Leistungsorientierte Krankenanstalten Finanzierung*), as the focal point of its reform of the former KRAZAF system. This is a partial form of supply side cost sharing akin to the diagnostic-related group approach. Payment is to be made to the hospital by giving the same price to a single diagnostic, with a catalogue of diagnostics each priced by a number of "points", each point having a particular monetary value in the base year. These points will be calculated by collecting data on services rendered nation-wide, and attaching a national average resource cost to each service. A national data bank has accordingly been developed and preparatory work completed, with pilot projects in some Länder giving valuable insights. This system has several merits. It eliminates the incentive, embedded in the previous flat per-day charge, to prolong hospital stays in order to cross-subsidise resource-expensive earlier days by less expensive later days, as hospitals will now face the full marginal costs of each individual case over and above the national average. It also contributes to better hospital budgeting; each treatment will be given at least a normative valuation, in contrast to the prior system where hospital managers had no information on the relative costs of different procedures. However, this system also gives an incentive toward underprovision of services. To guard against this danger, as well as to minimise financial risks for hospitals, the points system will be amended by each state to cover exceptional cases or hospitals with higher costs. But there are legitimate fears that such supplements could *de facto* lead to a return to the old passive financing system.[35]

LKF by itself does not provide a strong incentive for hospitals to be globally efficient. This is because this reform leaves untouched the basic problem of the public hospital "soft budget constraint". Recognising this, the government's reform programme collects all hospital financing into funds at the individual state level. However there is the problem of what sanctions hospital-owners should apply in the case of overruns. Initial experiments with budgeting in certain Länder failed simply because the budgets were not adhered to by the hospitals.[36] Second, there is no assurance that the individual or collective hospital budget allocations are the right ones to meet society's health care needs. Finally, the value of points will vary from year to year in line with budgets of the Länder health funds, which could reduce the managerial value of the system.

The first-best solution would be to introduce limited forms of competition into the hospital sector within a context of active public purchasing – either by the public health funds or the new Länder funds. Recent reforms in a number of countries suggest that a first main component should be strengthening the role of insurers/payers from simply passive funders to active *purchasers* of hospital services, acting as *agents* for patients, together with bidding for contracts by providers of services. The ability or at least the threat of moving funding promotes an environment of contestability in which hospitals will have a strong incentive to seek improvements in quality, efficiency, cost control, and other elements which may be needed to win health funding. This contrasts markedly with the current situation where hospitals "compete" to outspend the others on new capacity and high-tech equipment. Such managed competition and contracting would also elicit more realistic pricing practices; where providers have to compete for customers on the basis of price, there will be an incentive to cost individual procedures and to bring prices into line with marginal cost. This will promote a more rational allocation of resources within the hospital, and provide incentives for greater process innovation. Such a framework would thus provide greater assurance that the switch to LKF would have the desired effects on cost saving. Furthermore, the payers as major buyers could hold down prices in the hospital sector through the exercise of "monopsony power" in the purchase of hospital services, as they already do for ambulatory care and pharmaceuticals. Germany is considering the switch to a competitive contracting system in 1997 and others have already adopted a similar approach.

For this approach to work in Austria would require significant changes in institutional arrangements. Political realities have already decided that there will be nine Länder funds as successor institutions to the KRAZAF. An important step forward has been to avoid the need to have consensus in the funds and to give the respective state a working majority. This may make decisions as to the closure and restructuring of hospitals within the framework of the national plan less difficult to take. Financial incentives for maintaining the plan are also an important element. Ultimately, however, once such tasks are completed, it could be desirable to phase out the Länder funds altogether and put all hospital financing back into the hands of the public health funds. This would mean not only returning to the funds the control over their own contributions to the Länder funding pools, but also channelling all present federal, state, and local VAT-based (KRAZAF) contributions to the health funds as subsidies.[37] Although an appropriate distribution and risk-sharing formula would have to be found, the important point is that resources be distributed to the health funds and not to the hospitals directly, and that the nature of this distribution be depoliticised.

An accompanying reform would reduce tax-sharing with the Länder. Instead, public hospital financing should be made to depend principally on revenues raised within each Länder, in order to increase accountability to local hospital users (as in the Swiss cantons). In some countries, hospital investments are funded by local bond issues which have to be pre-approved by the voters. And there needs to be a plan to co-ordinate payments across Länder to compensate for the cross-border use of hospital services. (This would be relatively easy in a purchaser-provider system with subsidiary contracts with other hospitals). The practice of cross-subsidisation of hospital deficits by private insurance will terminate due a recent constitutional court ruling that this practice is unconstitutional; at the same time, tax deductibility of private insurance premia is due to expire in 1997. These reforms should contribute to greater transparency of hospital funding.

Most importantly, hospital managers need to recognise the cost of capital in their budgeting practices in order to reduce the current incentive to excessive capital intensity, as capital is for the moment written off immediately and perceived as being free. Purchaser/funders will be more closely involved in major capital investment decisions, taking into account regional needs and forcing hospitals to engage in economic sharing of expensive equipment (as already exists among private hospitals) – provided the right political and institutional framework is in place. The new structural commission which is due to start in 1997, and which has responsibility for developing a nation-wide hospital and major investment plan, will have an important role to play. However, funding and capital decisions still remain separated bureaucratically and this may not prove to be efficient in the longer term.

As regards the remuneration of doctors' services, the existing system of a mixed fee-for-service and lump-sum payment system is already the one most favoured by most health care policy experts – lump sum being akin to DRGs in that the provider bears the marginal cost of treatment and thus has an incentive to keep his patients healthy in the first place, and fee-for-service providing a work incentive in case they do get sick. However reimbursement methods vary widely by Land with some relying too heavily on flat fees or imposing declining-scale fees, so that incentives may not yet be appropriate for increased work effort.[38] Under the hospital reforms proposed above, by contrast, the insurance funds would have the incentive to discourage the practice of excessive referrals, because they would pay the marginal cost of hospital services they are purchasing (apart from any risk-sharing arranged with providers through the LKF contract method), rather than a fixed per day reimbursement rate as before. In addition, they would be motivated to give more contracts to the ambulatory sector where care is cheaper and more efficient. Under the present reform their direct interest in hospital efficiency will be even further diminished, since a flat annual sum will replace fees for service. The incentives for excessive referrals thus remain. The requirement to consult with the new state funds is not an adequate replacement for an appropriate incentive structure.

To strengthen the social insurance funds' incentives to act as efficient purchasing agents, it might be considered whether competition could usefully be introduced into the insurance market itself. For example, the social funds could be charged with providing a basic guaranteed package, funded out of income-dependent social security contributions as presently, but would then be allowed to offer higher-grade products in competition with the private insurers, for an extra price to the customer. Also, patients might be free to choose among the alternative social health funds for their basic coverage (Germany is about to test this approach). Such proposals have in fact been made for Austria.[39] The idea is that by giving a profit motive to insurers, they would be more motivated to bargain for lower prices from health care providers and lower their own administrative costs, rather than increasing insurance contribution rates. Also, customers would be more engaged in risk and cost sharing. However, there are problems such as how to adjust for risks across the different groups of insured (since premia for the basic plan would still be based on income), and the possibility of yet another layer of supply-induced demand if insurers decide to collude with one another. It also weakens the monopsony power of the insurer/purchasers. The experience of the United States, where insurers compete fully but merely pass through rising costs into higher premia, is not encouraging.

Deregulation of the health care and pharmaceuticals markets

Attempts to reform the hospital sector could be frustrated if not complemented by deregulation of the ambulatory care sector, allowing this sector to expand and take over many of the services currently provided less efficiently by hospitals. Liberalisation of market entry is particularly essential, together with new forms of doctor co-operation, as well as of doctor-hospital co-operation.

To some extent pharmaceutical costs have been held in check by the monopsonistic power of the social insurers, which has acted as a countervailing force to the monopoly rents created by patent protection and industry control in the past over wholesale distribution, as well as formal price controls. Nevertheless, pharmaceutical price *levels* are above EU averages, suggesting that at least significant one-time gains could be had from deregulation. This is a complex question, however, given the government's implicit objective of keeping prices high enough to stimulate innovation in this sector. Moreover, in the future, innovations in drug therapy will increasingly need to replace surgery and other interventionist treatments as an efficiency measure.[40] Nevertheless, the following might be considered:

- Free up the prices of older drugs. This would allow more differentiation between old and new drugs, retarding the constant shift to newer drugs and allowing more "process innovation" in the form of mixtures of old and new drug therapies to lower costs.
- Self-medication is still underdeveloped in Austria given the small number of pharmaceuticals that can be sold without a prescription, but its expansion is usually considered to be an element of overall health cost reduction. The pharmaceutical industry and pharmacies, and the government and social insurance funds, plead that greater scope be given to self medication. Doctors, on the other hand, are in general against more self-medication (as this diminishes their control), citing risks of abuse and excessive long-term use without adequate medical supervision, but acknowledge its usefulness in the realm of preventive medicine.
- Generic drugs, which are rarely approved on the pretext that their "isometric structure" is not equal to that of the parent drug, should be allowed in order to lower costs.
- Overall costs of dispensing drugs could be reduced by deregulation of the retail sector. Competition among pharmacies should be stimulated by EU regulations which permit advertising of prescription drugs, but this can be augmented by allowing non-prescription drugs to be sold in a wider variety of retail outlets, and easing restrictions on market entry.

The role of the federal government

Current reform proposals envisage an immediate role for the central government in controlling the actual funding of the system at least in relation to hospital investment spending (Box 4). However, in light of the above discussion, health care resource allocations, both for current and capital uses, would be better left to the joint insurance-provider "market" for contracts. The central government's comparative advantage rather lies in the following:

- A federal authority should assume a new role in monitoring the performance of the social health funds as purchasing agents, to make sure society is getting the best value for its health-care money.
- In this connection, it should co-ordinate a national data bank to diffuse information on "best practice" which could help to reduce the extreme uncertainty facing medical practitioners and guide wiser purchasing decisions by the funders.[41] It should also steer research efforts, both in the government and in universities, to evaluate the therapeutic and cost benefits of constantly changing technologies. As with other forms of basic research, there may not be a sufficient pay-off for this task to be adequately undertaken by commercial interests.
- An adequate disability care policy will be imperative in view of future demographic changes. To contain the costs of long term care, the treatment of such cases has to be shifted from the hospitals to long-term or home care facilities. This will involve not only endowing new facilities, but also changing the incentives of local authorities in charge of social assistance. This will require a reassessment of personnel needs, the demand for nurses and home care workers being likely to rise at the expense of doctors
- Prevention deserves more attention than hitherto given. This includes developing effective public health programmes to alter life-styles (with respect, for example, to smoking and alcohol consumption, road and workplace safety, stress management, nutrition), working to reduce environmental risks, and integrating preventive care measures into health care purchasing policies.

Perhaps most fundamentally, there is a need for setting *health* objectives and targeting desired improvements. These objectives would be taken by the purchasers in their own objectives, which might bring a better balance between preventive and curative care.

In sum, the recent reform proposals which will come into force in 1997 represent a significant step towards better control, while the accompanying budgetary measures should help to reduce pressure from the demand side through increased co-payments. The current set of reforms may nonetheless still be considered an interim measure which relies heavily on bureaucratic interventions and political good will. These may well be effective in containing the expansion of health spending for a while but experience in other countries suggests that budget pressures could re-emerge quite quickly. Moreover, as far as allocative efficiency is concerned, the performance-oriented reimbursement system is second best to a solution where competition is introduced through active public purchasing. Time has, nevertheless, been gained during which longer-term reforms can be considered. These should ultimately include the development of managed competition via the creation of institutions not only to finance health services but to purchase them. Such a system would cover both hospitals and ambulatory treatment, so as to solve the dysfunctions in the present system whereby cases are passed to hospitals which should be handled in other ways.

IV. Implementing the OECD Jobs Strategy

Introduction

The level of unemployment in Austria, including youth and long-term unemployment, has remained significantly lower than in most OECD countries. However, as in other countries, unemployment has increased with cyclical downturns and in the recovery phase has failed to drop back to previous cyclical lows. Employment growth since 1976 has been due partly to a rise in public employment while unemployment rates have been kept low by substantial recourse to early retirement and invalidity pensions. This has led to increasing strains on the budget, but even abstracting from fiscal considerations, there are pressures for labour market policies and institutions to adjust to increased globalisation and to competition from both EU economies and the reform countries of east and central Europe. Present projections do not point to a significant improvement in the labour market in the medium term.

Faced with what appear to be some significant structural weaknesses, an economic strategy which seeks to increase labour utilisation and to reduce the current levels of unemployment, needs to embrace a broad range of structural measures aimed at increasing the capacity of labour and product markets to adapt. In this medium-term context, macroeconomic policies have a key supportive role to play in creating the conditions for sustained non-inflationary growth. As far as monetary policy is concerned, Austria's hard-currency policy – involving a fixed relation to the Deutschemark – has established a credible framework for the steady deceleration of inflation, thereby creating a favourable background for economic activity. Fiscal consolidation still has some way to go, both in terms of reducing the deficit and in lowering the claims of government on resources. However, it is evident that fiscal consolidation and the hard currency policy will function most effectively if measures are also undertaken to improve the performance of labour and product markets. Aggregate real wage flexibility is high and has underpinned the hard currency policy, but may not be sufficient in the future for an economy facing rapid structural change and the need to increase labour utilisation. With respect to fiscal policy, social transfers including pensions do not appear to be viable in the long run unless, among other things, the functioning of the labour market is improved: inadequate growth of employment creates a vicious cycle of rising taxes and social security contributions which, in turn, lead to slower economic growth and lower employment, while fiscal consolidation remains under pressure.

This Chapter follows up the general structural policy recommendations of the *OECD Jobs Study* with specific recommendations for Austria. Its structure is as follows. The first section contains an overview of the Austrian labour market and employment performance over the last two decades. The specific policy requirements to emerge from the study are discussed in the second part, while a review of recent policy actions and an assessment of the scope for further action are given in the final two sections.

Labour market and employment performance

From a historical perspective, the comparatively low rate of unemployment in Austria results from the fact that unemployment has increased less than elsewhere during recessions: it is not due to larger unemployment falls during upturns. Migration flows have contributed to this cyclical damping of unemployment during the 1980s, though in the 1990s the effect has been pro-cyclical. More generally, the labour force has remained very cyclically sensitive. But employment has typically been more stable than elsewhere, reflecting the following factors which are interlinked:

- output has been less volatile in Austria than elsewhere;
- labour productivity has shown relatively strong pro-cyclical movements reflecting labour hoarding;
- average real wages have responded strongly to rising unemployment.

The rate of unemployment (not standardised) has increased from around 2 per cent in 1980 to 6 per cent in 1996[42] (Figure 22). The share of long term unemployment in total unemployment has risen (Figure 22), and trend measures

Figure 22. **LABOUR MARKET INDICATORS**

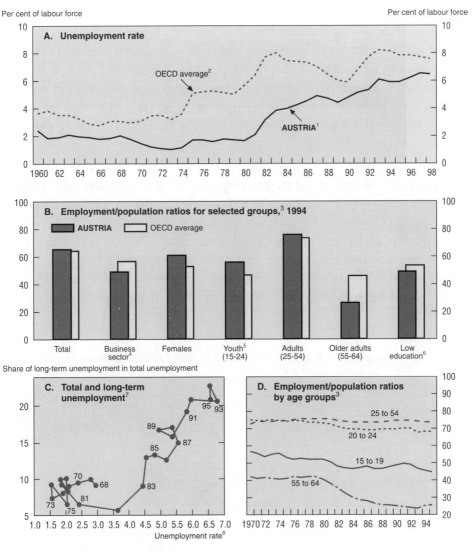

Per cent of labour force

A. Unemployment rate

OECD average[2]

AUSTRIA[1]

Per cent of labour force

1960 62 64 66 68 70 72 74 76 78 80 82 84 86 88 90 92 94 96 98

B. Employment/population ratios for selected groups,[3] 1994

AUSTRIA   OECD average

Total | Business sector[4] | Females | Youth[5] (15-24) | Adults (25-54) | Older adults (55-64) | Low education[6]

Share of long-term unemployment in total unemployment

C. Total and long-term unemployment[7]

95 93
91
89
87
85
83
70
68
73 75 81

1.0 1.5 2.0 2.5 3.0 3.5 4.0 4.5 5.0 5.5 6.0 6.5 7.0
Unemployment rate[8]

D. Employment/population ratios by age groups[3]

25 to 54
20 to 24
15 to 19
55 to 64

197072 74 76 78 80 82 84 86 88 90 92 94

1. Registered unemployment as percentage of total labour force.
2. For countries for which data are available.
3. Defined as the percentage of each population group that is employed.
4. Business sector employment divided by working-age population.
5. The minimum age for youth differs across country (either 14, 15 or 16).
6. In 1992. Completed less than upper secondary education.
7. Long-term unemployment is defined as individuals looking for work for one year or more.
8. Registered unemployment as percentage of total dependant labour force.
Source: WIFO; OECD.

111

of structural unemployment increased steadily through the 1980s (Figure 23). With the significant exception of the Okun measure (the ratio of the unemployment rate to capacity utilisation), the trend increase slowed in the 1990s, but this should not be taken as a sign of easing pressure on the labour market[43]; extensive resort to early retirement and invalidity pensions has reduced the labour force (Figure 24), leading to an exceptionally low employment rate for older workers (Figure 25). On the other hand, after experiencing severe problems at the beginning of the 1980s, the participation rate of youths has increased and is above the OECD average.

Structural problems are suggested both by the secular increase in the level of long-term unemployment and by its composition. Since 1980 the proportion of long term unemployed (according to the Austrian definition, those unemployed for longer than 6 months) has increased from around 17 per cent to 31 per cent in 1994 (Figure 22). Those without employment for over one year (the OECD definition) comprised about 19 per cent of the unemployed. While these figures are lower than in other countries, early retirement and other measures have reduced the measured rate considerably. With rising age the incidence of

Figure 23. **STRUCTURAL ASPECTS OF THE LABOUR MARKET**

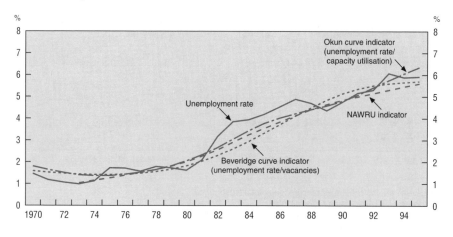

1. The trends of the three indicators are based on yearly estimates of unemployment rates which have a) resulted in a normal vacancy rate, b) stabilised wage inflation or c) led to a normal rate of capacity utilisation. These estimates have subsequently been smoothed using a Hodrick-Prescott filter.
Source: OECD.

Figure 24. **REASON FOR LEAVING EMPLOYMENT FOR PERSONS AGED 50 TO 64 YEARS**

Per cent of the age group

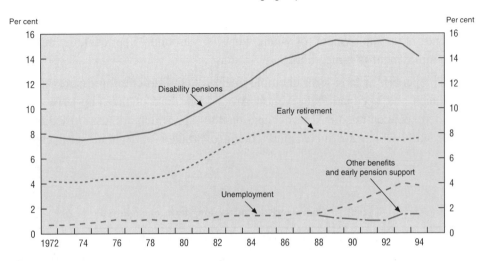

Source: Ministry for Labour and Social Affairs.

Figure 25. **INCIDENCE AND DURATION OF UNEMPLOYMENT BY AGE GROUP**

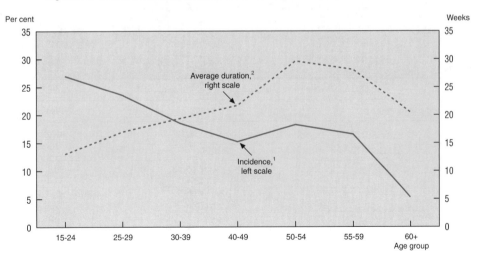

1. Unemployment as percentage of employed.
2. Duration in weeks.
Source: WIFO.

unemployment declines but the average duration increases significantly (Figure 25). The incidence of long term unemployment among the unemployed over 50 years old amounts to around two-fifths (Table 22). By contrast, while the incidence of unemployment for young workers is around 25 per cent, the duration of unemployment is quite short.

The pattern of long term unemployment reflects structural pressures at both the branch and occupational levels.[44] Around one half of the long-term unemployed are concentrated in four occupational groups which are less skilled and/or reflect skills which are increasingly being overtaken by technological change.

Table 22. **Characteristics of the long-term unemployed**

A. Percentage of total unemployed in group (yearly average) (1994)		
By age	Unemployed 6 months to 1 year	Unemployed for longer than 1 year
15-18	5.4	1.2
19-24	8.1	3.7
25-29	11.7	10.6
30-39	13.0	15.6
40-49	14.9	19.4
50-54	18.7	38.4
55-59	17.5	45.8
60 and older	19.1	34.0
Total	13.4	18.5
Men	12.4	18.4
Women	14.6	18.5
B. Percentage of total unemployed longer than 6 months		
By selected occupations	1981	1990
Miners	2.0	48.9
Building	21.6	31.8
Electrical	11.9	33.3
Leather	23.6	30.1
Textiles	18.4	32.4
Clothing	13.6	31.5
Chemicals	15.6	39.5
Machinists	28.1	43.2
Retail trade	12.8	32.7
Office jobs	14.9	33.7
Pulp and paper	17.0	46.2
Total	16.1	31.5

Source: G. Biffl, "Langzeitarbeitslosigkeit", WIFO, *Monatsbericht,* 1/1996.

The long-term unemployed are also drawn disproportionately from industries undergoing adjustment arising from international competition: textiles, leather and clothing as well as tourism. Given their occupation and industrial concentration, women have increasingly suffered from long term unemployment. An indication of the challenges arising from technological change is the rising incidence of long term unemployment among office occupations, which affects women in particular.

A marked feature of Austrian labour market performance over time has been the rapid growth of public sector employment, which accounts for a large share of employment: about 22 per cent of total employment is in the government sector excluding state-owned enterprises. Growth of total employment has been partly due to a steady rise in public employment since 1976, whereas the present level of business sector employment, despite a marked recovery in the late 1980s, is only marginally above its level in 1976 (Figure 26) and the share of such employment in the total is below the OECD average. State-owned firms in the manufacturing sector now account for around 17 per cent of that sector's employment, having fallen by about a half[45] since the 1980s as a result of continued privatisation.

Labour force growth averaged about 0.7 per cent per year between 1970 and 1993, with a period of particularly rapid growth at the beginning of the 1990s associated with the decision to increase the inflow of unskilled migrants to relieve cyclical labour shortages (Figure 27). As a result, in 1994 almost 9 per cent of wage and salary earners were foreigners. Since 1991 tight controls have been introduced to control the inflow of foreigners: employers may not receive permits if nationals have recently been dismissed, while foreign workers are often not permitted to change their jobs without prior approval. Male labour force participation has tended to decline and is low by international standards. Offsetting this development, female labour force participation has increased from 57 per cent in 1984 to 63 per cent in 1994. The increase in female labour force participation is, however, low in comparison with other OECD countries. Part-time employment is quite low by international standards;[46] in particular, only 23 per cent of married women are employed part-time. This may be partly due to the comparatively small share of services in overall employment.

Figure 26. **EMPLOYMENT BY SECTOR**

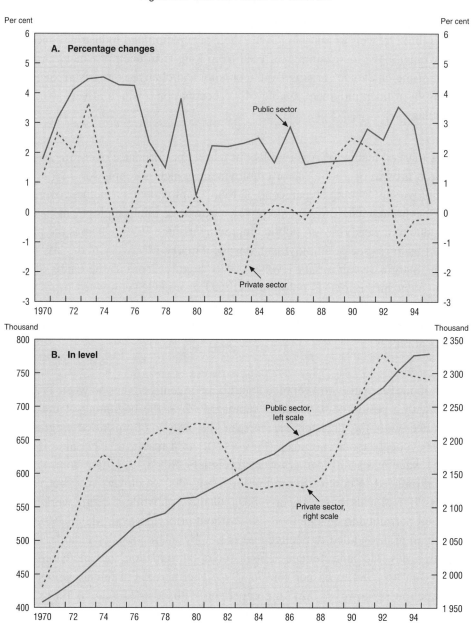

Source: OECD.

Figure 27. **FOREIGN AND TOTAL EMPLOYMENT**

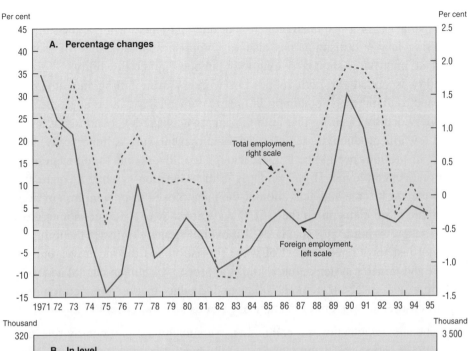

A. **Percentage changes**

Total employment,
right scale

Foreign employment,
left scale

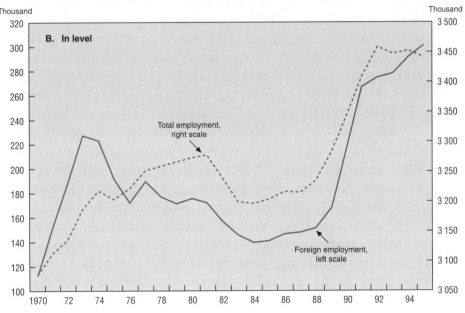

B. **In level**

Total employment,
right scale

Foreign employment,
left scale

Source: WIFO.

117

Policy requirements

A strategy for a sustained reduction of unemployment while at the same time increasing labour utilisation has also to comprise a broad range of measures aimed at improving short-and long-term labour market flexibility. Short term flexibility is called for both to prevent workers from falling into unemployment and to avoid their remaining in unemployment. To a large degree, this has to be provided by ensuring that both the aggregate wage level and relative wages adjust towards productivity levels at full employment. Just as importantly, labour market institutions need to be flexible enough to allow people to re-enter employment once unemployed. High standards in the education system, adequate training of the work force and activation of the unemployed to prevent loss of human capital are basic elements in the *OECD Jobs Strategy* to foster economic growth and to secure rising living standards. An overall strategy to foster flexibility thus calls not just for a reassessment of wage formation and the incentives built into the tax and transfer systems, but also of the process of human capital acquisition including active labour-market policy and product-market competition which should ensure an efficient allocation of resources in the economy at large.

The above elements of a comprehensive strategy are particularly relevant in view of the scope and nature of the employment problem confronting Austria now and in the foreseeable future. The performance of the Austrian economy over several decades has been impressive, leading to a remarkably high standard of living, excellent industrial relations and social cohesion. Labour market institutions are highly centralised and have participated closely in the formation of economic policy, as well as in the direction of state-owned enterprises. This structure has been associated with capital-intensive growth, but has been characterised by a lack of technological dynamism, with employment partly maintained by the growth of the public sector. Although the labour market has been able to deliver sufficient macroeconomic wage flexibility to achieve moderate wage growth and to support the hard currency policy, the globalisation of economic activity demands greater heterogeneity, both between enterprises and amongst employees, demanding more flexibility from centralised institutions. Indeed, the labour market has already started to adjust to these new forces, with more decentralised market solutions arising spontaneously in the form of *de facto* agreements between works councils and enterprises to adopt more flexible work practices, albeit without a firm institutional and legal basis. The imminent need to absorb greater numbers of older workers as a result of reduced early retirement and falling public sector employment reinforces the need both for greater flexibility and for technological dynamism. These in turn will require institutional flexibility. A synopsis of the recommendations made below, which address these issues, can be found in Box 6.

Enhancing the ability to adjust and adapt

Despite the existence of considerable flexibility, empirical studies point to three key features of the Austrian labour market which would make it difficult for unemployment, once it has occurred, to fall again naturally. First, wages respond to unemployment but the longer unemployment lasts the less is its influence: long term unemployment exercises only a small effect on real wage developments.[47] Second, the pattern of relative wages appears to be quite stable and only weakly related to differences in performance at the firm and sectoral level.[48] Third, employment adjusts to labour demand only gradually, with adjustment in the short run occurring through hours of work.[49] Taken together with product market distortions, the ability of the labour market to adjust in response to pressure stemming from both internal and external developments (''shocks'') could be limited. Underlying these features are a variety of institutions which determine not only the behaviour of the social partners but also individual economic actors. Many of these factors are not directly under the control of policy makers, requiring rather a consensus between all social partners and the governing political parties with respect to policy and institutional change. It is nevertheless appropriate for this section to examine these factors from the policy perspective.

The wage formation system

After Japan, Austria has the highest (estimated) degree of macroeconomic real wage flexibility among OECD countries,[50] because the system of centralised wage bargaining has emphasised aggregate productivity and international competitiveness in assessing wage demands. However, the similarity between the two countries may also be related to the fact that the wage system is based to some extent on tenure, although age is also an important factor. In Austria white-collar workers are subject to tenure-based remuneration while some skilled workers (*Facharbeiter*) and craftsmen (*Meister*) are also classed as white-collar workers

119

Box 6. **The OECD Jobs Strategy:**
a synopsis of recommendations for Austria

The *OECD Jobs Study* sets out a strategy based on nine recommendations for improving the ability of OECD economies to cope with structural change, through enhancing the ability to adjust and to adapt, and increasing the capacity to innovate and to be creative. The nine distinct policy areas covered included the macroeconomic policy framework and the creation and diffusion of technological know-how. With respect to labour and product market flexibility it identified the need for initiatives in the following areas: working-time flexibility, the entrepreneurial climate, wage and labour cost flexibility, employment security provisions, active labour market policies, labour force skills and competencies, and unemployment and related benefits systems.

The Austrian labour market already exhibits considerable macroeconomic flexibility and labour force flows are significant. However, the cost of supporting early retirement has been high. As part of the fiscal consolidation package the government has taken a number of measures which improve the framework for the labour market. These include increased disincentives to early retirement and a tightening of qualifications for drawing unemployment benefits by the seasonally unemployed. However, while these steps are welcome they also increase the need for further complementary reforms if labour market performance is to be improved under conditions of continuing structural adjustment.

Following the detailed review of labour market and employment performance, and the assessment of policy requirements, this chapter identifies the need for Austria to move ahead in the following areas:

Increase wage and labour cost flexibility

Greater wage differentiation with respect to firms should be encouraged by permitting the more general use of opening clauses allowing adjustments for local wages and working conditions in wage contracts. The existing system of centralised bargaining between the social partners leads to a high aggregate level of macroeconomic wage flexibility, but wages at the enterprise level can only be adjusted upwards relative to the agreed minimum, and measured wage differentiation is relatively stable and related mainly to the different age/tenure composition of sectors and to product market imperfections. Market signals to facilitate employment during a period of restructuring are thus likely to be distorted.

The employment of older workers needs to be promoted. Increased wage flexibility should complement other policy measures such as retraining by lowering the relative wages of older workers, but for this to be agreed in wage bargaining, further significant reductions need to be made in the financial incentives for early retirement.

(continued on next page)

(continued)

Reform unemployment and related benefit systems

Further measures are required in order to raise the effective age of retirement. The steps undertaken as part of the 1996 and 1997 budget to reduce the widespread resort to early retirement are in the right direction but the immediate impact on the labour market might be to increase unemployment, so that complementary labour market measures are required.

The subsidy provided by the unemployment insurance system to seasonal employment in tourism needs to be curtailed.

The operation of social assistance programmes needs to be examined to determine whether the incentives to take up work can be strengthened by, for example, raising the level of earnings which are permissible while receiving benefits. To control budget expenditures, the amount which can be earned before benefits are cut has been reduced for a number of programmes, but as benefit levels have not been lowered, this could result in very high marginal effective tax rates at lower levels of income. These reduce incentives for such households to earn more income (*i.e.* poverty trap), or to seek and accept normal jobs (*i.e.* unemployment trap). These traps could be significant, and consideration needs to be given to increasing earnings allowances while at the same time reducing benefits more rapidly so as to limit the number of people affected.

To facilitate active labour search by the older unemployment the reference wage for the calculation of benefits should more closely reflect their employment opportunities. Wages for many rise steeply with tenure and age implying that some older unemployed workers will have to accept a significant wage cut to become re-employed. However, benefit entitlements are based on past income so that there is little incentive to do this. The reference wage could be reduced annually to more closely reflect employment opportunities at lower wages.

Increase working-time flexibility

Arrangements for increased work-time flexibility need to be facilitated, since flexible working practices appear to be underdeveloped. Working practices should be a matter for collective bargaining, in conjunction with wages and other conditions and subject to opening clauses, but the rules governing overtime and weekend work are restrictive.

The further liberalisation of shop opening hours is welcome, but to be effective more regulatory room must be given to the social partners to adjust working conditions accordingly.

Part-time work needs to be facilitated. To gain flexibility employers and employees have resorted increasingly to work contracting (*Werkverträge*); such flexibility is desirable, although contracts should not be a means of avoiding taxes and charges. Current measures to control the tax avoidance aspects of the system more closely should not be allowed to inhibit their contribution to labour-market flexibility.

(continued on next page)

(continued)

Reform employment security provisions

Dismissal protection provisions need to be liberalised, with the object of encouraging new hiring by reducing the uncertainty and costs of dismissal. Dismissal protection appears to be restrictive and provisions which protect older workers, or those with long company service, may inadvertently increase barriers to re-employment.

The regulations governing fixed-term contracts need to be liberalised. Extension or renewal at present automatically converts the contract to an indefinite-term one which, in the context of dismissal protection provisions, might discourage new hiring.

Improve labour force skills and competencies

The apprenticeship scheme has become increasingly narrow both occupationally and by sector and is in need of reform. While the apprenticeship system has been effective in the past in promoting youth training, the trades on which it is based have become too narrow. Too few places are provided by industry.

Full-time vocational training has been successful but needs continuous updating to respond to new demands of the economy. Students need the possibility of being able to move on to tertiary institutions and not have the paths closed.

The new higher level vocational schools (Fachhochschule) appear promising and this initiative deserves to be pursued with vigour. There is no reason why they should only focus on niche training.

The university system is in urgent need of reform to make it more competitive and to increase the benefits accruing to the economy. In particular the system of tenure and promotion needs to be liberalised to allow resources to be allocated according to changing needs. Links between universities and industry should be developed, so as to increase the transfer of knowledge between the academic and business sectors.

Greater competition needs to be promoted in the area of retraining. Such services are provided on an extensive scale by the federation of employers and the federation of trade unions, but a more contestable market in the provision of training would be useful.

Enhance the creation and diffusion of technological know-how

Access to venture capital markets need to be fostered. In a small open economy it is probably unreasonable to expect an indigenous venture capital market to develop, so that efforts need to be made to link Austria more closely to pan-European efforts in this direction.

Greater diffusion of technology is necessary to shift the specialisation of Austrian industry and employment to higher value-added production. The regrouping or merger of the public research institutes (*Forschung Austria*) could yield positive spillovers if oriented to industry needs.

(continued on next page)

(continued)

Nurture an entrepreneurial climate

The establishment of new enterprises needs to be encouraged. The rate of new company start-ups is comparatively low, suggesting the absence of a risk-taking culture. This suggests the need for a general approach encompassing greater opportunities for private involvement in public service provision and greater equality of treatment between enterprises and non-profit bodies.

Bankruptcy laws need to be reformed so as to allow reorganisation. The current law does not allow reorganisation, and places a heavy stigma on bankruptcy. In the past, subsidies have been used to prop up ailing firms, and now that these are being phased out, the system needs a means of coping with a rising bankruptcy rate.

Increase product market competition

A major deregulation effort is necessary to eliminate regulatory barriers to entry in the trade and craft sectors. The administrative requirements for opening a new enterprise need to be significantly simplified and the requirements to enter trades need to be relaxed (*Gewerbeordnung*), at a minimum by defining occupations more widely.

A competition-oriented regulatory framework for the network industries needs to be put in place (in particular, telecommunications and electricity). An important first step has been put in place with the decision to privatise ultimately the telecommunications carrier, while the electricity markets will have to be progressively opened up. The need now is to create the framework conditions for the industries to develop.

Barriers to entry in the provision of local services need to be lifted and the treatment of local and private suppliers placed on an equal footing. Under the pressure of budget consolidation local services are being corporatised. While this could lead to some efficiency improvements, these will not be ensured until a competitive environment is created.

An independent competition authority should be established. With entry into the EU competition policy has changed fundamentally, and an independent authority could help to increase transparency further.

---

for the purpose of remuneration. High aggregate real wage flexibility tends to be observed with tenure-based wage systems because the cost to individual workers of losing their jobs is high, so that flexibility serves to preserve their tenure-based premia.

Flexibility of average real wages has been reflected in the counter-cyclical development of real wages and the wage share of business-sector value added. Such flexibility has, however, not ensured that wage trends have always matched productivity gains in the medium term (Figure 28). During the 1970s, the wage share of the business sector steadily increased as the growth of real compensation exceeded productivity gains; business sector employment then fell and the growth of value added declined. This situation was reversed during the 1980s and business sector employment growth recovered. The wage share increased sharply prior to the last recession, but has since declined. This tendency for the wage share to become excessive arises in part because the pressure for wage adjustment in the enterprise sector has been dissipated by the growth of public sector employment and by early retirement. In addition, the longer-term unemployed appear to have exercised a diminishing influence on wage outcomes. From the perspective of future growth and employment it is, however, also necessary to consider the wage bargaining system as a factor: central wage bargaining is oriented toward aggregate rather than branch productivity but at both branch and enterprise level those with high profitability have usually had to negotiate still higher effective wage increases. Employment creation in profitable expanding sectors could thus be impaired, while the fact that enterprises with low profitability cannot negotiate reductions below the minimum agreed wage means that their productivity can only be increased through a shakeout of labour. This process creates problems in an economy subject to the need for more rapid structural change.[51]

The structure and dispersion of wages is also an important determinant of employment generating capacity, and in this respect the Austrian wage-bargaining system has permitted a comparatively high degree of wage dispersion (Table 23). However, tenure and human capital effects account for much of the variation:[52] once adjustments are made for these factors the dispersion of wages appears more characteristic of Europe than of the United States, the high measured wage dispersion being due to a great extent to a different age composition of workers between sectors (Table 24). Moreover, research suggests that the dispersion of sectoral and branch wages is stable over time, although recently, in the face of higher unemployment and increased immigration, this has started to change.[53] The earnings distribution has only shown a slight tendency to shift in favour of higher earners (Figure 29) and against low earners during the 1990s. While low wage dispersion – after taking into account individual human capital characteristics – is indicative of a competitive labour market in equilibrium, it can also mean that differentials are insufficient to stimulate employment in the

Figure 28. **REAL WAGE, PRODUCTIVITY AND LABOUR SHARES
IN THE BUSINESS SECTOR**

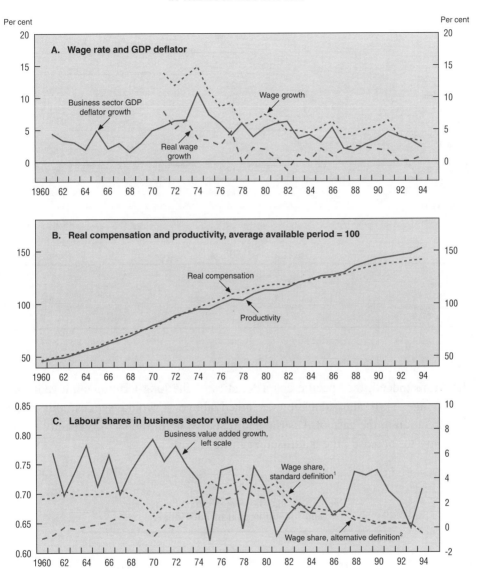

1. Calculated by imputing a wage compensation to self-employed equal to average compensation for wage earners.
2. Calculated by imputing a wage compensation to self-employed rising from 70 per cent of average compensation
    in 1960 to 100 per cent in 1993.
Source: OECD.

Table 23. **International comparisons of wage dispersion by branch and sector**

	Coefficient of variation in per cent	
	Industry	Manufacturing and private service sector
	Hourly wages	
Japan	24	35
United States	25	30 [1]
Canada	24	28 [2]
Austria	**19**	**27** [1]
United Kingdom	18	21 [3]
Finland	17	
Germany (West)	14	21 [2]
Switzerland	14	18
Belgium	15	
France	12	18 [4]
Netherlands	13	17
Norway	16	15
Italy	12	
Denmark	13	14 [1]
Sweden	10	10 [1]

1. 1987.
2. 1986.
3. 1988.
4. 1982.
Source: Guger (1993).

short run. Indeed, the specific characteristics of the long-term unemployed – by sector, age, skill and education as noted above – would suggest this latter interpretation in the case of Austria, and if so, would diminish the capacity of the economy to increase labour utilisation in the future.

Table 24. **Wage dispersion corrected for age and human capital of individuals**

	Coefficient of variation
United States	0.140
Sweden	0.013
Germany	0.072
Norway	0.052
Austria	**0.066**

Source: Hofer (1995).

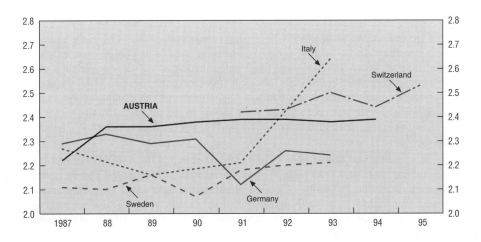

1. Ratio of upper earnings limit of the 9th decile of male workers to the upper limit of the first decile.
Source: OECD.

The combination of average wage flexibility and low dispersion for similar workers (Table 24), which is a characteristic of Europe more generally, reflects the institutional features of the labour market, which make for a high level of centralisation. Although in 1990 trade union density was only 46 per cent, the coverage rate for collective agreements negotiated within the framework of the chamber system (see Box 7) was the highest in the OECD at around 98 per cent.[54] The boundaries of the trade unions are drawn very widely – there are only 14 unions and one union covers all white-collar workers – so that conflicts between various groups of workers are settled internally and do not lead to inter-union competition. This might be one factor explaining the constancy of wage dispersion: unions have accepted the existing wage structure and have not followed a ''solidaristic'' approach characteristic of Scandinavia by which wage agreements were linked to a leading sector. At the same time, it has been easier for the unions to accept the principle of seniority which in turn has led to a high measured dispersion of sectoral wages. Wage agreements have usually only set minimum conditions with authority given to individual works councils to improve only the terms of the agreement. Thus, high profitability enterprises – including those in the past supported and subsidised by the government – have usually paid rates above the award rates resulting in substantial inter-firm wage differences which moved pro-cyclically. Structural features such as branch capital intensity and level of exports also have an influence, but these characteristics are linked to industrial concentration and state ownership, suggesting that an element of wage dispersion may derive from rent sharing activity in the past, which could have reduced overall employment.[55]

In response to increasing commercial pressures, including the privatisation of many previously state-owned enterprises and more binding budget constraints on the remainder, wage drift (the difference between centrally-negotiated wages and actual wages) has fallen significantly since the mid 1980s (Figure 30). In the

Figure 30. **DECLINING WAGE DRIFT IN INDUSTRY**[1]

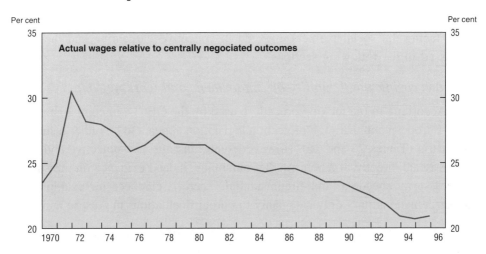

1. Data refer to January of each year and include the construction sector until January 1975.
Source: Wirtschaftskammer, Vienna.

current downturn, which comes at a time of heightened international competition, there is also anecdotal evidence that a number of work councils are also accepting adjustments downwards to centrally-negotiated agreements. This is technically speaking illegal, but the pressure on some small and medium enterprises to adjust labour costs is quite intense. In addition, there is also pressure to relax work practices in order to preserve employment. This spontaneous development has been underpinned by the failure to effectively establish opening clauses in centralised wage contracts. In the 1993 wage round an opening clause was agreed which allowed firms to set aside the 2.8 per cent wage increase if they undertook investment to increase or to secure jobs. Negotiations were supposed to take place centrally, or at least be approved centrally if negotiated with the works council. However, the possibility was only used by some 70 enterprises.

In sum, although the wage-bargaining system has provided a great deal of macroeconomic flexibility linked to the acceptance by the social partners of the hard-currency policy, pressures nevertheless exist to increase flexibility at the enterprise level. However, the implementation of such flexibility depends on the strengthening of market signals. Arrangements concerning employment conditions, dismissals, early retirement, as well as eligibility for – and generosity of – unemployment and related social welfare benefits, condition the economic pressures facing the social partners engaged in collective bargaining and these are discussed in the following sections.

Increasing the flexibility of employment and working time

According to the ranking procedure used by the OECD, in comparison with other European countries job protection legislation appears to be rather restrictive in Austria (Tables 25 and 26). However, such rankings are subjective and difficult to relate directly to labour market outcomes; indeed evidence on the subject is necessarily anecdotal and circumstantial. There is evidence for example that labour demand adjusts only sluggishly to output fluctuations in Austria and there

Table 25. **Summary of job protection legislation in Europe in the late 1980s**

	Summary rankings by main area [1]			
	Regular procedural inconveniences	Notice and severance pay for no-fault dismissals	Unfair dismissal	Overall ranking for strictness of protection against dismissals
Portugal	12.0	15.0	16.0	16.0
Spain	15.0	14.0	13.0	15.0
Italy	3.0	16.0	15.0	14.0
Austria	**10.0**	**10.0**	**11.0**	**13.0**
Greece	8.0	12.0	10.0	12.0
Sweden	11.0	8.0	9.0	11.0
Finland	14.0	9.0	4.0	9.5
Germany	13.0	2.0	12.0	9.5
Norway	6.5	6.0	14.0	8.0
Netherlands	16.0	1.0	8.0	7.0
France	9.0	7.0	6.5	6.0
Belgium	4.5	13.0	3.0	5.0
Denmark	1.0	11.0	5.0	4.0
Ireland	6.5	3.0	6.5	3.0
United Kingdom	4.5	5.0	1.0	2.0
Switzerland	2.0	4.0	2.0	1.0

1. All rankings increase with the strictness of employment protection. The summary rankings for each sub-heading are ranks of the unweighted average of the ranks of each variable shown in Table 26 and the overall ranking is the rank of the unweighted average of the first 3 columns.

Source: D. Grubb and W. Wells, "Employment regulation and patterns of work in EC Countries", *OECD Economic Studies,* 21, Winter 1993; M. Emerson, "Regulation or deregulation of the labour market: policy regimes for the recruitment and dismissal of employees in the industrialized countries", *European Economic Review,* 32, pp. 775-817, 1988; R. Lilja, T. Santamaki-Ki-Vuori and G. Standing, *Unemployment and Labour Market Flexibility: Finland,* ILO, 1990; G. Standing, *Unemployment and Labour Market Flexibility: Sweden,* ILO, 1988.

Table 26. Indicators of the "strictness" of employment protection legislation in Europe in the late 1980s

Values of the indicators[1]

Key	Regular procedural inconveniences		Notice and severance pay for no-fault individual dismissals						Strictness of provisions for unfair dismissals			
	Procedures	Delay to start of notice	Notice period after			Severance pay after			Definition of unfair dismissal	Trial period	At 20y	Reinstatement
	Scale 0 to 3	Days	Months						Scale 0 to 3	Months		Scale 0 to 3
			9m	4y	20y	9m	4y	20y				
Austria	**2.0**	**5.0**	**0.8**	**1.2**	**2.5**	**0.0**	**2.0**	**9.0**	**1.0**	**1.0**	**9.0**	**1.0**
Belgium	1.0	3.0	2.0	3.6	11.4	0.0	0.0	0.0	0.0	3.3	12.5	0.0
Denmark	0.5	0.0	1.6	2.8	5.0	0.0	0.0	1.5	0.0	3.0	9.0	1.0
France	1.5	12.0	1.0	2.0	2.0	0.0	0.4	2.7	0.0	1.2	15.0	0.0
Germany	3.0	10.0	1.0	1.0	4.5	0.0	0.0	0.0	2.0	6.0	18.0	2.0
Greece	2.0	1.0	0.6	1.7	9.0	0.3	0.9	4.6	1.0	2.0	9.0	2.0
Ireland	1.5	3.0	0.2	0.5	2.0	0.0	0.5	3.9	0.0	12.0	24.0	1.0
Italy	1.5	0.0	0.3	1.1	2.2	0.7	3.5	18	0.0	0.8	32.5	3.0
Netherlands	3.0	35.0	0.6	1.0	5.3	0.0	0.0	0.0	1.0	2.0	5.3	1.0
Portugal	2.0	17.0	0.8	2.0	9.1	0.2	1.7	9.3	3.0	1.0	20.0	3.0
Spain	2.25	40.0	1.0	3.0	3.0	0.2	1.3	6.0	2.0	1.7	35.0	0.0
United Kingdom	1.0	3.0	0.2	0.7	2.8	0.0	0.9	4.6	0.0	24.0	10.8	0.0
Finland	2.0	56.0	2.0	2.0	6.0	0.0	0.0	0.0	0.0	4.0	20.0	0.0
Norway	1.5	3.0	1.0	2.0	5.0	0.0	0.0	0.0	2.0	1.0	15.0	2.0
Sweden	2.0	7.0	1.0	4.0	6.0	0.0	0.0	0.0	1.0	6.0	32.0	2.0
Switzerland	0.5	1.0	1.0	2.0	3.0	0.0	0.0	0.0	0.0	3.0	20.0	0.0

1. Situation in the late 1980s. The definitions of the indicators shown here are listed in the next note, and some underlying assumptions are described in more detail in D. Grubb and W. Wells, "Employment Regulation and Patterns of Work in EC Countries", OECD Economic Studies, 21, Winter 1993. Information in this table relates to **individual** dismissals (provisions applying to large-scale plant closures may differ) and relates, where relevant, to an average across provisions for manual and non-manual workers and an average across provisions for personal (individual) reasons and provisions for technical (economic) reasons.

2. The variables tabulated under each key are as follows:
   Procedures: procedures to be followed when issuing a regular dismissal notice: 1 for a statement in writing to the employee of reasons for his dismissal, 2 for notification to a third party (works council or local employment exchange) and 3 when prior permission for dis-missal must be obtained from the third party.
   Delay to start of notice: the delay between a decision to dismiss and the time that notice can become effective after following required procedures in days (e.g. notification by registered letter is assumed to involve 3 days).
   Notice period, 9m, 4y, 20y: the lapse between issuance of a dismissal notice and the effective cessation of employment, in months. The columns refer to workers who have been with the employer 9 months, 4 years, and 20 years respectively.
   Severance pay, 9m, 4y, 20y: a lump-sum payment to the dismissed employee at the time of cessation of employment: the three columns differ as for "notice period" above.
   Definition of unfair dismissal: scored 0 when worker capability or redundancy of the job are adequate grounds for dismissal, 1 when social considerations, age or job tenure, must be, when possible, influence the choice of which worker(s) to dismiss, 2 when retraining to adapt the worker to different work must be attempted prior to dismissal, and 3 when worker capability can never be a basis for dismissal.
   Trial period: the maximum length of the period after hiring during which an appeal against dismissal on grounds of unfairness cannot be made.
   Compensation at 20y: the compensation payable to a worker who has been unfairly dismissed after 20 years with the employer.
   Reinstatement: scored 0 if, following a court judgement of unfair dismissal, reinstatement is never granted, 1 if reinstatement is "rare", 2 if reinstatement is "possible" and 3 if the employee always has the option of reinstatement.

Source: D. Grubb and W. Wells, "Employment Regulation and patterns of Work in EC Countries", OECD Economic Studies, 21, Winter 1993; M. Emerson, "Regulation or deregulation of the labour market: policy regimes for the recruitment and dismissal of employees in the industrialized countries", European Economic Review, 32, pp. 775-817, 1988; R. Lilja, T. Santamaki-Ki-Vuori and G. Standing, Unemployment and Labour Market Flexibility: Finland, ILO, 1990; G. Standing, Unemployment and Labour Market Flexibility: Sweden, ILO, 1988.

is direct evidence[56] that this could be related to high costs of employment adjustment arising in part from legal requirements. In addition, employment protection is more stringent for older workers and this was reinforced in 1993 with additional legal protection (*Beschäftigungssicherungsgesetz*), including explicit penalty payments. The unemployment rate for older workers has nevertheless continued to rise, as has the duration of unemployment spells. Anecdotal evidence points to an unwillingness to take on older workers, partly on account of restrictive conditions of dismissal.

Although comparable data are lacking, the incidence of flexible work arrangements appears to be low in Austria. Only 10 per cent of employees work regularly at night and shift-type work on a regular basis covers only 11 per cent of the work force, a pattern which appears to have been relatively stable over time.[57] Labour hours are limited by legislation. Although there are many exemptions, in accordance with the EU directive, the legal maximum number of hours per week is 50 with the daily maximum 10 hours. The law also defines the threshold for overtime as 8 hours and 40 hours respectively with a legal premium for overtime of 50 per cent. Collective agreements can and do alter these conditions in favour of the employee. A minimum period of two months for averaging working time is specified, subject to hours not exceeding legal norms, but collective agreements may lengthen this period and sometimes devolve bargaining powers to the enterprise level.

Employment contracts are usually of unlimited duration, with a short probationary period. Fixed term contracts are permitted under certain conditions, but in 1994 only 4.8 per cent of employees were covered by such contracts, concentrated in a small number of seasonal sectors. An important regulation restricting fixed term contracts stipulates that if such a contract is extended beyond the original term, it is to be considered of unlimited duration. A second restriction concerns successive fixed term contracts; these are treated as unlimited contracts unless they are justified by economic and social considerations.

The incidence of part-time work is relatively low in Austria. This is often attributed to the industrial structure and to the relatively low labour force participation rate of women since there appear to be few legal or financial barriers to its further development. However, other reasons might be important. Although there are no reliable statistics, many Austrian firms appear to make great use of work contracts with self-employed (*Werkverträge*). This has the advantage to the firm of circumventing employment legislation, while for both the employee and employer the advantage is sometimes to avoid paying high social security contributions. As a result, many such self-employed persons may not be adequately covered by social security.

Taxes and transfers

As in other European countries Austria is characterised by a well-developed system of social security, social expenditures amounting to some 29 per cent of GDP in 1993; in 1980 the share was around 26 per cent and the rise during recent years owes much to labour market-related problems such as early retirement and unemployment benefits. This section focuses on the labour market incentive effects of the system: the incentives for accepting work or for actively seeking it, or for leaving or entering the labour force. On balance, the unemployment benefits system appears to be associated with some undesirable features resulting in both poverty and unemployment traps. Special benefits for older workers reduce incentives to remain in the labour force, and discourage the older unemployed from accepting jobs which are lower paid than their previous employment.

The tax/benefit system is summarised in Box 8[58]. The unemployment benefits system comprises unemployment benefits (UI) and, on exhaustion of these, unemployment assistance (UA). From the perspective of the unemployed the system provides income replacement for an almost unlimited period, although only 5 per cent of the inflows to unemployment remain on benefits for more than a year. Moreover, for some recipients the requirement to actively seek work in practice is weak. At the same time, the social assistance system ensures a subsistence level of income. Taken together, the incentive for active job search for some unemployed would appear to be relatively weak and reservation wages have been maintained at high levels in the face of structural change. The system may thus have contributed to unemployment persistence among marginal groups and also operates as a subsidy for seasonal workers in the tourist industry.

Statutory unemployment benefit replacement rates are not in themselves particularly high by international standards (Table 28), but once the combined tax and benefit system is taken into consideration – especially family allowances – net replacement rates for some segments of the population could be around 70 per cent, even after 5 years of unemployment. As in most other countries, net

Box 8. **The tax/benefits system**

Benefits for the unemployed

There are three systems affecting the unemployed – unemployment insurance (UI), unemployment assistance (UA, *Notstandshilfe*) and social assistance (SA) – and 95 per cent of the registered unemployed receive at least one of these benefits.

Unemployment insurance is compulsory for all except the self-employed and civil servants. To qualify for benefits a person must have worked and paid contributions for twelve months in the preceding two years. In the case of a repeat spell of unemployment, 26 weeks of work in the previous year (20 weeks up to 1995) or 52 weeks in the previous two years are necessary to requalify for benefits. Official training programmes do not requalify but subsidised jobs serve this role.

Benefits are paid for at least 20 weeks, but this rises to 30 weeks after 156 weeks of work in the last five years.

In addition, the benefits period is also age-dependent:

– 40-49 years – 39 weeks after 312 weeks of work in the last ten years
– from 50 years – 52 weeks after 468 weeks of work in the last fifteen years.

These periods can under special circumstances – *i.e.* participation in a special employment foundation (*Arbeitstiftung*) – be increased up to 3-4 years.

Unemployment benefits are tax-free and are defined as percentages of gross income during the previous twelve months. The replacement ratio is around 56 per cent (82 per cent for older workers prior to 1996 when the *Sonderunterstutzung* was abolished) of net income to which must be added family allowances for households with children. These are paid at a flat daily rate of Sch 21.40 per dependent and are means-tested for each additional family member. With a spouse not working and two children the replacement rate is increased by 8-12 percentage points depending on income. The highest income compensated at the maximum replacement rate is roughly 50 per cent higher than the average blue collar wage, while total benefits may not exceed 80 per cent of reference income. The average benefit paid in 1994 corresponded to slightly more than 50 per cent of the average manual worker's after-tax income. The level for an average production worker (APW) was Sch 279 249 per annum in 1994.

Family supplements are reduced against the other partners income above Sch 14 000 per month. The basic benefit is not affected by other income or earnings from the beneficiary himself not exceeding Sch 3 600 per month. Any earnings above that level destroy all benefits entitlements.

Benefits for involuntary short time work, replacing income in the same proportions as unemployment benefits, are also available on condition that the working time reduction is due to temporary, non-seasonal, difficulties.

(continued on next page)

(continued)

Persons who remain unemployed after exhausting their unemployment benefit entitlements are transferred to *unemployment assistance (Notstandshilfe)* which they can continue to collect indefinitely although they must reapply annually. The level of UA depends on previous income and is means tested, mainly with respect to the spouse's income. The replacement rate is 92 per cent of the recipients UI, or 95 per cent for low-income groups. This corresponds to a replacement rate of 51 to 54 per cent of after-tax work income, plus family allowances if applicable. Benefits are not affected by other income or earnings not exceeding Sch 5 621 per month. Family·income above that amount is deducted on a one-to-one basis from the benefit. For people aged 50-54 this limit is raised by 100 per cent and for people over 55 years by 200 per cent.

Social assistance is also paid to those classed as unemployed – as well as to other persons – and it is estimated[1] that around a half of recipients were in this category in 1994. Assistance is administered and financed locally subject to rules established by the Länder, and there are no national SA standards. The prevailing Länder norms for benefits to single persons have ranged from 45 to 60 per cent of the lowest net earnings of full time workers covered by collective agreements. This corresponds to roughly one-third to two-fifths of an average production worker's after tax wage. The norms for a five person household are roughly twice as high. The actual replacement rate is further increased by compensation for the actual costs of housing (*Wohnbeihilfen*).

Social assistance is not affected by other income or earnings not exceeding Sch 1 400 per month, above which all entitlements are withdrawn. Entitlements depend on household resources rather than those of the individual or nuclear family. Officially, other relatives have a duty under family law to render financial support. Under some circumstances assistance will have to be repaid if the finances of the family improve.

The tax system

The tax unit is the individual and there is a progressive tax system with five rates ranging from 10 to 50 per cent in 1994. For the APW the marginal tax rate is about 42 per cent. Tax allowances include social security contributions in their entirety. Tax credits include a general credit of Sch 8 840, a wage earners credit of Sch 1 500, a wage earners transport credit of Sch 4 000, a sole earners tax credit of Sch 5 000, tax credits for children of Sch 4 200 for the first, Sch 6 300 for the second, and Sch 8 400 for the third. A worker with low income may have a negative income tax. This cannot exceed the wage earner's tax credit and is limited to 10 per cent of social security contributions.

Not all labour income is taxed in the same manner. Overtime, shift work and bonuses (13th and 14th monthly salaries) are subject to special rules. A special flat rate of tax of 6 per cent applies to bonuses and other remuneration, limited to one sixth of current income in cases where tax is deducted at source. An amount of Sch 8 500 of

(continued on next page)

(continued)

bonuses is tax free and if the total amount of bonuses is below Sch 23 000 p.a. they are not taxable.

The taxation of income including interest and dividends is low and only moderately progressive due to a number of tax concessions which lowers the tax rate for high incomes substantially. Indirect taxes and social security contributions which have a clearly regressive effect on income distribution comprise 70 per cent of all tax revenues. Thus overall the degree of progression is only moderate.[2]

---

1. See *The Public Employment Service in Austria, Germany and Sweden,* OECD, Paris, 1996.
2. A. Guger (ed.), *Umverteilung durch öffentliche Haushalte in Österreich,* WIFO, Vienna, 1995.

Table 27. **Unemployment and recipients of income support**

Average stocks in 1994

Category (1 000 persons)	
Population aged 15-64 years	5 330
Labour force	3 699
Unemployed according to household surveys[1]	166
PES-registered unemployment	
UI beneficiaries	128
UA beneficiaries	67
SA beneficiaries[2]	15
Others	5
Total	215
Early retirement	
Early pensions	356
Other schemes[3]	26
Total	382
Extended paid leave after childbirth[4]	120

1. *Mikrozensus.*
2. Approximate estimates by the OECD, covering SA recipients registered as unemployed excluding those with both SA and UI or UA.
3. *Sonderunterstützung.*
4. *Karenzurlaub.*
Source: Various national sources and OECD estimates.

Table 28. Unemployment benefit replacement rates by duration of unemployment and family circumstances,[1] 1991

Duration categories	First year			Second and third year			Fourth and fifth year			Overall average
Family circumstances	Single	With dependent spouse	With spouse in work	Single	With dependent spouse	With spouse in work	Single	With dependent spouse	With spouse in work	
Australia	28	50	0	28	51	0	28	51	0	26
Austria	**42**	**45**	**25**	**40**	**43**	**0**	**40**	**43**	**0**	**31**
Belgium	52	52	47	36	52	30	36	52	30	43
Canada	58	58	58	13	25	0	13	25	0	28
Denmark	73	74	72	61	67	54	21	43	0	52
Finland	58	58	56	44	44	27	30	30	0	38
France	58	58	58	37	37	30	28	28	0	37
Germany	37	41	37	33	36	0	33	36	0	28
Greece	44	53	44	4	4	4	0	0	0	17
Ireland	38	52	38	26	41	5	25	39	0	29
Italy	7	8	7	0	0	0	0	0	0	3
Japan	25	25	25	0	0	0	0	0	0	8
Netherlands	70	70	70	56	56	56	34	48	0	51
New Zealand	28	47	0	29	49	0	29	49	0	26
Norway	62	62	62	41	41	41	14	14	14	39
Portugal	65	65	65	37	40	37	0	0	0	34
Spain	70	70	70	30	30	30	0	0	0	33
Sweden	80	80	80	6	6	6	0	0	0	29
Switzerland	63	72	63	0	0	0	0	0	0	22
United Kingdom	19	31	19	17	27	0	17	27	0	18
United States	24	26	21	5	10	0	5	10	0	11

1. Benefit entitlement before tax as a percentage of previous earnings before tax. Data shown are averages over replacement rates at two earning levels (average earnings and two-thirds of average earnings). For further information, see OECD, *The OECD Jobs Study: Evidence and Explanations*, Chapter 8.

Source: OECD Database on Unemployment Benefit Entitlements and Replacement Rates.

Table 29. **Replacement rates¹ for single-earner households, 1994**

Average effective tax rate at the average production worker (APW) level of earnings

	Replacement rates in first month of unemployment: no social assistance			60th month of unemployment: including social assistance
	Net replacement rates (after tax and other benefits)			
	Couple, no children	Couple, 2 children	Couple, 2 children, housing benefits (excluding Austria)	Couple, 2 children, housing benefits
Austria	**57**	**69**	**69**	**78**
Australia[2, 3, 4]	49	64	71	71
Belgium	64	66	66	70
Canada	63	67	67	47
Denmark[5]	69	73	83	83
Finland	63	75	88	98
France	69	71	80	65
Germany	60	71	78	71
Ireland[3]	49	64	64	64
Italy	37	47	47	11
Japan[3]	43	42	42	68
Netherlands	77	77	84	80
New Zealand[3, 4]	48	64	70	70
Norway	67	73	73	83
Spain	75	74	74	46
Sweden[2, 5]	81	84	89	99[2]
Switzerland	77	89	89	71
United Kingdom[3]	35	51	77	77
United States[6]	60	68	68	17

Note: In the first month of unemployment it is assumed that families possess enough assets to be ineligible for social assistance. In the 60th month it is assumed that they no longer have such assets and so social assistance (SA) is assumed to be paid where it is higher than other benefits to which they may still be entitled. The replacement rates reflect a strict application of legal provisions rather than common practice, where these differ. For more details see source. For Austria it is assumed that private rents amount to 20 per cent of the APW and that social assistance comprises only payments covering such housing costs.

1. It is assumed that the worker is 40 years old, and started work at 18. The replacement rates are for the first month of unemployment, after waiting periods have been satisfied. This entitlement is then multiplied by 12 to give an annualised equivalent, on which tax is calculated. The person is fully unemployed. Social assistance is calculated according to a "typical rates" for the country concerned. This may involve making assumptions about housing costs.
2. Benefit amounts for couples are calculated on the basis of both spouses actively seeking work.
3. Figures for Australia, Ireland, New Zealand and the United Kingdom are for 1995. Unemployment benefits parameters for Japan are for 1996.
4. There is no social insurance in Australia or New Zealand. All figures in the table, refer to the assistance benefit.
5. Social assistance is only available when there is a "social event" such as unemployment. Low earnings are not themselves a social event.
6. The taxes and benefits are calculated using the rules applying in Detroit, Michigan. All figures include AFDC and Food Stamps. If these are treated as being equivalent to social assistance, columns 3, 4 and 5 would read 60, 59 and 59 at the level of APW.

Source: "Making work pay", *Employment Outlook*, OECD, Paris 1996.

Table 30. **Replacement rates for single-earner households, 1994**

Replacement rates at two-thirds of the average production worker (APW) level of earnings

	Replacement rates in first month of unemployment: no social assistance [1]			60th month of unemployment including social assistance
	Net replacement rates (after tax and other benefits)			
	(1) Couple, no children	(2) Couple, 2 children	(3) Couple, 2 children, housing benefits (excluding Austria)	(4) Couple, 2 children, housing benefits
Austria	58	74	74	100 [2]
Australia[3, 4, 5]	66	76	78	78
Belgium	**75**	**76**	**76**	91
Canada	64	67	67	61
Denmark[6]	92	93	95	95
Finland	**67**	**83**	**89**	100
France	79	81	88	83
Germany	**60**	**70**	**77**	80
Ireland[4]	67	70	70	70
Italy	36	45	45	14
Japan[4]	**49**	**48**	**48**	86
Netherlands	79	78	84	95
New Zealand[4, 5]	70	80	86	86
Norway	**66**	**75**	75	100
Spain	74	78	77	66
Sweden[3, 6]	**82**	**85**	**89**	121 [2]
Switzerland	**75**	**87**	**87**	97
United Kingdom[4]	52	67	90	90
United States[7]	66	60	60	19
Average (unweighted)	68	73	77	80

Note: In the first month of unemployment it is assumed that families possess enough assets to be ineligible for social assistance. In the 60th month it is assumed that they no longer have such assets and so social assistance (SA) is assumed to be paid where it is higher than other benefits to which they might still be entitled. Figures in **bold** indicate those cases where families would be entitled to SA on the basis of their income were they not to have been assumed to have been disqualified by an assets test. The replacement rates reflect a strict application of legal provisions rather than common practices where these differ.

1. It is assumed that the worker is 40 years old and started work at 18. The replacement rates are for the first month of unemployment, after waiting periods have been satisfied. This entitlement is then multiplied by 12 to give an annualised equivalent on which tax is calculated. The person is fully unemployed. Social assistance is calculated according to a ''typical rate'' for the country concerned. This may involve making assumptions about housing costs.
2. It is assumed that private rents amount to 20 per cent of the APW. Such housing costs are assumed to be covered by social assistance with no other payments. If rent support were to be so high, replacement rates would near 100 per cent.
3. Benefit amounts for couples are calculated on the basis of both spouses actively seeking work.
4. Figures for Australia, Ireland, New Zealand and the United Kingdom are for 1995. Unemployment benefit parameters for Japan are for 1996.
5. There is no social insurance in Australia or New Zealand. All figures in the table refer to the assistance benefit.
6. Social assistance is only available when there is a ''social event'' such as unemployment. Low earnings are not themselves a social event.
7. The taxes and benefits are calculated using the rules applying in Detroit, Michigan. All figures include aid to families with dependent children (AFDC) and food stamps. If these are treated as being equivalent to social assistance, columns 1, 2 and 3 would read 59, 52 and 52 at two-thirds of APW.

Source: OECD database on taxation and benefit entitlements.

replacement rates are somewhat higher for the lower paid (Tables 29 and 30). In addition, net replacement rates for some older workers (*i.e.* those on *Sonderunter-stützung* up to 1996) are higher, since statutory replacement rates for benefits are around 80 per cent. Moreover, since wages are heavily related to both tenure and age, an unemployed older worker could face employment opportunities at wages substantially lower than those used for calculating unemployment benefits (*i.e.* earnings over the last twelve months of employment). Hence, measured in terms of new income earning opportunities the net replacement rate for some groups is likely to be high and it could even be above 100 per cent. Thus, among older workers and the most poorly paid, which are the sectors of the work force in which unemployment problems are most acute and the need for structural change the greatest, the incentive system could favour long job search and a slow change in reservation wages.

An important feature of the unemployment benefits system is the means test. Private earned income (net of income and social security taxes) exceeding Sch 3 600 per month (15 per cent of APW) destroys all entitlements to unemployment benefits. Receipt of unemployment assistance (*Notstandshilfe*) and social assistance also affects the incentives facing the partner: family net income of Sch 5 621 (23 per cent of the earnings of an average production worker (APW) is deducted one for one from all benefit entitlements. The fact that unemployment benefits are reduced causes strong disincentives to work more than a small number of hours whilst on benefits. At about 8 hours of work or 20 per cent of the APW, all family types face sharply reduced income from work effort (Figure 31), the marginal effective rate of tax being above 100 per cent. A one-earner couple with two children on unemployment benefit would have to succeed in finding a job paying about 73 per cent of the APW wage to bring net earned income up to the level equal to UI plus Sch 3 600 per month. This unemployment trap is quite dramatic for other family types also, but much less for the spouse of a benefit recipient.

Recipients of social assistance face a means test on all resources within the extended family, including parents, grandparents and even brothers and sisters, accounting perhaps for the low take-up relatively to the presumed number of needy people. In addition, there is a wealth test in some Länder and benefits may have to be repaid if the financial situation of the family improves. Accurate data on the number of social assistance recipients do not exist, but it is evident that

Figure 31. **NET INCOMES FROM INCREASING WORK EFFORT[1]**
FOR HOUSEHOLDS ON UNEMPLOYMENT INSURANCE
Schillings

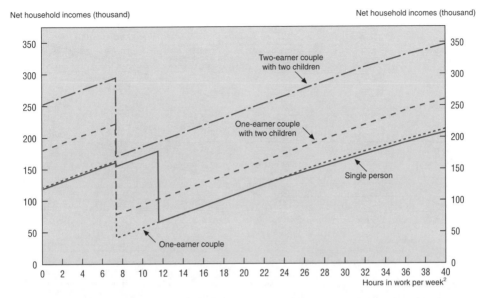

1. In 1994. Net incomes of different household types on UI, not including SA. All earners are increasing their hours worked from zero to 40 hours per week at APW pro-rata pay. In the case of two-earner household the UI beneficiary is increasing hours worked at APW *pro-rata* pay, and the spouse is working 2 days a week at APW *pro-rata* pay. The children are aged 5 and 11.
2. Number of hours worked per week by APW is 40.
Source: OECD.

there may be substantial poverty traps, such that it does not pay some recipients to accept low-paid work. To illustrate this, Figure 32 has been constructed on simplified assumptions that, apart from a basic allowance, social assistance also covers support for rents which cost around 10 per cent of earnings. Under these simplified but realistic assumptions the poverty trap operates in a range up to 70 per cent of the APW wage for a family with two children.

Recipients of unemployment-related transfers must be "willing" to work, which means that they must seek jobs at their own initiative, and not merely wait for offers from the employment service. There is no general specification of what constitutes proof of job search so that the practical significance of the requirement depends on the employment offices involved. The job willingness require-

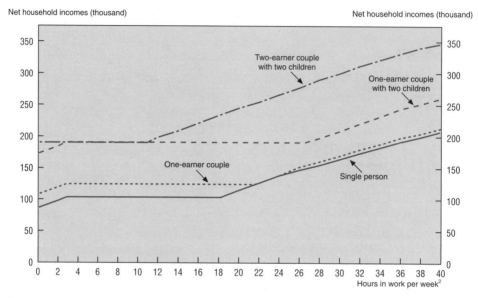

Figure 32. **NET INCOMES FROM INCREASING WORK EFFORT**[1]
FOR HOUSEHOLDS ON SOCIAL ASSISTANCE

Schillings

Net household incomes (thousand)

Net household incomes (thousand)

Two-earner couple
with two children

One-earner couple
with two children

One-earner couple

Single person

Hours in work per week[2]

1. In 1994. Net incomes of different household types, including SA entitlements. At zero hour of work the household is entirely dependent on SA. All earners are increasing their hours worked from zero to 40 hours per week at APW pro-rata pay. In the case of two-earner household the UI beneficiary is increasing hours worked at APW *pro-rata* pay, and the spouse is working 2 days a week at APW *pro-rata* pay. The children are aged 5 and 11. The private rents covered by SA equal 10% of the APW (= 279 249 schillings).
2. Number of hours worked per week by APW is 40.
Source: OECD.

ment is in practice suspended – but not formally waived – for groups of job seekers covering about a fourth of all the unemployed.[59] In general, though, benefit recipients must visit the public employment service at least once a month for counselling and calls to attend are sometimes used as a formal check of availability. Job offers and training proposals are also used to test availability.

Jobs which are deemed suitable (*zumutbar*) must be accepted if a penalty is to be avoided. The principle of occupational protection applies for recipients of unemployment benefits – though not for recipients of unemployment assistance – but only to the extent that the public employment service finds that working in a different occupation would jeopardise a subsequent return to a previous career.

Any collectively agreed wage must be accepted and temporary jobs are also deemed acceptable. However, lack of child care is accepted as a reason for refusing jobs only for job-seekers with families where jobs are far away from home. Sanctions can be justified by quits and dismissal for bad behaviour, refusal to accept job offers and training. For job refusal benefits are cancelled for six weeks on the first occasion and thereafter for eight weeks. Sanctions are relatively common but in one fifth of the cases they have been subject to appeals – with a similar proportion leading to reversed decisions.

Early retirement

The labour force participation rate for older workers in Austria is amongst the lowest in any OECD country, due to the extensive use of early retirement: only 24 per cent of the population aged 55 to 64 years are in the labour force. The statutory retirement age is 65 for men and 60 for women, but only 15 per cent of men and 30 per cent of women who retired in 1994 had reached the statutory retirement age. There are three avenues to early retirement: disability, contribution period, and unemployment. Disability pensions are granted using medical criteria alone excluding the labour market situation but as Figure 24 shows clearly, the rapid decline in the number of new retirees on account of disability indicates that previously this channel in fact was much broader. Anyone who has paid contributions for 35 years can obtain a full old-age pension before the normal retirement age from the age of 55 for women and 60 for men. The rules were changed in 1993, making them more liberal: reduced working capacity is now taken into account for early old age pension as well as for disability pensions. This accounts for the dramatic fall in recourse to disability pensions (Figure 24). Moreover, periods of child care which could be counted as contribution years were increased, leading to the surge of early old-age pensions for women since 1994.

As many as 30 per cent of all new pensioners in Austria in 1993 received unemployment-related benefits in the period immediately preceding retirement. There was until 1996 a special pre-retirement benefit (*Sonderunterstützung, SU*) which was higher than the normal unemployment benefit available from the age of 54 for women and 59 for men, or four years earlier in some industries. There was an obligation to be available for work but the law relating to SU benefits gave considerable room for manoeuvre to ignore the requirement. As a result, the *de facto* age of retirement was lower than it appeared from pension statistics.

Non-wage costs and social security contributions

Measured in a common currency, nominal hourly compensation in Austria is amongst the highest in the world (Table 31), while if thirteenth and fourteenth

Table 31. **Structure of labour costs in manufacturing**

1994

	Hourly labour cost in schillings	Direct wages	Proportion of direct wages (per cent)
Germany (West)	309	170	55.06
Switzerland	292	192	65.66
Belgium	263	136	51.59
Norway	256	172	67.25
Japan	253	150	59.09
Austria	**248**	**125**	**50.47**
Netherlands	245	136	55.55
Denmark	242	198	81.98
Luxembourg	229	158	68.98
Finland	225	122	54.16
Sweden	218	128	58.84
France	203	106	51.87
United States	197	138	69.93
Italy	191	95	49.76
Germany (East)	187	109	58.35
Canada	186	134	72.19
Australia	164	119	72.50
Ireland	156	111	71.18
United Kingdom	155	111	71.40
Spain	142	78	54.52
Greece	86	52	60.21
Singapore [1]	70	47	67.74
Portugal	65	36	55.83
Korea [1]	60	42	70.04
Chinese Taipei [1]	60	46	77.48
Hong Kong [1]	52	43	82.42
Hungary [1]	32	16	50.00
Poland [1]	24	13	54.78
Czech Republic [1]	21	13	59.80
Slovakia [1]	19	11	58.89
Thailand [1]	19	15	82.33
Malaysia [1]	18	14	76.28
Bulgaria [1]	12	7	57.14
Romania [1]	9	6	62.69
Indonesia [1]	8	6	79.82
Russia [1]	6	4	58.70
China [1]	5		

1. 1993.
Source: Helmut Hofer and K. Pichelman, Lohnbildung und Wettbewerbsfähigkeit in Österreich, Institute for Advanced Studies, Vienna, 1996.

month wages and salaries are treated as normal wages, the share of the non-wage labour cost component is about the same as in other OECD countries. Social security contributions are a major component of indirect wage costs, accounting for around 45 per cent of gross wages and salaries: employers pay about 25 per cent for wage earners and 22 per cent for salaried employees in addition to 4.5 per cent of wages which are paid to the Family Assistance Fund, while employees pay about 17 per cent of their gross wages or salary for social insurance.[60]

For a number of years Austria has sought to minimise the growth of social security contributions, even at the cost of greater transfers from general government revenues to the social security system. Nevertheless the average tax wedge including indirect taxes has steadily increased since 1989, markedly so for taxes on wages and salaries, in the case of both employers and employees (Figure 33, Panel B). Empirical studies suggest that direct taxes and contributions levied on wages have been passed forward to some extent in the form of higher product prices, thereby lowering labour demand.[61] The *OECD Jobs Study* concluded that policy makers should not expect long-run effects on employment from substituting direct labour-based taxes and contributions by indirect taxes, but empirical work in Austria suggests that there may be some grounds for expecting short term gains from such a shift, and even long-run ones to the extent that the tax base is extended to the inactive population.

Active labour market policies

Active labour market programmes (ALMPs) are quantitatively less important in Austria than in most other OECD countries: in 1994 spending on ALMPs was only 0.2 per cent of GDP (Figure 34), while the annual participant inflows were equivalent to 2.3 per cent of the labour force. Around 15 per cent of the outflow from unemployment go to ALMPs rather than normal jobs. Adult training dominates the ALMP effort, the European Social Fund paying about a quarter of ALMP spending. Training programmes are primarily available to unemployed workers and those at risk of becoming so, although 10 per cent of entrants in 1994 were neither unemployed nor judged at risk. Since 1995 the European Social Fund has financed a programme targeted at those groups at special risk of becoming unemployed. Apprenticeship training is important in Austria but is regarded as general education and not as labour market policy. There is no fixed

Figure 33. **TAX WEDGES ON WAGES**

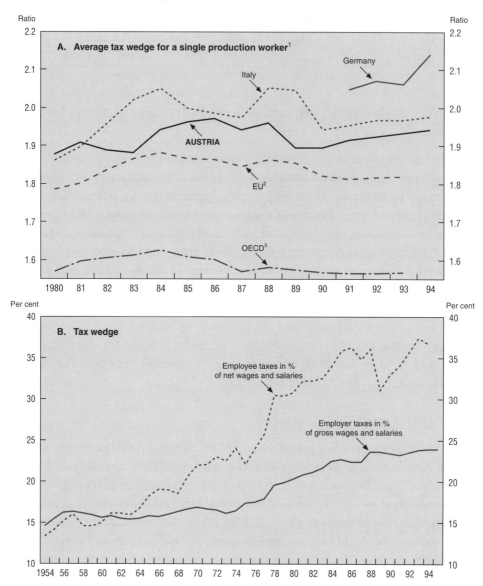

1. Total labour costs divided by net take-home pay for an average single production worker whithout children plus indirect tax rates.
2. EU 15 less Ireland, Portugal and Spain.
3. Czech Republic, Ireland, Mexico, New Zealand, Norway, Portugal, Spain, Switzerland and Turkey excluded.
Source: WIFO; OECD, *National Accounts.*

Figure 34. **LABOUR MARKET MEASURES**
Active and passive measures in 1995, per cent of GDP

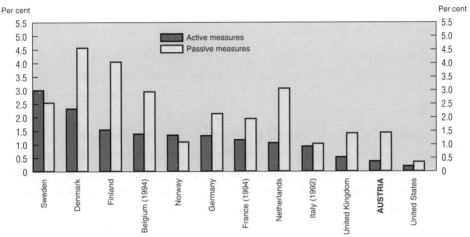

Source: OECD.

definition of the kinds of training which can be supported, apart from a short list of exclusions: these include full apprenticeship qualifications and master craftsmen (*Meister*) courses. The courses often last less than six months and are increasingly organised as modules.

With respect to training, Austria's legal and institutional framework has been more flexible since 1994, when the public employment service became autonomous, although ministry officials have retained some powers to issue instructions. Tripartite boards at national, Land, and local level require that important decisions are taken by a majority of two-thirds, plus one member, a feature designed to encourage consensus as well as to harness knowledge of local conditions. Overall, the market for providing training services is not very competitive: local markets for adult training are dominated by a few big providers (the unions and the employers' federation), who focus on different market segments. Moreover, the same organisations are also represented on the decision-making boards of the labour office which, in addition to contracting out training, also provide the investment capital for many centres. Although this might facilitate efficient planning of training programmes, there is nevertheless a risk of conflict of interest as the social partners are involved in funding decisions affecting their own training facilities. In addition, the development of effective competition might remain restricted.

Some older studies to evaluate training programmes showed mixed results,[62] but one study found that the average duration of unemployment was substantially shorter after participation in a training programme.[63] More generally, effectiveness appears to increase in line with the focus of a programme.

Subsidised work schemes have remained relatively unimportant in Austria although a number of job-creation schemes are in operation. One programme (*Aktion 8000*), which was launched in 1985, permitted the placement of long-term unemployed persons in work of public interest with local and regional governments and non-profit organisations, which then receive a 66 per cent wage subsidy for up to a year. Evaluations show that for about one half of the participants employment continued for several more years.[64] The programme, however, remained modest, with 2000 to 4000 participants in most years, and has now been replaced by broader measures.

Increasing the knowledge base, efficiency and innovative capacity

Reflecting the nature of the post-war catch-up process, a significant part of labour productivity increases during the 1960s and early 1970s (one half prior to 1973) reflected total factor productivity growth, driven by technological progress and other intangible elements such as human capital.[65] In the more recent period, as the productivity gap between Austria and the wealthiest OECD countries narrowed, TFP growth has slowed sharply and its contribution to labour productivity growth has declined (to about one third). While a slowing also occurred elsewhere, in other European countries it was from much higher rates of total factor productivity growth. Indeed, during the 1980s Austria's rate of TFP growth fell to among the lowest in Europe and well below the OECD average. The fact that Austria's labour productivity growth remained at the OECD average was due to continuing strong capital for labour substitution, a feature related to the above-average share of investment in GDP, which was encouraged by capital subsidies including low interest rates. This pattern of development is reflected in the factor-intensity of trade, with differentiated and knowledge-based goods under-represented (Table 32) and in the fact that technological progress

Table 32. **Factor intensities in manufacturing production and trade[1]**

Per cent of total in 1992

	Output[2]		Exports		Imports		RCA index[3]
	Austria	OECD	Austria	OECD	Austria	OECD	Austria
Resource-intensive industries	30.6	34.7	15.8	15.7	12.6	18.3	1.46
Labour-intensive industries	21.0	16.1	18.4	12.5	19.4	17.2	1.30
Scale-intensive industries	32.5	31.8	31.9	32.4	32.2	29.7	0.91
Differentiated goods	12.1	9.5	26.9	24.0	23.8	20.5	0.96
Science-based industries	3.0	7.9	7.0	15.3	12.0	14.3	0.54
Total	100.0	100.0	100.0	100.0	100.0	100.0	. .

1. See *OECD Survey of Austria* (1995) for classification of manufacturing industries.
2. In 1990.
3. RCA = revealed comparative advantage, defined as ratio of exports to imports for Austria, divided by the ratio of exports to imports of the OECD as a whole, for each category.

Source: OECD, *Foreign trade by Commodities.*

appears to have been process-related, rather than based on product innovation and differentiation. Moreover, technological progress appears to have been embodied in capital equipment, mainly imported, with the coverage ratio low by international standards (Table 33).

The apparent weakening of growth dynamics and the developments in factor intensities suggest a need for growth to be based more broadly on human capital (*i.e.* knowledge based) and on increased innovation. The barriers to such a change are, however, quite severe, since institutions have not adapted to newer

Table 33. **Indicators of R&D**

	Gross domestic expenditure on R&D as a percentage of GDP		Total number of researchers (university graduates) per cent of labour force		Technology balance of payments: coverage ratio	
	Mid-1980s	Mid-1990s	Mid-1980s	Mid-1990s	Mid-1980s	Mid-1990s
Austria	**1.23**	**1.5**	**2.3**	**2.5**	**0.2**	**0.29**
Belgium	1.62	1.66	3.2	4.3	0.86	0.94
Denmark	1.19	1.8	2.8	4.7	0.98	
Finland	1.36	2.31	3.7	6.1	0.06	0.14
Netherlands	1.99	1.87	3.8	4.3	0.89	1.01
Sweden	2.55	3.05	4.4	6.8	2.19	8.89
Switzerland	2.28	2.68	4.4	4.6		
EU	1.77	1.91	3.5	4.6		

Source: OECD, *Main Science and Technology Indicators.*

patterns of growth, while policy instruments are diffuse. This section first examines the nature of the innovation system which has arisen – covering the way knowledge is produced, disseminated, adopted and put to use – and then considers the link with the education system more generally. The final section considers competition: if the structure of growth is to be changed it will have to be driven by the competitive process as influenced by the regulatory and legal structure.

Technology and innovation

Viewed from a long-run perspective, the importance of heavy industries in manufacturing has been reflected in a specialisation in lower-technology output[66] and a dependence on imported technology. Research and development expenditures represented 1.5 per cent of GDP in 1993 compared with Germany's 2.5 per cent and 2.2 per cent for the OECD as a whole. The share of business research spending (51 per cent of the country's R&D expenditures) has not changed since 1971, while the number of graduates per thousand of the work force was only 2.5 in comparison with an EU average of 4.2 (see Table 33). As in many smaller OECD economies, Austria's higher education sector absorbs a large share (32 per cent compared with the OECD average of 16 per cent) of the country's R&D expenditures. The business sector performs around 60 per cent of research compared to close to 70 per cent for the OECD. This pattern of indicators is in part related to the large number of SMEs, but nevertheless points to a relatively low level of innovative capacity. There is ample evidence that investment in R&D facilitates the absorption of knowledge produced elsewhere,[67] while studies of technological diffusion conducted at the firm level indicate that a firm's R&D activity both enhances its capacity to monitor and assess technological developments and reduces the cost of imitation and technology transfer. In Austria, surveys indicate that the ability of SMEs to utilise external resources in the innovation process is limited.[68] Insofar as innovative activity does take place in SMEs, it is primarily in the area of process innovation; product innovation – product differentiation, quality improvement and the flexibility of production – appears to be less important.[69]

During the 1980s, the Austrian government implemented a series of programmes to promote application and diffusion of advanced manufacturing technologies in industry, principally through direct supports in the form of grants and subsidised loans. Experience with such programmes was mixed,[70] in part because of the failure to upgrade training and managerial skills. Survey data on the use of advanced manufacturing systems in 1989, for example, revealed that 85 per cent of Austrian firms viewed shortages of higher- and multi-skilled workers as the main problem in adopting advanced micro-electronics.[71] Such problems have been especially acute for smaller firms. Small and medium-sized enterprises (SMEs) are the dominant source of employment, with around 84 per cent of Austrian manufacturing jobs being in establishments with less than 100 workers. Job turnover has been highest in the smallest firms (less than 20 employees), which have experienced the highest net job creation.[72]

In addition to shortages of skilled labour, lack of access to venture capital has been cited as a significant obstacle to the creation of technology-based start-ups. Relatively weak firm creation is confirmed by low entry rates for Austrian firms (around 9 per cent between 1984-1992 compared with 12 per cent for Italy).[73] There are legal and taxation barriers to the effective development of venture capital markets in Austria and companies appear unwilling or unable to tap wider European markets: in 1995 there were only four projects undertaken by European venture capital investors in Austria.[74]

The government is addressing these problems by seeking to strengthen linkages between public and private research, and by enhancing skills development in industry. Channels for technology transfer include the Seibersdorf Research Centre and the Christian Doppler Laboratories, which maintain joint research projects with industry. The Association for the Promotion of Modernisation of Production Technology links the research needs of large and small firms. The promotion of technology diffusion, particularly among SMEs, is focusing more on ''soft'' supports such as consultancy services to upgrade management skills and technology planning. A Techno-Counselling Programme has been established under the Federal Ministry for Economic Affairs to advise firms on the managerial and organisational aspects of deploying new technologies. The Integrated Production Innovation Programme also provides training in technology-oriented management for enterprises.

Upgrading skills and competencies

With the exception of university qualifications, Austria ranks as a country with a well-qualified labour force: the vast majority have gone through secondary vocational education or apprenticeship and have solid vocational education, while almost a quarter of the working population took part in further vocational instruction during the period 1984 to 1989, often at their workplace. Apart from older workers, who have acquired competencies though work experience, comparatively few persons have failed to complete upper secondary education or to acquire a vocational education: the proportion of the workforce with only a school leaving certificate declined from 41 per cent in 1981 to 26 per cent in 1992. Among younger persons, the levels of educational attainment are rising rapidly, with two-fifths of 18-19 year olds now enrolled in higher education; after the period of compulsory schooling (to age 15) three quarters move to vocational training and about a half of these into the apprenticeship programme. Thanks to a well diversified school curriculum, and the fact that pathways for both technical/vocational education as well as academic instruction are of high quality, early school leaving is not widespread. The existing vocational and apprenticeship system continues to ensure a smooth transition to work for most young persons. Nevertheless the system is subject to numerous pressures which have a bearing on labour market performance.

Around 40 per cent of the work force have as their highest qualification level an apprenticeship in the dual system, but recently enterprises – both large and small – have been displaying a marked reluctance to offer new positions. Many industrial firms keep the number of apprentices low, preferring to recruit from vocational schools. There are several reasons for this. While the system must be rated highly, it suffers from narrowness in the specification of some skills and, unlike Germany, apprenticeships do not provide access to all industrial trades, including those with a high technological content. Indeed the Austrian system is highly compartmentalised, so that apprenticeships are increasingly viewed by young people as a dead end. About 20 per cent of apprenticeships relate to office professions, retailing and hairdressing, while only 10 per cent were in the electrical engineering area. Moreover, although 65 per cent of all apprenticeships are in SMEs, in manufacturing comparatively few training places are available in small firms which has meant that the system has adapted slowly to their changing qualification requirements. One reason for the declining number of apprenticeships is the cost, which is in part related to labour market regulations: from the perspective of labour law, apprentices are treated as minors until the end of their training which restricts hours of work, and because apprenticeship is regarded as education the employer is committed to carrying through training to completion. By one estimate, the net cost of training by enterprises – taking into account lower wages and productivity – is Sch 6 billion per year and for individual enterprises the gross cost for a complete apprenticeship is around half a million schillings.[75] Public financial support for the system is limited, with support for apprentices amounting to only Sch 6 000 per annum (covering the funding of part-time vocational schools – *Berufsschule*) while for higher education government direct support per student is in the order of Sch 60 000 for general education to Sch 95 000 per annum for vocational and technical education (the annual wage of the average production worker is Sch 279 000).

To overcome some of the problems in the present apprenticeship system – as well as to respond to challenges arising from technological change – there has been pressure to reduce the number of trades and to broaden the amount of general training offered. While appealing in principle, such an approach raises a number of difficulties. Broader definitions of trades would probably further reduce the participation of SMEs in the scheme, since they would not be able to offer all the required work experience. More general training would also reduce the role of work experience, increase costs and lead to reduced numbers of training places. As a compromise there have been moves to collect some trades under common training titles enabling sharing of common curricula as well as some professional mobility later. With respect to increased general training the problem is that time spent at work places would decline and costs would correspondingly rise. Indeed, it is argued by the employers' federation that this tendency is already present to an unwarranted degree.

The recent development of the *"Fachhochschulen"* (polytechnics) has introduced another option for tertiary study and a means for extending the availability of high-quality technical training beyond apprenticeship level. Measured in terms of student numbers and interest, they are already clearly filling a gap for reasonably short post-secondary, vocationally-oriented education. Although experience is limited, several issues are already arising. Permission is only being given by the authorities at present for niche courses, which will in no way compete with universities and which will not be recognised in Europe. The original proposal envisaged more general technical education. Moreover, admissions appear to be regulated too stringently, further compartmentalising the education system rather than opening it up. In particular, the path for apprentices appears to be relatively restrictive. These deficiencies serve to segment the tertiary education system and reduce the pressure on the universities to reform.

The most pressing education reform need in Austria relates to the university sector. As noted above, Austria has a comparatively low number of graduates in the work force, due to long study periods and high non-completion rates. However, from the perspective of growth and employment the deficiencies are more profound. The universities receive the bulk of research funding, yet the pattern of research appears to bear little relationship to the needs and structure of the economy.[76] One reason for this has been the linear approach to technological change, which has dominated post-war thought with respect to the role of the universities: new products and processes will ultimately arise out of the "purest realms of science", for whose development the universities were ultimately responsible. This paradigm has increasingly been overtaken by technological development and economic pressures. As a result, the contribution by the university sector to the innovation potential of the economy has been relatively limited. In addition, the system remains rigid with respect to fields of study on offer, curriculum, and duration of studies. It absorbs scarce resources, yet the drop-out rate for students and the average length of study are both relatively high.

Product market competition

Previous *OECD Economic Surveys* have documented a pervasive lack of competition in the Austrian economy. State-owned industries have been protected and subsidised, the entrance into trades and professions tightly controlled, and the service sector, including network industries, highly protected. This lack of competition resulted not only in generally higher prices than in other more open economies but also reduced the growth dynamic and structural changes in the economy. Services developed more slowly than in other countries, while the structural change required of any high wage economy toward higher value-added goods associated with technological innovation was retarded. Slow adjustment to new opportunities, combined with continued quite strong process innovation and capital deepening in established sectors has meant that employment creation has been low, leading to depressed levels of labour utilisation and ultimately to unemployment. As stressed in recent *Surveys,* this situation is in the course of changing significantly with increased privatisation, and especially since the entry into the EU.[77] The beneficial effects on employment and on dynamism in general will emerge gradually. But significant barriers to competitive behaviour remain, which are reviewed in this section.

A notable feature of the Austrian economy is the low rate of business start-ups. This might be due in part to the general absence of a risk-taking entrepreneurial behaviour, but it is certainly also due to a restrictive legal and regulatory framework. Two related areas are particularly notable: restrictions on entry into trades (*Gewerbeordnung*) and the requirements for setting up an enterprise. The former have been a characteristic feature of Austria and although they have been partially liberalised, such regulations still control entry into some 153 trades (*e.g.* commercial agents, business consultants, plumbers, electricians) and governs their behaviour once established. Demarcation lines are often restrictive (*e.g.* on a building site some four different occupations will be needed in fitting a bathroom) and current members of the profession can, in some cases, exercise *de facto* insider power to influence the number of new entrants: proof of qualification is often necessary and must be approved by the appropriate control body. With respect to normal business start-ups, there is a web of regulations and applications to start a business, and in some cases it can take from one year to eighteen months to obtain final approval.[78] After receiving approval of qualification, the potential entrepreneur must then receive permission to open business premises, and have these inspected by different authorities. For most requirements, several state organs with overlapping competencies are often involved. Moreover, with some investment decisions further delaying approvals are also necessary.

Competition via the entry of new enterprises is also held back by the widespread provision of services by local governments and the Länder, as well as by special regulations favouring non-profit organisations. With respect to the latter, since 1993 trade and industrial co-operatives have not been subject to the law governing cartels and vertical restrictions, insofar as these restraints can be justified by the special purpose of the co-operative. Local governments have tended to favour self provision of services and market testing appears not to be undertaken to any great extent. In order to meet the Maastricht fiscal criteria there is currently a tendency for the provision of many services to be incorporated, so as to be shifted off-budget together with some level of debt. While this move could in principle open the way for more effective management and for greater competition, as owners local government are faced with a conflict of interest. As a result, new entrants and greater competition could be discouraged.

Barriers to exit are also important. In particular the current bankruptcy law is rather restrictive in the area of corporate reorganisation, which would allow enterprises to dispose of assets and activities at an early stage of the process. In the past, subsidies have allowed firms not to restructure or to do so at their own pace. Budgetary pressures and international commitments make this course of action no longer feasible so that the legal framework needs to be brought up to date.

In other regulatory areas there has been some progress toward making the system more competitive: price controls have been lifted in all but a few sectors (see Chapter III for a description of controls in the pharmaceuticals sector and pharmacies) and limitations on sales and rebates in the retail sector lifted. Shop opening hours are controlled, with opening possible to 7.30 p.m. on week days and to 9 o'clock once in the week. However, hours of opening are in practice much shorter, with 6 p.m. being normal even in tourist areas where special regulations allow opening up to 10 p.m.[79] Lack of competition has been one reason for this, but even more important are wage agreements which specify large premia: 70 per cent for work between 6.30 p.m. and 7.30 p.m. and 100 per cent after 8 p.m. Work hours and opening hours are still closely connected in the relevant wage agreements. With accession to the EU, competition in the retail/wholesale sector has increased, as has foreign ownership. Consolidation in the sector is now underway in response to these challenges.

Since the entry into force of the EEA agreement, European competition law has been directly applicable in Austria and this has led to important changes in the regulatory environment. The number of registered cartels has decreased by around a half and they currently number less than 25, mainly in traditional sectors and industries (e.g. welded wire mesh, corrugated board, wood-building slabs). There are around 1 200 reported vertical agreements, and since joining the EU at the beginning of 1995 the four main block exemption agreements have also been taken over. These relate to exclusive dealing agreements, exclusive purchasing agreements, motor vehicle retail agreements, and franchising agreements. A far-reaching reporting requirement has increased the transparency in this field of competitive restraints. Merger controls have also been in force since the end of 1993. However, despite wide-ranging reform of competitive regulations,

Figure 35. ELECTRICITY, TELEPHONE AND GAS PRICES FOR INDUSTRY

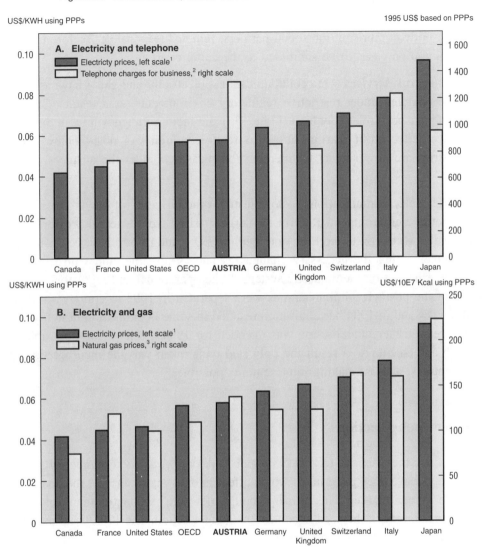

US$/KWH using PPPs

1995 US$ based on PPPs

A. Electricity and telephone
- Electricty prices, left scale[1]
- Telephone charges for business,[2] right scale

US$/KWH using PPPs

US$/10E7 Kcal using PPPs

B. Electricity and gas
- Electricity prices, left scale[1]
- Natural gas prices,[3] right scale

Note: Cross country comparison is impaired by exchange rate fluctuations.
1. In 1995, except for Canada 1994. The prices shown exclude taxes, except for Canada and OECD. In US$ based on PPPs.
2. January 1996. OECD basket of business telephone charges. The values express the average annual price for a business user (for 2 911 calls), in 1995 US$ based on PPPs, excluding tax.
3. In 1995, except for Germany 1994. The prices shown exclude taxes, except for Canada, US and OECD. In US$ per 10E7 Kcal (Gross Calorific Value basis) using PPPs.
Source: IEA Statistics (1996); OECD, *Communications Outlook.*

157

following accession first to the EEA and then to the EU, the administration of competition law has remained unchanged. The Joint Committee for Cartels, an expert body comprising the social partners, remains responsible for formulating an opinion on cases to be submitted to the cartel court.

Network services – telecommunications, electricity and gas – have as elsewhere operated under restrictive regulatory environments, as a result of which prices have been relatively high (Figure 35) and factor efficiency low. In the case of electricity, profit margins are also relatively high. As noted below these industries are now subject to liberalisation measures under the auspices of the EU.

The telecommunications sector illustrates the difficulty of moving to a more competitive environment. Reform has largely arisen from external pressure – in particular accession to the EEA and then the EU – and reform has been confined to implementing the necessary changes as late as possible, and with the least possible impact on the domestic system.[80] The operational and regulatory activities of the post/telecommunications were separated in 1993 to comply with EU directives and in 1994 harmonisation resulted in some liberalisation of non-voice services. Further liberalisation was intended for 1994 but it was not possible to reach agreement. As a result the only step undertaken was the incorporation of the entities, at least making joint ventures possible.

Recent policy actions

Since the previous *OECD Economic Survey of Austria,* a number of policy measures have been undertaken which affect in one way or another the operation of the labour market. The primary though not sole reason for many of these measures has been the need to control the budget deficit. The 1995 fiscal package contained the following measures:

- With respect to public employment, some employment benefits were abolished and pension contribution rates for civil servants were raised by 1.5 percentage points.
- In the field of unemployment insurance, entitlements for unemployment benefits and special help for long term unemployment (*Sondernotstandshilfe*) were restricted and family benefits were reduced by Sch 100 per

month to Sch 1 500 on average. Unemployment benefits for those on higher incomes were cut, the minimum age for support of older unemployed in a few special sectors (*Sonderunterstützung I*) was raised, and the support for older unemployed in general (*Sonderunterstützung II*) was abolished.

– Contribution rates by self-employed persons and farmers to social insurance were increased.

The 1996/1997 fiscal consolidation package introduced a number of measures which aim to increase the effective age of retirement, improve work incentives, and shift family support from regressive tax benefits to progressive tax allowances. The measures include:

– Incentives for early retirement in the public sector have been eliminated and a full pension will be available only from the 60th year.

– To lower the rate of growth of family subsidies, a range of benefits were reduced which will save some Sch 6 billion annually.

– Funds for active labour market measures were frozen at 1995 levels, although expenditures will increase due to additional funds from the European Social Fund.

– A bonus-malus system was introduced to encourage employment of older workers and to discourage their dismissal: with the employment of older workers, indirect labour costs will be reduced through lower social insurance contributions. By contrast, dismissal of older workers carries with it a fine unless the dismissal is related to a number of special conditions including the closure or partial closure of a plant. The one-off penalty payment is difficult to calculate but based on a monthly salary of Sch 39 000 would amount to Sch 4 680 for a 50-year old worker and Sch 49 140 for a worker of 55 years of age. This is small relative to the much lower wage rate of younger workers – while the penalty payment might prove to be a significant cost for firms but one not sufficient to prevent layoffs.[81]

– With respect to unemployment benefits the qualifying period was increased from 26 to 28 months and the earnings history for the calculation of benefits has been increased from 6 to 12 months. Measures have also been undertaken to deal with seasonal unemployment by requiring working hours to be averaged over time.

- Access to social assistance will also depend on the time spent in employment.
- With the aim of increasing the actual age of retirement, the number of months of contributions necessary for early retirement has been increased from 420 to 450 months and early retirement of older workers on account of long term unemployment has been eliminated (SUG II). Time spent in education will not be counted unless additional contributions are made at a favourable rate. The annual increase in pensions has been temporarily lowered and the increase confined to the lowest basic pension. The minimum income which can be earned before pensions are reduced has been lowered. Moreover, incentives for later retirement have been strengthened by changing the form of the tables determining pensions (*Anwartschaftsprozenttabelle*).
- Stricter controls of invalidity pensions have been introduced.
- The special payment (*Sonderunterstützung*) of up to 25 per cent of unemployment benefits for older workers (women above the age of 54 and men above the age of 59) has been cancelled as from April 1996. In compensation, the basis for calculating emergency help has been widened by increasing the value of deductibles.
- In March 1996 a special programme was started to encourage the employment of long term unemployed which ran until August 1996 (*Sonderprogramm zur Einstellungsförderung für Langzeitarbeitlose*). The subsidy amounts to 20 per cent of the wage for a year – the 20 per cent amounts to the employer's social security contributions. The wage must correspond to the relevant collective agreement.

There have been a number of initiatives in the area of R&D and in competition policy. These include:

- The government adopted the *Working Agreement on Research and Technology Policy.*[82] (1994-98) which incorporates many recommendations of the *OECD Technology/Productivity Job Creation Study*. The concept provides the basis for rationalising R&D support programmes in Austria. The emphasis is on the promotion of business research spending and technology diffusion rather than direct R&D support. The two main mechanisms are the Research Promotion Funds and the Innovation and Technology Fund (ITF). Responsibility for the Research Promotion

Funds is now with the Ministry for Economic Affairs and the focus has shifted from support of traditional sectors (*e.g.* wood and textiles) to areas such as micro-electronics, environmental protection, information technologies and software development. The Innovation and Technology Fund (ITF), which is now under the joint authority of the Ministry for Economic Affairs and the Ministry of Science, Transport and the Arts, promotes technological innovation in industry through grants and loans. A new ITF programme, *Technologies for the Information Society,* was initiated in 1995 to speed computerisation of the public and private sectors. These schemes have largely replaced the *Top-Aktionen* scheme, which for fourteen years provided long-term loans and investment financing for innovation projects in industry.

– In addition, a "clusters policy" has been introduced to address high unemployment in specific regions, such as Styria and Upper and Lower Austria, stemming from a concentration of declining heavy industries such as steel. In these regions, government programmes are targeted to supporting horizontal, vertical and diagonal relationships between suppliers and customers, larger and smaller firms, manufacturers and service providers in related industries. The aim is to speed technology diffusion and exploit local advantages and resources among a regional network of actors. The focus has thus far been on the wood and paper, electronics and chemicals sectors.

– With respect to the regulatory and competitive environment, the new coalition agreement from 11 March 1996 establishes a number of goals in the area of accelerating administrative decisions, deregulation and liberalisation. In addition, privatisation is to be pursued. Progress is, however, most advanced in those areas where EU initiatives have been forcing the pace: in network industries.

– With respect to electricity, subject to special consideration for hydroelectric power and rigorous environmental requirements, Austria is committed since July 1996 to following EU-wide liberalisation directives. Austrian reluctance to accept the more liberal EU alternative was based on the desire to avoid imports of nuclear energy which would undermine national policy in this area. The import/export regime will be handled by the single buyer model. Initial market opening will cover customers using more then 100 GWH which will mean an initial market opening of around 23 per cent. Reorganisation of the grids and local generators – often owned and operated by lower levels of government – will be necessary. The government has recently become concerned about the level of energy prices and has threatened regulatory measures rather than an intensification of competition.

- The gas industry already has a high degree of market opening and liberalisation. Nevertheless prices remain surprisingly high. The government is currently participating in EU negotiations for further liberalisation.
- Dissolution of the parliament in late 1995 delayed further structural reforms of the post/telecommunications sector. However, disagreements among the coalition parties as to the form that the separation of the postal service from the Ministry should take also contributed to the delay. A bill was finally passed by the Parliament in April 1996 incorporating the post office and allocating ownership rights to the Ministry of Finance. Regulatory authority was delegated to the Ministry of Science, Transport and the Arts. The law specifies that preparations have to be made to list the company on the stock exchange by the end of 1999 but the bill did not seek to break up the post office into separate areas such as post, telecommunications, transport, etc. An important step was taken in 1995 with the opening to tender of a second mobile telephone network, awarded in 1996. The new network involves the payment of a licence fee, and in order to prevent competitive distortions the Post will also have to pay such a fee. Current regulatory arrangements provide for a price commission comprising among others the social partners. Little progress has been made in setting a new regulatory regime.

Assessment and scope for further actions

Although the Austrian authorities have embarked on an ambitious programme of structural reform, there are a number of areas where reforms are either too modest or not at present contemplated. Further progress is needed in the following areas if the benefits of integration into the world economy are to be realised and labour utilisation increased:

- The challenges facing Austria requires additional institutional flexibility on the part of the social partners. Economic pressures require increased powers to adjust settlements emerging from central wage agreements, possibly in a downward direction, with respect to wages and employment conditions at the enterprise level – and indeed *de facto* this is already taking place. The government needs to support such increased flexibility, which is consistent with the maintenance of the system of social partnership. In particular, it should remove possible barriers to and generally facilitate the development of opening clauses in wage contracts.
- Another possibility for the government to take the initiative in this area concerns the overdue reform of legislation covering working hours. Provisions in this area could account for the prevalence of contracts for self-employed persons (*Werkverträger*) in Austria. The law should set only the broad framework and leave it to centralised wage agreements to decide the extent to which the adoption of flexible working practices can be determined at the enterprise level. The government should resist demands to place all responsibility at the central level.
- The government has been concerned to encourage employment of older workers, but particularly in the face of a steep wage/age profile, and employment protection, employers are still reluctant to expand employment of older workers. Moreover, generous benefits do not encourage flexibility on the part of those less qualified older workers who need to adjust to lower-paid jobs after losing their age and seniority-based wages. Some form of in-work benefit might be helpful, but should be introduced in the light of overall reforms of the tax/benefit system. In addition, consideration might be given to a gradual reduction in the reference wage for unemployment benefits as in Germany so as to more accurately reflect employment opportunities.
- On balance, job protection provisions do not favour increased employment. Given existing dismissal protection provisions, the possibility of extending fixed-term contracts needs to be liberalised.
- Recent moves to control the abuse of contracts for the self-employed (*Werkverträge*) aimed at differentiating contracts which are similar to labour contracts from those which are not, and at excluding some sectors, could go in the wrong direction.

- The measures taken to increase the effective age of retirement represent a modest step in the right direction. Further measures are necessary in the long term.
- Although the empirical evidence is only tentative at this stage, it appears that the tax/benefit system results in poverty and unemployment traps, making it uneconomical to look for part-time work or to accept lower-paid full-time jobs. While such traps are often the unavoidable consequence of means-testing, they should be substantially reduced. One way to do this would be to spread out the current withdrawal of benefits, which is at present quite sudden, by allowing for only a gradual loss of benefit as earnings rise. Alternatively, the rather low earning disregard before benefits are reduced could be raised substantially, while reducing benefits rapidly so as to avoid high marginal effective tax rates over a wide range of income.
- Unemployment benefits for seasonal workers remain in need of reform since they continue to represent an implicit subsidy for the tourism sector.
- Active labour market measures are modest in Austria and need to be expanded. Experience with highly targeted programmes has been favourable, so that any new measures should remain focused on groups at risk of becoming unemployed long-term.

The Austrian education system has generally performed well and qualifications in the population at large have improved significantly since the early 1980s. Further measures are necessary in view of the need to improve the innovation system:

- With respect to the apprenticeship system, efforts will have to be made to control costs so as to maintain the vitality of the scheme. This is preferable to imposing an equalisation tax on non-participating enterprises which would serve only to increase the overall non-wage cost. One way to lower costs would be to lower regulatory barriers confronted by firms wishing to offer training posts, and increase the time which should be spent in the work place. The quality of the system needs to be continually monitored but there are some areas requiring speedy rectification. If the level of trainees is to be kept high, clear possibilities need to be given for trainees to go on to higher education including vocational schools and the new polytechnics. Greater collecting of skills under a common general training programme would be useful, although it should not be so wide as to reduce the value of specific work experience. With respect to the technological content, consideration should be given to extending to other Länder and occupations the four year high technology training scheme which has been pioneered in Voraalberg. The OECD review of education concluded that "... The modernisation of the apprenticeship system should include more general and theoretical training and provide for some groupings among the 225 trades taught in order to develop a multi-skilled and adaptable labour force. This modernisation probably requires some flexibility in the regulations so that greater allowance can be made for the range of apprenticeships and their particular requirements".[83]

– As stressed in the OECD *Review of National Policies for Education,* the universities need to recognise the broadly vocational aspirations of most of their students, and the demands of the economy. The complexity and difficulty of central control of university curricula needs to be diminished. The universities are not over-inclined to reform and the system enhances this reluctance rather than rewarding initiative and innovation. There is a need to enhance the completion rates of students and reduce the length of their studies. The funding of the universities should be related more closely to the functions that they serve, and need to be radically reformed the functions of academic staff and their remuneration.

– The introduction of the *Fachhochschulen* has made it imperative to identify clearly the role of the universities and of their staffs. Initial steps in this area appear to have resulted in too restrictive an approach to the *Fachhochschulen,* limiting them to offering niche courses which do not compete with universities. Their role needs to be widened, especially with respect to direct R&D contacts with industry. Greater transferability of credits needs to be established between vocational/technical studies and academic studies.

– A greater emphasis needs to be given to establishing industry-near innovation-oriented research institutes.

– Venture capital markets remain underdeveloped in Austria and attention needs to be devoted to removing tax and regulatory barriers. More important, however, is to investigate why Austrian firms have failed to make use of existing opportunities in European venture capital markets.

In addition to making labour markets more efficient and the innovation system more effective, there are several areas in both manufacturing and in private and public services where there is still a clear need to strengthen competition and to promote efficiency through regulatory reform:

- The EU regulatory framework in the telecommunications area is still fluid, so that the opportunity exists for the Austrian authorities to create a transparent and liberal regulatory regime. Reorganisation of the postal services needs to go further than recent legislation, which failed to separate operating entities: the postal service needs to be hived off from telecommunications and bus services. A financial system has to be created to compensate the companies for public service activities, in order to prevent cross subsidisation which will become increasingly difficult in a competitive environment. New institutions are required to enforce competition and to oversee price regulation. Crucial for success will be clear rules to provide competitors with access to the line networks at a reasonable price and to provide for transferable telephone numbers. The government's decision to issue a third mobile licence in 1997 is welcome.
- Deregulation and the simplification of administrative procedures have been on the list of the government's priorities for some time but more needs to be achieved and the costs of regulation systematically investigated. Entrance to the trades needs to be liberalised and the procedures for founding a new enterprise simplified. Shop opening hours are already more liberal than the actual use by enterprises. New legislation is nevertheless needed which addresses the labour market barriers to longer and more flexible shop opening hours.
- Although competition has increased and competition policy is more rigorous with entry into the EU, much still needs to be done to promote competitive behaviour. In particular market contestability needs to be improved: the provision of services by communes and Länder needs to be made more contestable through more stringent application of public tendering provisions. All enterprises – profit or non-profit, public- or privately-owned – need to be placed on a common basis. In view of the changing international environment, consideration also needs to be given to creating an independent competition authority.

Notes

1. Defined as the ratio of registered unemployed to the estimate of the work force including self-employed. Other definitions are used by the authorities. See Annex II for a discussion of different concepts.

2. The results for 1994 and 1995 show that there were some problems in forecasting the timing of the revenue effects. In 1995, revenue from abolished taxes (from assessments of former years) was higher than expected. The loss of tax on industry and trade (*Gewerbesteuer*) is estimated to have been less than Sch 13 billion, of wealth tax (*Vermögensteuer incl. Erbschaftsteueräquivalent*) almost 10 billion and of the special tax on banks nearly 2 billion. The wage tax was about Sch 12.5 billion lower than it would have been without the reform. However, the compensating measures yielded considerably less than originally calculated (Sch 2.5 billion for income tax and about Sch 10 billion for corporate tax).

3. Both revenues and expenditures are effected by the exclusion from the federal budget of the Post Office from May 1996 onwards. Though outlays for personnel will still be contained in the federal budget, they will be fully refunded by the Post Office. The Bund will also continue to pay pensions for employees of the Post Office and these will only be partially covered by contributions from the Post and Telekom Austria, implying a budgetary burden of an estimated Sch 4.8 billion in 1996 and Sch 8.1 billion in 1997. In 1996 and 1997 the Post and Telekom Austria will pay concession charges to the Bund, and from 1997 onwards dividends. In addition, the company is obliged to pay corporation tax. Overall, in 1996 budgetary outlays and receipts for the Post Office are expected to be balanced, but since in the past the revenues of the Post Office exceeded its outlays (Sch 9.7 billion surplus in 1995) the new regulation implies a longer-term deterioration for the federal budget. In 1997 the Post and Telekom Austria is expected to contribute to the federal budget with a surplus of some Sch 10 billion, about the same amount as in 1995.

4. As an instrument for more efficient budget control and policy-making the government is setting up national accounts compatible accounting systems (satellite systems according to the standard of the most recent system of national accounts, SNA 1993) covering major fields of public sector activity, mainly personnel, education, family support, unemployment, pensions, health care, subsidisation, taxation and relations to other public sector entities and to the EU. The accounts will make transparent on a programme by programme basis the flow of spending and revenues between individual government units and destinations, as well as additional data that are relevant for programme evaluation.

5. Another study which focused only on comparable medicines found a considerably smaller price difference of around 10 per cent. See "Arzneimittelpreise und Struktur der österreichis-

chen Pharmawirtschaft im International Vergleich'', *Schriftenreihe des Wirtschaftsförderungsinstitutes,* 258, Vienna, 1995.

6. Prices for medical services are subject to severe measurement problems. For example, hospital prices may be measured by the cost of one day in hospital, or of specific operations (*e.g.,* appendectomies). See Newhouse, J. P., ''Medical care costs: how much welfare loss?'', *Journal of Economic Perspectives,* 6, 3, (1992). Insofar as such problems are present in all OECD countries, however, cross-country comparisons may still have some merit.

7. ''New Directions in Health Care Policy'', *Health Policy Studies* No. 7, OECD, Paris, 1995, p. 13.

8. Because of the unavailability of data for Turkey and the lack of time series data for the three newest members of the OECD, Mexico, the Czech Republic and Hungary, these four countries are omitted from all calculations below the ''OECD average''.

9. However, private insurance has cross-subsidised the public system up to the present since charges have borne no relation to marginal costs.

10. *New Directions in Health Care op. cit.,* Table 7.

11. It has been estimated that 10 per cent more doctors lead to 11 per cent more costs, as cases per insured rise 6.6 per cent, consultations per case rise 2.9 per cent, and the number of services per visit rises 1.6 per cent. C. Karsch, ''Die Nachfrage nach Gesundheit'', *Wirtschaftspolitische Blätter,* No. 6, 1993, Vienna.

12. For example, Austria now has two ''gamma knives'' for special surgical procedures, where one is enough to service 10 million people (Austria has 8 million people). Germany (80 million people) has no gamma knives as there they are considered too expensive.

13. It should be noted that in Switzerland, contributions to the sickness funds tend to be flat-rate rather than income-related, making the system highly regressive. Also, in the Netherlands, social insurance coverage stops after a certain maximum income level, above which people must purchase private insurance, giving a mixed system.

14. The alternative systems are the national health service model, found in the United Kingdom and characterised by universal coverage, national general tax financing, and public provision of services; the national health insurance model, such as in Canada, where universal coverage is financed by national general taxation and health care is provided by a mix of public and private suppliers; and the private insurance system as in the United States, where government financial involvement is limited to certain groups such as the elderly and the indigent, though supply can be private or public.

15. *The reform of health care systems: A review of seventeen OECD countries,* Health Policy Studies, No. 5, Paris, OECD 1994, Chapter VII.

16. This definition of costs excludes outlays for the building, equipping, and expansion of the hospital; depreciation charges; pension costs; and extra expenses due to a university function for hospitals. However, the law leaves open the possibility to reshuffle expenditures so that smaller investments can be declared as ''running costs'' in order to claim a higher daily charge.

17. Only in Salzburg and Vorarlberg does the law explicitly require the Länder to adopt these cost-covering charges — and, even so, only ''when possible''.

18. The states' contribution to KRAZAF depends on their own revenues which in turn are related to VAT revenues collected by the federal government through the system of fiscal equalisation.

19. In GDP data this is categorised by the OECD as education rather than health spending.

20. Taking the subset of doctors with contracts, however, the distribution is far more homogenous, with the exception of the polar cases of Vorarlberg (1 per 1 325) and well-served Vienna (1 per 680).

21. There are many doctors who are both employees of a hospital and have their own practice; these are classified as practising physicians.

22. Unusually long working-lives in specialist practice may have contributed to this apparent surplus: in 1993, one-fifth (and in some specialities, such as pulmonary disease, as many as one-third) of practising specialists were over the age of sixty-five – in a country where the average retirement age is fifty-eight.

23. See Altmann A. and E. Theurl, "Budget Konsolidierung und Krankheitsreform", *Wirtschaftspolitische Blätter,* 1992, 2, Vienna.

24. The foreign trade law, customs tariff law, and pharmaceutical import law also regulate the import of pharmaceuticals.

25. Nonetheless, drugs which are not on the register are still reimbursable by the funds if they are prescribed (or approved) by the head doctor of a health fund (*Chefarzt*).

26. The concession/licensing obligation has been lifted for most other service industries with entry into the EC, but an exemption exists in this area. See *1995 OECD Economic Survey of Austria.*

27. See *Gesundheitswesen in Österreich,* Winter 1994, Chapter V, p. 158.

28. The "raw" retail price margin is calculated as: 40 per cent up to a wholesale price of Sch 812; 35 per cent up to Sch 1 150; 30 per cent up to Sch 1 500; and afterwards a flat margin of Sch 450, or 20 per cent, whichever is higher. For antibiotics, insulin, serum, etc., *i.e.* drugs requiring an injection, the margin stays at 40 per cent.

29. See Zweifel, P., "Technischer Fortschritt und Gesundheitswesen", *Wirtschaftspolitische Blätter,* 6/1993.

30. *New Directions in Health Care Policy, (op. cit).*

31. This presumption is corroborated by experiments run in the United States. A plan with a large deductible of up to $1 000 in the 1970s reduced total expenditures on health care by 31 per cent relative to a plan with full coverage. See R. Ellis and T. McGuire, "Supply-side and demand-side cost sharing in health care", *Journal of Economic Perspectives,* 7, 4, 1993.

32. See, for example, Karsch (*op. cit.*) and F. Schneider, "Anreizorientierte Systeme im Gesundheitswesen unter besonderer Berücksichtigung des stationären Sektors", *Wirtschaftspolitische Blätter* 6, 1993.

33. See, for example, Marmot *et al.* (1991), "Health inequalities among British civil servants: The Whitehall II study," *Lancet,* 337. Also see footnote 5 above.

34. This is what happened in Italy after the reforms of the 1980s. See *New Directions in Health Care Policy, op. cit.*

35. See H. Ivansits and W. Eichhorst, *Zur Krankenanstalten Finanzierung in Österreich,* Arbeiterkammer, Vienna, 1993.

36. See E. Mayer-Deyssig, *Gesundheitswesen in Österreich,* Verband der Versicherungsunternehmungen Österreichs, Vienna, 1994. This is the initial experience in New Zealand as well.

37. Such subsidies might be economically justified in terms of keeping social insurance contribution rates and hence labour costs low.

38. For example, an experiment to try to improve incentives of doctors was run in the state of Kärnten. Instead of the previous quarterly flat per patient fee, doctors were asked to rate the cost-intensity of their services as low, medium, or high, and were reimbursed on that basis. It turned out that an abnormally high number of cases were classified as high cost – since patients never saw the bill there was no check on the veracity of the doctors' classification. This shows that in benefits-in-kind systems with fee for service, supply side moral hazard can be high. See Bodenhöffer and Riedel (1995) and also E. Theurl, "Ärztehonorierung und optimale medizinische Versorgung", *Wirtschaftspolitische Blätter,* 6, 1993.

39. See Schneider (1993), *op. cit.*

40. Case studies have shown that government-imposed rationing of pharmaceuticals leads to increased use of hospital care. A recent study conducted in the United States shows that the number of hospital days, bed-days, and surgical procedures, and in some cases mortality, declined most rapidly for those diagnoses with the greatest number of drugs prescribed and the greatest novelty in the use of drugs. The estimates imply that a $1 increase in pharmaceutical expenditure is associated with a $3.65 reduction in hospital care expenditure. See Lichtenberg, F., "The effect of pharmaceutical utilisation and innovation on hospitalisation and mortality," *NBER Working Paper* No. 5418, January 1996.

41. Phelps argues that this is perhaps the most cost-effective action the government could take in the field of health care (C. Phelps, "Diffusion of information in medical care", *The Journal of Economic Perspectives,* 6, 3, 1992).

42. See Annex II for a discussion of the issues involved in measuring unemployment in Austria.

43. One study indicates that the NAIRU has continued to increase through 1994, and this trend is likely to have continued. See Hofer, H., and K. Pichelmann, *Lohnbildung, Arbeitskosten und Wettbewerbsfähigkeit in Österreich,* Institute of Advanced Studies, Vienna, 1996.

44. For a detailed analysis see Biffl, G., "Entwicklung der Langzeitarbeitlosigkeit in Österreich und Massnahmen zu ihrer Bekämpfung", *WIFO Monatsberichte, 1/1996.*

45. Biffl, G. and Pollan, W., "The Austrian Labour Market", *WIFO Working Papers,* No 75, 1995.

46. *OECD Employment Outlook,* 1996, Table E, p. 192.

47. Hofer and Pichelmann, *op. cit.,* 1996.

48. Hofer and Pichelmann, *op. cit.*

49. For evidence on the slow rate of labour demand adjustment Stephen Nickell, "Labour market dynamics in OECD countries", *Centre for Economic Performance Discussion Paper,* 255, LSE, August 1995.

50. Layard, P.R.P., Nickell, S.J. and Jackman, R., *Unemployment: macroeconomic performance and the labour market,* Oxford University Press, 1991.

51. For an empirical description of the process by which higher productivity enterprises should not be expected to pay higher wages but to expand more strongly, see W. Salter, *Productivity and Technical Change,* Cambridge, 1964.

52. Accounting for gender differences between industries also reduces significantly the dispersion of wages in Japan. See R.E. Rowthorn, "Centralisation, Employment and Wage Dispersion" *The Economic Journal* No. 102, May 1992.

53. See Hofer, H., "Eine Untersuchung über die Ursachen der sektoralen Lohnunterschiede in Österreich", *Institute for Advanced Studies, Research Memorandum 311,* Vienna, 1992. For a similar explanation Barth, E., and J. Zweimüller, "Labour market institutions and the industry wage distribution: Evidence from Austria, Norway and the US", *Empirica, 19,* 1992.

54. *OECD Employment Outlook,* OECD, 1994, Chapter 5.

55. H. Hofer, "Über die Ursachen der sektorale Lohnunterschiede in Österreich", Institute of Higher Studies, Vienna, *mimeo, 1995.* The issue of higher wages in state-owned industrial enterprises during the 1970s and 1980s was also raised in E. Walterskirchen, *Unemployment and labour market flexibility: Austria,* International Labour Office, Geneva, 1991.

56. See for example S. Nickell, *op. cit.*

57. "Arbeitsbedingungen", *Statistische Nachrichten,* Vienna, 8/1996, p. 612.

58. See also *Social Report Austria,* Ministry of Labour and Social Affairs, Vienna, 1995, for a detailed description of all features of the system.

59. See *The public employment service in Austria, Germany and Sweden, op. cit.* The job search requirement is not formally waived on grounds of age, but its enforcement would appear to be minimal. In some cases where workers are approaching the minimum age for early retirement, options may be discussed by the employment office with unions and employers resulting in a tacit agreement to pay unemployment benefits without enforcing job search.

60. The breakdown of social insurance contributions is 6.8-10.4 per cent for health insurance, 22.8 per cent for pension insurance, 6 per cent for unemployment insurance, and 1.3 per cent for accident insurance. In addition, 4.5 per cent of total wages is paid to the Family Assistance Fund.

61. Hofer and Pichelmann *op. cit.,* 1996, estimated pass forward coefficients of 60-70 per cent but with an extended estimation period (1968-1994) this coefficient declined to some 30-40 per cent.

62. *OECD Employment Outlook,* 1993.

63. Blumberger, W., *et al., Facharbeiterintensivausbildung: Karriereverläufe,* Institut für Berufs- und Erwachsenenbildungsforschung, Linz, 1993.

64. Lechner, F. *et al., Aktion 8000: Anforderungsgerecht,* Vienna, 1995.

65. See *OECD Economic Survey of Austria,* 1995, p. 66 and Table 17.

66. However, within product groupings it is likely that Austrian firms specialise in higher value-added products.

67. See G. Hutschenreiter, Joerg, L., and Polt, W., *Mapping knowledge flows within the Austrian system of innovation,* draft, Vienna, 1996.

68. Hutschenreiter, G., *et al., op. cit.*

69. Innovation expenditures – which include outlays for construction and design, patents, licences and marketing – are about the same in Austria as in other countries: 4.8 per cent of turnover in 1990 as opposed to 5.4 per cent in Germany. The major international difference is that in R&D expenditures. This supports other evidence that process innovation is more important in Austria than in many other countries.

70. Polt, W. (1992), "Technology Development and Technology Programmes in Austria, Finland and Other Small Open Economies", in *Mastering Technology Diffusion: The Finnish Experience,* edited by Vouri, S. and Anttila, Y., The Research Institute of the Finnish Economy, Helsinki, 1992.

71. OECD (1993), "Surveys on the Diffusion of Micro-Electronics and Advanced Manufacturing Systems", *STI Review* No. 12. OECD (1996), *Science, Industry and Technology Outlook: 1996.*

72. Hofer, H. and Pichelman, K. (1995), *Verarbeitungsmechanismen von Reallokationsschocks,* Institut fur Höhere Studien, Vienna.

73. Exit rates are also low but the net rate of firm creation remains relatively modest. See OECD *Economic Survey of Austria,* 1995, Table 22.

74. "Venture and development capital", *Financial Times Survey,* 20 September 1996.

75. Stepan A., G. Ortner and M. Oswald, *Die betrieblichen Kosten der Berufsausbildung,* Institut für Bildungsforschung der Wirtschaft, Bildung und Wirtschaft, No. 4, 1994, Wien.

76. The research profile of Austrian universities has a strong focus on medical and natural sciences which differs from the specialisation pattern on industry. See Hutschenreiter *et al., op. cit.*

77. At the end of 1995, Austria had implemented only 1 063 out of the required 1 262 single market directives (84 per cent) which placed it second last out of member countries. However, this was mainly due to delays in implementing directives in the agricultural sector. With respect to free movements of services, persons and capital, as well as financial services, implementation is almost complete.

78. For a description of the problems faced by a would be entrepreneur see C. Gassauer-Fleissner and W. Kalny, " Deregulierungsbedarf im Zuge einer Unterenehmensgründung", *S.O.S. im Regelwald,* D. Neumann-Spallart (ed.) Signum, Vienna, 1996.

79. Shop opening hours have been extended from January 1997 and exemptions for family enterprises have been introduced. At the same time, the law covering working hours has been amended so that Saturday work will be compensated by a full day on the following weekend.

80. See H. Leo "Liberalisation and regulation in the telecommunications sector", *Austrian Economic Quarterly,* 1/1996 and the references therein for a history of liberalisation.

81. As quoted in *Industrie,* No. 14, April 1996, p. 9.

82. WIFO *et al., Technologiepolitisches Konzept 1996 der Bundesregierung,* July 1996.

83. *Reviews of National Policies for Education, Austria,* OECD, Paris, 1995.

Annex I

The Austrian health insurance system

Health insurance funds

Membership of the public health insurance funds is compulsory and covers the whole population except for members of certain professions (such as notaries and architects) and convicts. Participants do not have the option of choosing their own insurance scheme, since the decisive factor is normally membership of an occupational group. There are 24 health insurance institutions, 15 nation-wide funds organised on occupational lines, and 9 regional funds on the Länder level (Figure A1). Despite the multiplicity of funds there are four basic types of health insurance institutions – for wage and salary earners,[1] civil servants, farmers, and small traders, respectively – each with their own legal regime governing the contribution rate, payment method and co-payment requirement (if any). In addition to the health insurance funds, there is a general accident insurance institute and three pension insurance funds. These also contribute to health care financing, the former via payments for medical costs due to accidents, and the latter via medical costs associated with disability rehabilitation.[2] All insurers are self-managing public corporations whose activities are coordinated by an umbrella association, the *Hauptverband*, of Austrian Social Security Institutions.

The main benefits and reimbursement methods of the health schemes are as follows:

– The insured is free to consult any *doctor* whether under contract to the health insurance scheme or not. In the case of the former, the doctor's fees are paid directly by the health insurance institution and the consumer never sees the bill, while in the case of the latter, the patient must pre-pay the doctor but may claim reimbursement up to the amount that would have been paid by the insurance funds to a doctor under contract. Both the number of doctors under contract and the level of reimbursable fees are determined by a bargaining process between the *Hauptverband* and the doctors' association. The doctor consulted, in turn, has virtually free choice of method of treatment, and has an unrestricted right to refer the patient to a specialist or hospital. Patients are free to change their primary care doctor, but not more than once a quarter or month (depending on the insurer). Wage and salary earners have no co-payment requirement, while civil servants, farmers, and small traders normally have to make a 20 per cent co-payment.

Figure A1. **THE AUSTRIAN SOCIAL INSURANCE STRUCTURE**

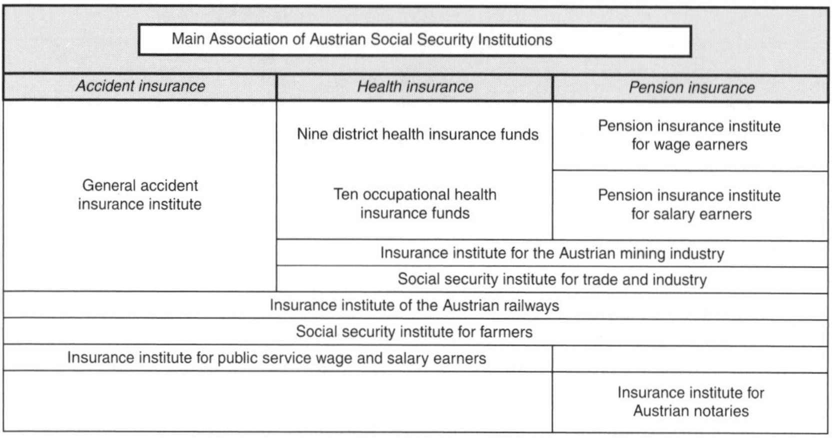

Main Association of Austrian Social Security Institutions		
Accident insurance	*Health insurance*	*Pension insurance*
General accident insurance institute	Nine district health insurance funds	Pension insurance institute for wage earners
	Ten occupational health insurance funds	Pension insurance institute for salary earners
	Insurance institute for the Austrian mining industry	
	Social security institute for trade and industry	
Insurance institute of the Austrian railways		
Social security institute for farmers		
Insurance institute for public service wage and salary earners		
		Insurance institute for Austrian notaries

Source : Hauptverband der österreichischen Sozialversicherungsträger, *Soziale Sicherheit* (1994).

- For reimbursement of *medicines,* there is a flat prescription charge of 32 schilling per prescription (as of 1994), which is adjusted every year in line with the rise in the CPI, and works out at an average 20 per cent of total prescription charges. There are guidelines on financial considerations in prescribing medicines and therapeutic aids, and only medicines on an approved list are reimbursable without explicit authorisation from the *Hauptverband.*
- The insurance funds reimburse *hospitals* in three ways: 1) a partial (about 40 per cent) percentage reimbursement of the flat per day in-patient care charge; 2) fixed payments to the hospital funding pool, which grow in line with contributions; and 3) full reimbursement for treatment in a hospital's outpatient department. Treatment should in principle be given at the nearest hospital that has a contract with the health insurance funds (all public and most private hospitals have such contracts). There is a small copayment for in-patient care: Sch 58-64 per day up to a maximum of 28 days per year per insured person, and 10 per cent (20 per cent for farmers) of the first four week of costs of care for dependants.

Public health insurance also provides *cash benefits* for sickness and maternity. A sickness benefit is available from the fourth day of an incapacity to a maximum of 78 weeks per individual case of sickness, depending on the fund (the legal minimum is 26 weeks), covering 50 per cent of earnings up to the 43rd day of illness, and 60 per cent thereafter. The maternity allowance fully compensates for earnings for the duration of the period during which the mother is not allowed to work (currently 4 months). The insurers recover half of the cost of this latter benefit from the state, however.

Table A1 shows that the biggest expenditure item of the social funds has been hospital financing, both direct and indirect (via the KRAZAF), followed by physicians' services and cash benefits. Preventitive care and home care command relatively small amounts of resources, despite the general recognition of their growing importance in controlling health costs.

Administrative costs are low by international standards. While this may reflect certain factors linked to the mode of payment (directly to the doctor in most cases), it also arises because of the relatively few controls over health care spending.

Contributions are based on income earned by the insured, but only up to a certain threshold, which varies by scheme and is periodically raised.[3] Contribution rates also differ across funds, the differences being largely historically based, with employers normally covering half (Table A2). To cover the cost of health insurance for pensioners, contributions are provided from the funds of the pension insurance organisations; pen-

Table A.1. **Social insurance funds' financing of health expenditure**

Billion schillings

	1988	1989	1990	1991	1992	1993	1994
Benefits-in-kind	**56.2**	**59.2**	**62.6**	**67.5**	**73.6**	**80.6**	**87.0**
Health insurance	51.9	54.6	57.8	62.2	67.9	74.2	80.2
Physicians' services	16.9	17.9	19.1	20.6	22.2	24.4	26.6
Dentists' services and dentures	5.6	5.7	5.9	6.3	7.1	7.9	8.4
Hospital care	15.7	16.5	17.2	18.1	19.4	20.9	22.3
Pharmaceuticals	8.6	9.2	9.8	10.8	12.1	13.3	14.4
Home care	1.5	1.6	1.8	2.0	2.1	2.0	2.1
Maternity care	0.9	0.9	1.0	1.1	1.2	1.3	1.3
Preventive care programmes	1.5	1.6	1.6	1.8	2.3	2.9	3.2
Transport costs	1.1	1.2	1.2	1.4	1.5	1.7	1.8
Accident insurance	2.1	2.1	2.3	2.5	2.7	3.0	3.2
Pension insurance	2.3	2.5	2.6	2.7	3.0	3.5	3.6
Transfers	**16.1**	**17.8**	**19.7**	**23.9**	**30.2**	**28.7**	**29.3**
Money transfers to interprises [1]	5.7	6.3	6.9	7.4	7.8	7.1	7.0
Money transfers to private households [2]	7.0	7.4	8.1	10.1	11.9	11.3	12.1
Transfers to KRAZAF	3.4	4.1	4.7	6.3	10.5	10.3	10.3
Administrative costs	**3.5**	**3.6**	**3.8**	**4.1**	**5.3**	**5.7**	**6.0**
Total	**75.9**	**80.6**	**86.2**	**95.5**	**109.2**	**115.0**	**122.3**

1.   According to the provisions of the *Entgeltfortzahlungsgesetz*.
2.   Mainly *Krankengeld* (sickness payments) and *Wochengeld* (maternity leave payments).
Source :   Ministry of Finance.

175

Table A.2. **Rates of contribution**

		Share	
		Employer	Employee
Non-self-employed			
Health insurance [1]			
Salary earners	6.80	3.40	3.40
Wage earners	7.90	3.95	3.95
Other insured persons [2]	9.10	4.55	4.55
Civil servants	7.10	3.15	3.95
Accident insurance			
Wage and salary earners	1.30	1.30	
Civil servants	0.47	0.47	
Pension insurance			
Wage and salary earners	22.80	12.55	10.25
Miners	28.30	18.05	10.25
Self-employed small traders			
Health insurance [1]	9.30		
Accident insurance	Sch 864 p.a.		
Pension insurance	12.50		
Self-employed professionals			
Health insurance [1]	9.30		
Accident insurance	Sch 815 p.a.		
Pension insurance	20.00		
Farmers			
Health insurance [1]	6.40		
Accident insurance	1.90		
Pension insurance	12.50		

Maximum contribution basis for 1994

Schillings

Wage and salary earners, self-employed professionals, and others	36 000
Self-employed small traders	42 000
Farmers	42 000
Civil servants	36 000

1. Including 0.5 per cent additional contribution to hospital financing.
2. Includes groups such as home helpers, tourist guides, and employees of extraterritorial organisations.
Source: Hauptverband der Österreichischen Sozialversicherungsträger, Soziale Sicherheit (1994).

sioners have a contribution of 3.5 per cent (retired civil servants, 3.95 per cent) deducted from their pension. Contribution rates are low by international standards, and are determined by the legislature after the social insurance authorities submit financial reports. Insofar as contributions may not fully cover the benefits payable, the Bund assumes liability for the deficit in the form of a guarantee and provides a contribution to the health and accident insurance of farmers. Until recently, the funds have tended to run small surpluses, thus building up reserves, but in 1995 the funds incurred deficits which are projected to increase further.

Private insurance

Around 34 per cent of the Austrian population holds a *private insurance* contract, with 14 per cent holding a standard supplementary hospital cost/ambulatory doctor contract and 21 per cent holding a special variant that offers a daily cash allowance in the case of a hospitalisation (*Krankenhaus-Tagegeld-Versicherung*). In the former, the insurer maintains a corresponding contract with the hospital, guaranteeing that he will pay the hospital directly in full for the extra costs of a stay in the "special class" (*Sondergebühr*), allowing for both a higher level of comfort and free choice of treating doctor in hospital. Past hospital practice, due to terminate in 1996 as the result of a recent constitutional court ruling, resulted in private insurees being charged not only for extra amenities received in the special class, but also for a part of the hospital financing gap. Payments to hospitals have thus grown from 20 per cent of total expenditures in 1980 to 35 per cent in 1993, a 5-fold absolute increase to Sch 4.1 billion (Table A3). In 1994, payments to doctors for in-patient care amounted to 5 billion, or 44 per cent of all expenditures, having grown about as strongly as payments to hospitals and likewise representing an implicit cross-subsidy to cover hospital labour costs and physician "rents". Though benefits also allow for the choice of a non-contract doctor in private practice, such payments were far less significant (Sch 401 million).

In contrast to the organisation of social insurance, there is free choice in the selection of private insurer and the premium is set freely by the latter in accordance with insurance market principles (depending on level of benefits, sex, and age). At the same

Table A.3. **Coverage and financing by private insurance**

	1980	1985	1990	1991	1992	1993	1994
Per cent of population covered	36.1	37.5	37.3	37.3	36.7	36.2	34.4
Hospital cost coverage plans	–	–	14.4	14.4	14.4	13.8	13.6
Hospital day-money plans	–	–	22.8	22.7	22.3	22.4	20.8
Total expenditures (billion schillings)	4.2	6.6	8.6	9.4	10.2	11.1	11.5
of which: (in per cent)							
Hospital doctors' fees for "special class"	24.2	36.1	41.9	42.6	42.9	42.4	44.5
Hospital charges for "special class"	20.1	36.6	34.0	35.4	35.1	36.1	34.6
Other	55.7	27.3	24.1	22.0	22.0	21.5	20.9

Source: Association of Austrian Insurers, *Gesundheitswesen in Österreich,* Summer 1994, and submission to the OECD.

time, the sector is regulated by the Ministry of Finance, to the effect that after an initial waiting period, the insurer is not allowed to terminate contracts; on the other hand, the insured is free to terminate contracts once a year after a waiting period of two years. Another feature of private, as opposed to social, insurance is the practice of "profit sharing": at least 85 per cent of the insurer's profits are to be put aside in a special profit/loss account as a set-aside for profit sharing with insured customers; these profits are then distributed among policy holders according to a formula, chiefly depending on the extent to which medical services were not used in the previous year, as a premium refund. This device gives customers an incentive for economies (something completely lacking in the social insurance). Premium payments were, until 1997, 50 per cent tax deductible but this has now been reduced to 25 per cent. Furthermore, employers can take out private supplementary health insurance for their employees by voluntary agreement, and the premiums are also tax deductible up to a ceiling (Sch 4 000 per annum).

Notes

1. This group also includes the liberal professions, the unemployed and the military.
2. This includes stays in convalescent homes, rest homes, spas and sanatoriums, and rehabilitation therapy in hospitals.
3. For the pension of self-employed small traders, funds are also raised from the trade tax (*Gewerbesteuer*), and for farmers from a levy on agricultural and forestry enterprises.

Annex II

Measuring the rate of unemployment

The best-known definition of unemployment is that used by the Labour Office and is defined as the ratio of registered unemployed to the dependent employment, both being derived from social security records. In the first half of 1996 the rate of unemployment according to this definition was 7.0 per cent. The OECD, by contrast, defines the rate of unemployment as the registered unemployed relative to the total labour force, including the self-employed (see *Economic Outlook* 59 for details) and over the same time period the rate amounted to some 6.2 per cent. A third measure is based on Survey data provided by the microcensus up to 1994. The rate of unemployment according to this definition was considerably lower than for the former two approaches. Finally, since 1996 the microcensus has been adapted to the norms of the EU (which do not correspond fully to those of the OECD) and unemployment under this definition amounts to some 4.3 per cent.* No time series is, however, available.

In nearly all countries, measures of the rate of unemployment differ according to whether administrative or survey sources have been utilised but the development over time is usually similar. This is not true for Austria since 1984 (Figure A2), with the labour force survey indicating a relative constancy of the rate of unemployment until around 1993 after which the three time series indicate a similar development. The labour force survey produces both lower estimates of the level of unemployment and much higher levels of employment – particularly the self-employed – than administrative records suggest. While this could be expected, it is nevertheless difficult to reconcile the sample survey results with those obtained by the full census, raising doubts about the sampling properties of the labour force survey. Moreover, the definitions used by the labour force survey have varied over time making it unsuitable for time series analysis.

In view of these considerations, and given the need to use a sufficiently long and consistent time series in order to identify labour market trends, this *Survey* refers to the definition of unemployment utilised for the *Economic Outlook*.

---

* See ''International vergleichbare Daten zur Arbeitslosigkeit in Österreich 1994'', *Statistische Nachrichten,* 5/1996.

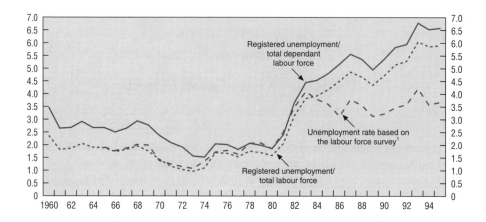

1. Breaks in 1974 and in 1994.
Source: OECD, *Quarterly Labour Force Statistics, Main Economic Indicators*; OECD Analytical Data Bank.

Annex III

Chronology of main economic events

1995

January

Austria accedes to the EU.

March

The Austrian national bank lowers the discount rate by $1/2$ percentage point to 4 per cent and the Lombard rate by $1/4$ percentage point to 5.25 per cent. The Gomex open market rate is reduced by $1/4$ percentage point to 4.45 per cent.

April

Following the resignation of the Minister of Finance in March, the government is reorganised.

July

To comply with the Treaty on European Union, the Austrian national bank redefines the minimum reserve requirements. Short-term government paper (*Bundesschatzscheine*) ceases to be regarded as an acceptable asset for required minimum reserves. To compensate for this tightening, minimum reserve rates are simultaneously lowered; for sight deposits by 2 percentage points to 7 per cent, for short-term time and savings deposits by 1.5 percentage points to 5.5 per cent, and for long-term time and savings deposits and securities with maturity below 24 months by 2 percentage points to 4 per cent.

August

The Austrian national bank lowers the discount rate by $1/2$ percentage point to 3.5 per cent and the Gomex open market rate by 0.1 percentage point to 4.35 per cent.

A hiring freeze comes into force in the public sector.

September

A further drop in minimum reserves comes into force: for sight deposits by 2 percentage points to 5 per cent, for short-term time and savings deposits by 2.5 per cent to 3 per cent, and for long-term time and savings deposits and securities with maturity below 24 months by 1 percentage point to 3 per cent. The Austrian national bank also lowers the Gomex open market rate three times by 0.1 percentage points to 4.05 per cent.

The tariff partners in the metal industry agree on wage increases for workers and salaried employees: from November onwards minimum wages are increased by 3.8 per cent, and actual wages (*Istlöhne*) by 3.8 per cent or by a minimum of Sch 650. In addition, a lump-sum payment of Sch 2 500 is paid. Workers become entitled to immediate sickness benefits to be paid by employers for up to six weeks. Under certain conditions normal weakly working time can be extended to 56 hours without an obligation to pay overtime.

October

The negotiations between the two coalition parties about the 1996 budget fail. The Parliament endorses new elections and passes a law increasing the government's borrowing authority for the 1995 budget.

The Austrian national bank restructures the system of commercial bank refinancing by reducing the share of refinancing provided by standard facilities. A supply-oriented tender repurchase system is introduced.

November

The members of the Economic Chamber (*Wirtschaftskammer*) are polled on whether membership should remain legally obligatory. In each state a majority votes affirmatively.

December

In the national parliamentary elections the parties obtain the following shares of votes: Social Democratic Party of Austria (*Sozialdemokratische Partei Österreichs*) 38.3 per cent, Austrian People's Party (*Österreichische Volkspartei*) 28.3 per cent, Free Party of Austria (*Freiheitliche Partei Österreichs*) 22.1 per cent, Greens (*Grüne*) 4.6 per cent and Liberal Forum (*Liberales Forum*) 5.3 per cent. The final distribution of seats in the Parliament is: 71, 52, 42, 9, and 9.

The Austrian national bank lowers the Gomex open market rate in two steps by 0.1 by 0.2 percentage points to 3.75 per cent. The discount rate is lowered by $\frac{1}{2}$ percentage point to 3.0 per cent.

1996

January

The Minister of Finance resigns and is succeeded by Mr. Klima.

The hiring freeze in the public sector is extended until April.

The Austrian national bank lowers the Gomex open market rate by 0.1 percentage point to 3.65 per cent. The national bank starts to invite commercial banks to bid for volume tenders with a maturity of one week in weekly intervals. In two subsequent weeks tenders are offered at rates of 3.65 and 3.55 per cent.

February

In the public sector agreement is reached to raise wages by lump sum payments of Sch 2 700 in 1996 and Sch 3 500 in 1997.

The Austrian national bank lowers the Gomex open market rate by 0.15 percentage point to 3.5 per cent. The rate for volume tenders is lowered by 0.25 percentage points to 3.3 per cent.

March

Following the elections of December 1995 a new government is formed, based on a coalition between the Social Democratic Party and the People's Party.

A programme by the Labour Market Service to reduce long-term unemployment comes into force. Companies hiring registered long-term unemployed obtain a refund of 20 per cent of the gross wage for up to one year.

The members of the Labour Chamber (*Arbeiterkammer*) are polled on whether membership in the Labour Chamber should remain legally obligatory. In each state a majority votes affirmatively.

The government announces a plan to spend Sch 90 billion over the next four years on infrastructure projects to combat unemployment.

A zero wage round for 1997 is agreed for the employees of the Austrian Railways.

April

Parliament approves the combined budgets for 1996 and 1997, and passes the pertinent laws. Overall, the package contains savings relative to the government's base-line of Sch 100 billion for the Federal government and Sch 113 billion at the general government level. Of these, two-thirds are to be realised by spending restraint and one third via raising revenues. The package aims at reducing the general government deficit to not more than 3 per cent of GDP in 1997.

A ''bonus malus'' regulation promoting employment of elderly employees comes into force. For companies hiring unemployed aged 50 or older, unemployment contributions are reduced or eliminated. If an elderly employee is made redundant the company is required to pay a fine to the unemployment insurance system.

The Austrian national bank lowers the discount and Lombard rates by 0.5 percentage point each to 2.5 per cent and 4.75 per cent, respectively.

The tariff partners in the textile sector agree on new working time regulations. The weekly working time may total 48 hours without an obligation to pay overtime premia, provided the average weekly working time in a reference period of 26 weeks does not exceed 40 hours.

May

The tariff partners in the construction sector agree on a yearly working time model which allows the extension of regular working time to 45 hours in the summer. Working time in excess of 39 hours is compensated by reduced working time in the winter. Holiday payments by employers are increased.

The Austrian national bank lowers the rate for the volume tender by 0.1 percentage point to 3.2 per cent.

June

The Minister of Economics, Mr. Ditz, resigns and is succeeded by Mr. Farnleitner.

July

The Parliament passes a revision of the social security law which aims at fiscal consolidation of the health insurance.

Anonymous deposits of securities with banks are no longer allowed.

August

The government presents a plan to charge a user fee for motorways to come into effect in January 1997.

September

The Austrian national bank lowers the Gomex open market rate by 0.1 percentage point to 3.4 per cent, and the interest rate for the volume tender by 0.2 percentage points to 3.0 per cent.

New legislation restraining eligibility for early retirement comes into force.

October

Laws governing the reform of hospital financing are passed by the Parliament.

STATISTICAL ANNEX AND STRUCTURAL INDICATORS

Table A. Gross domestic product

Sch billion

	Current prices					1983 prices / Current prices, percentage distribution				
	1991	1992	1993	1994	1995	1991	1992	1993	1994	1995
Expenditure										
Private consumption	1 062.1	1 133.7	1 180.7	1 247.2	1 299.7	850.2	873.7	879.7	902.0	919.2
Public consumption	348.4	374.8	404.5	426.3	444.0	248.4	253.8	261.6	267.4	273.0
Gross domestic fixed capital formation	488.4	513.1	515.1	560.9	581.9	391.1	397.6	391.2	417.6	427.3
Construction[1]	279.9	305.5	323.5	351.1	359.0	219.1	231.5	238.2	251.4	251.2
Machinery and equipment[1]	208.5	207.6	191.6	209.8	223.0	172.0	166.1	153.0	166.2	176.1
Change of stocks, including statistical errors	10.9	6.0	9.8	34.7	50.4	9.6	8.7	12.6	27.2	40.4
Exports of goods and services	774.7	791.6	786.5	835.4	887.1	700.7	709.3	698.3	734.4	774.1
Less: Imports of goods and services	758.0	772.0	772.6	841.7	910.7	713.6	726.3	721.1	780.1	836.8
Gross domestic product at market prices	1 926.5	2 047.2	2 124.1	2 262.9	2 352.4	1 486.4	1 516.7	1 522.2	1 568.6	1 597.2
Origin by sector										
Agriculture, forestry and fishing	53.0	50.0	47.3	49.5	..	44.9	43.5	43.4	44.7	43.3
Manufacturing and mining	496.1	509.7	502.9	536.4	..	422.3	422.8	409.3	425.7	440.5
Construction	140.0	153.8	167.1	178.9	..	105.0	110.7	116.7	123.1	122.3
Other	1 237.4	1 333.7	1 406.7	1 498.2	..	914.1	939.6	952.8	975.1	991.1
Distribution of net national income										
Compensation of employees	1 027.4	1 095.6	1 141.3	1 182.1	1 227.0	71.7	71.9	72.4	71.2	70.1
Net income from property and entrepreneurship and savings of corporations	446.3	466.5	484.1	536.5	574.2	31.1	30.6	30.7	32.3	32.8
Direct taxes on corporations	39.7	47.1	44.8	33.3	40.6	2.8	3.1	2.8	2.0	2.3
Government income from property and entrepreneurship	40.8	45.7	41.1	44.2	53.5	2.8	3.0	2.6	2.7	3.1
Less: Interest on public and consumer debt	120.8	130.4	135.3	136.2	146.1	8.4	8.6	8.6	8.2	8.4
Net national income	1 433.4	1 524.5	1 576.0	1 659.9	1 749.2	100.0	100.0	100.0	100.0	100.0

1. Excluding VAT.

Source: Österreichisches Statistisches Zentralamt, and Österreichisches Institut für Wirtschaftsforschung (WIFO).

Table B. **General government income and expenditure**

Sch billion

	1987	1988	1989	1990	1991	1992	1993	1994	1995
Operating surplus and property income receivable	29.4	30.7	33.3	38.1	40.6	49.8	45.5	46.1	49.4
Casualty insurance claims receivable	0.3	0.3	0.4	0.4	0.4	0.4	0.4	0.4	0.4
Indirect taxes	245.2	254.9	271.4	287.9	305.8	325.8	339.1	366.4	334.6
Direct taxes	203.4	214.5	214.4	239.0	267.1	296.9	312.7	299.2	326.4
Compulsory fees, fines and penalties	3.9	4.1	4.4	4.9	5.1	5.1	5.6	6.1	6.5
Social security contributions	183.3	191.8	204.3	220.6	238.9	262.3	280.0	300.5	315.5
Unfunded employee welfare contributions imputed	39.6	41.1	43.4	46.0	49.8	53.1	56.3	54.2	55.6
Current transfers n.e.c. received from the rest of the world	0.7	0.6	0.6	0.7	0.9	0.7	0.7	0.8	9.3
Current receipts	705.7	738.0	772.3	837.5	908.6	994.2	1 040.3	1 073.7	1 097.8
Final consumption expenditure	280.4	288.4	302.9	319.9	348.3	375.2	405.0	425.7	442.5
Property income payable	58.4	61.8	66.4	73.1	81.9	87.5	92.0	91.8	102.0
Net casualty insurance premiums payable	0.3	0.3	0.4	0.4	0.4	0.4	0.4	0.4	0.4
Subsidies	47.4	45.1	45.1	47.9	60.9	63.3	68.0	57.4	60.4
Social security benefits and social assistance grants	161.5	167.8	176.4	188.7	199.9	212.5	229.6	247.3	261.5
Current transfers to private non-profit institutions serving household	87.0	85.2	86.4	94.1	103.7	117.1	142.3	150.7	151.5
Unfunded employee welfare benefits	63.4	66.0	70.1	74.5	80.8	85.9	91.5	95.7	100.2
Current transfers n.e.c. paid to the rest of the world	3.9	4.3	4.5	5.5	6.5	8.0	8.5	9.4	14.8
Current disbursements	702.2	718.8	752.4	804.0	882.3	949.9	1 037.3	1 078.5	1 133.3
Saving	3.5	19.2	19.9	33.5	26.3	44.3	3.0	-4.8	-35.5
Consumption of fixed capital	11.6	11.8	12.2	12.8	13.5	13.8	14.5	15.1	15.7
Capital transfers received net, from:	-26.8	-27.3	-23.1	-27.0	-29.0	-29.4	-37.5	-35.9	-44.1
Other resident sectors	-26.8	-27.3	-23.0	-26.9	-28.7	-29.1	-37.1	-35.4	-43.7
The rest of the world	0.0	0.0	-0.1	-0.1	-0.3	-0.2	-0.4	-0.5	-0.4
Finance of gross accumulation	-11.8	3.6	9.0	19.3	10.8	28.7	-20.0	-25.6	-64.0
Gross capital formation	50.7	50.7	55.2	57.3	63.0	67.7	67.5	70.4	72.7
Purchases of land, net	0.7	0.6	0.6	0.7	0.5	0.0	1.2	2.5	1.5
Net lending	-63.2	-47.7	-46.8	-38.7	-52.8	-39.1	-88.7	-98.5	-138.2

Source: Bundesministerium für Finanzen.

187

Table C. **Output, employment and productivity in industry**

	1987	1988	1989	1990	1991	1992	1993	1994	1995
Output in industry, 1990 = 100[1]									
Total industry	84.2	87.9	93.1	100.0	101.6	100.5	98.5	102.4	107.9
Investment goods	77.0	81.1	86.5	100.0	106.6	102.2	97.5	101.0	109.6
Consumer goods	87.9	87.8	93.4	100.0	100.6	99.0	97.8	98.7	98.4
Intermediate goods	80.7	87.8	93.6	100.0	100.6	100.9	97.5	104.5	111.4
Manufacturing goods	81.0	86.4	92.1	100.0	102.0	101.2	98.5	103.7	108.1
Employment, thousands[2]	543.6	532.6	536.3	544.8	538.9	520.5	487.4	470.1	465.7
Monthly hours worked[3]	140	141	140	139	138	138	138	140	139
Wages and productivity									
Gross hourly earnings for wage earners (sch.)	104.3	107.8	112.6	120.7	127.9	135.3	142.0	147.4	153.9
Gross monthly earnings, employees (sch.)	21 504.5	22 338.9	23 389.5	25 143.5	26 592.8	28 207.7	29 613.2	30 791.5	32 192.8
Output per employee (1990 = 100)	81.5	88.2	93.3	100.0	102.5	105.1	108.7	118.4	126.0

1. Break in the series in 1990.
2. Including administrative personnel.
3. Mining and manufacturing

Source: Österreichisches Institut für Wirtschaftsforschung, and Österreichisches Statistisches Zentralamt.

Table D. **Retail sales and prices**

(1990 = 100)

	1987	1988	1989	1990	1991	1992	1993	1994	1995
Retail sales	85.0	89.2	93.5	100.0	107.5	111.6	112.0	115.5	115.1
of which: durable	78.0	86.3	92.8	100.0	108.0	112.5	112.0	115.2	116.9
Prices									
Consumer prices									
Total	92.6	94.4	96.8	100.0	103.3	107.5	111.4	114.7	117.3
Food	95.2	95.9	97.1	100.0	104.1	108.2	111.3	113.4	112.8
Rent	91.1	93.3	96.1	100.0	105.0	111.0	116.8	122.8	129.8
Other goods and services	92.0	94.1	96.8	100.0	102.9	106.9	110.8	114.2	117.3
Wholesale prices									
Total	95.8	95.5	97.2	100.0	100.9	100.6	100.2	101.5	101.9
Agricultural goods	94.4	93.2	93.1	100.0	101.6	91.3	88.7	91.3	85.3
Food	102.3	101.5	100.8	100.0	102.6	107.8	108.8	109.9	103.0
Cost of construction (residential)	90.0	92.8	96.1	100.0	105.9	110.7	114.2	117.6	120.3

Source: Österreichisches Statistisches Zentralamt, and Österreichisches Institut für Wirtschaftsforschung.

189

Table E. **Money and banking**[1]

End of period
Sch billion

	1987	1988	1989	1990	1991	1992	1993	1994	1995
Interest rates (per cent)									
Discount rate	3.00	4.00	6.50	6.50	8.00	8.00	5.25	4.50	3.00
Average bond yield[2]	6.86	6.58	7.06	8.72	8.69	8.39	6.74	6.69	6.51
Money circulation and external reserves									
Notes and coins in circulation	102.9	108.4	117.8	124.7	133.4	141.2	149.8	158.3	158.6
Sight liabilities of the Central Bank	43.6	39.6	51.1	44.3	38.8	48.9	55.6	56.3	43.9
Gross external reserves of the Central Bank	114.9	123.4	132.8	130.3	140.1	167.4	202.4	208.3	201.6
of which: Gold	39.5	39.5	38.6	38.1	37.4	37.2	34.7	34.2	22.3
Credit institutions									
Credits to domestic non-banks	1 438.2	1 579.4	1 688.4	1 846.2	1 994.2	2 129.7	2 202.1	2 316.9	2 477.5
Deposits from domestic non-banks	1 259.2	1 312.3	1 404.3	1 503.8	1 613.9	1 680.3	1 751.9	1 850.8	1 941.6
Sight	129.1	142.2	146.5	155.9	170.8	180.9	207.2	222.0	266.4
Time[3]	176.3	174.4	198.8	185.8	172.4	136.9	118.0	131.4	123.6
Savings	953.7	995.7	1 059.0	1 162.1	1 270.7	1 362.5	1 426.7	1 497.4	1 551.6
Holdings of domestic Treasury bills	51.2	46.9	44.9	53.7	60.4	56.3	67.0	72.6	49.2
Holdings of other domestic securities	287.0	319.5	345.7	356.1	365.0	342.4	376.2	445.7	501.0
Foreign assets	751.7	816.9	842.0	843.9	846.8	915.9	1 012.4	1 039.5	1 138.5
Foreign liabilities	794.7	883.8	933.0	937.8	962.0	1 048.8	1 088.3	1 114.1	1 189.4

1. Totals may not add due to rounding.
2. Average effective yields on circulating issues.
3. Including funded borrowing of banks.
Source: Österreichische Nationalbank.

Table F. **The Federal budget**

National accounts basis
Sch billion

	Outturn								
	1987	1988	1989	1990	1991	1992	1993	1994	1995
1. Current revenue	354.8	389.2	404.7	437.6	475.0	520.6	539.2	556.0	570.8
Direct taxes of households	105.0	130.1	124.5	140.2	154.7	169.1	181.8	185.2	208.0
Indirect taxes	173.1	178.8	190.1	201.2	213.2	229	236.2	254.2	224.6
Corporate taxes	20.0	21.3	25.7	26.5	29.8	36.4	34.3	25.9	33.2
Income from property and entrepreneurship	22.4	23.1	24.9	27.6	29.1	33.6	30.1	33.2	38.0
Current transfers from abroad	0.3	0.3	0.2	0.3	0.4	0.2	0.2	0.3	8.9
Other	34.0	36.1	39.5	42.0	47.8	52.2	56.6	57.3	58.1
2. Current expenditure	392.1	403.7	414.7	441.4	494.6	525.0	584.1	602.4	633.3
Goods and services	102.0	104.3	109.0	113.7	124.3	131.2	140.8	148.4	155.0
Subsidies	37.5	34.7	34.1	35.2	47.4	48.8	53.5	43.7	42.9
Public debt	49.4	53.1	58.0	64.3	72.9	78.4	82.8	82.7	91.4
Transfers to abroad	1.0	1.1	1.2	1.6	2.0	2.1	2.7	3.5	8.7
Transfers to public authorities	96.3	105.5	105.5	111.0	121.4	125.4	140.0	152.0	163.6
Transfers to private households	67.6	65.0	64.5	70.6	77.8	87.2	108.6	113.3	109.7
Other	38.4	39.9	42.4	45.0	48.9	52.0	55.7	58.9	62.0
3. Net public savings (1 – 2)	–37.3	–14.5	–10.0	–3.8	–19.6	–4.4	–44.9	–46.4	–62.5
4. Depreciation	2.6	2.7	2.8	2.9	3.1	3.1	3.3	3.4	3.6
5. Gross savings (3 + 4)	–34.7	–11.8	–7.2	–0.9	–16.5	–1.3	–41.6	–43.0	–58.9
6. Gross asset formation	15.5	15.2	15.4	16.0	16.8	15.1	15.7	16.2	14.1
7. Balance of income-effective transactions (5 – 6)	–50.2	–27.0	–22.6	–16.9	–33.3	–16.4	–57.3	–59.2	–73.0
8. Capital transfers (net)	23.5	39.4	35.2	38.1	38.5	40.3	43.0	42.0	50.6
9. Financial balance (7 – 8)	–73.6	–66.4	–57.8	–55.1	–71.9	–56.7	–100.4	–101.4	–123.6

Source: Österreichisches Statistisches Zentralamt.

Table G. **Balance of payments**

Sch million

	1987	1988	1989	1990	1991	1992	1993	1994	1995
Trade balance[1]	-69 152	-68 227	-85 377	-90 168	-112 869	-106 365	-97 738	-116 363	-72 949
Exports	342 433	383 213	429 310	466 065	479 029	487 558	467 171	512 515	732 773
Imports	411 585	451 440	514 687	556 233	591 898	593 923	564 909	628 878	805 722
Services, net	44 003	43 139	61 829	73 148	77 546	85 900	87 832	76 904	47 539
Foreign travel, net	41 359	46 739	58 882	64 666	74 842	67 400	61 427	42 827	29 661
Receipts	112 012	124 599	141 750	152 441	161 178	159 640	157 520	150 183	147 140
Expenditure	70 653	77 860	82 868	87 775	86 336	92 240	96 093	107 356	117 479
Investment income, net	-10 861	-11 279	-12 318	-10 976	-17 562	-13 083	-11 533	-10 812	-9 992
Other services, net	5 566	7 227	9 861	9 615	20 266	31 583	37 938	44 889	27 870
Unclassified goods and services	23 717	22 575	28 490	30 681	36 349	30 456	14 377	27 100	
Transfers, net	-1 008	-429	-1 665	-26	-206	-11 649	-12 716	-8 258	-21 606
Current balance	-2 440	-2 942	3 277	13 635	820	-1 658	-8 245	-20 617	-47 016
Long-term capital, net	32 761	-14 634	6 110	-10 207	-24 383	7 871	75 318	9 285	78 907
Austrian abroad	-13 594	-49 629	-49 601	-56 894	-73 983	-72 389	-47 902	-71 887	-97 566
Foreign in Austria	46 355	34 995	55 711	46 687	49 600	80 260	123 220	81 172	176 473
Short-term capital, net	-19 757	20 188	10 456	8 942	24 818	13 182	-34 851	24 389	-14 274
Balance of capital	13 004	5 554	16 566	-1 265	435	21 053	40 467	33 674	64 633
Errors and omissions	-5 820	5 515	-8 414	-12 967	7 955	8 348	-5 612	-2 724	-3 345
Memorandum items									
Changes in reserves arising from allocation of SDRs, monetization of gold and revaluation of reserve currencies	-4 807	1 297	-2 737	-3 083	1 144	2 184	7 603	-4 829	5 842
Allocation of SDRs	-92								
Change in total reserves		9 351	8 830	-3 723	10 307	29 957	34 206	5 504	20 131
Conversion factor (Sch per dollar)	12.64	12.34	13.23	11.37	11.67	10.99	11.63	11.42	10.08

1. Until 1994 including non monetary gold and adjustments to trade according to foreign trade statistics. From 1995 due to Austria's the EU, a new collection method for obtaining data on merchandise trade within the EU has been introduced. The payments for merchandise deliveries include gross transit trade.

Source: Österreichische Nationalbank.

Table H. Merchandise trade by commodity group and area

Sch billion

	Imports					Exports				
	1990	1991	1992	1993	1994	1990	1991	1992	1993	1994
Total	558.1	593.0	594.7	565.1	632.0	467.7	480.0	488.0	467.3	514.3
By commodity group										
Food, drink, tobacco	27.7	29.5	29.1	29.2	33.0	15.2	15.2	15.9	15.9	18.6
Raw materials	25.3	25.4	24.6	22.0	26.6	24.4	21.5	19.9	18.4	22.1
Mineral fuels, energy	35.4	35.5	30.5	28.5	27.8	4.7	4.4	5.2	5.2	6.7
Chemicals	55.3	57.7	58.4	58.8	65.6	39.5	42.8	42.1	42.1	47.0
Machinery and transport equipment	211.6	232.1	234.8	213.1	239.9	175.6	184.0	189.7	182.4	200.5
Other	202.9	212.8	217.3	213.4	239.2	208.3	212.1	215.2	203.3	219.4
By area										
OECD countries	491.1	522.5	523.7	500.3	556.3	400.1	413.8	418.5	405.8	446.0
EC countries	396.7	416.0	418.8	391.5	432.0	317.1	326.9	332.7	306.2	333.3
Germany	245.5	255.0	255.2	234.2	252.8	175.1	187.5	194.5	182.3	195.9
Italy	50.5	52.4	51.3	50.9	55.9	45.8	45.0	42.9	36.9	41.8
France	23.4	25.8	26.3	24.8	29.8	22.2	20.9	21.4	20.7	23.4
United Kingdom	14.4	16.0	16.2	15.4	18.3	18.1	17.4	17.5	15.3	16.3
EFTA countries[1]	39.4	40.8	40.6	37.9	43.2	47.3	44.1	42.2	40.5	45.5
Switzerland	23.8	24.8	23.8	23.1	25.8	32.4	30.6	29.0	28.8	32.7
United States	20.2	23.4	23.5	24.9	27.6	15.0	13.6	12.9	15.4	17.9
Other OECD countries	34.8	42.3	40.8	46.0	53.5	20.7	29.3	30.6	43.6	49.3
Non-OECD countries										
Eastern Europe[2]	18.0	18.6	21.5	8.1	10.5	21.4	21.0	24.6	13.8	15.8
Africa[3]	13.8	12.9	11.0	11.3	10.4	7.5	7.7	6.4	6.4	7.9
Latin America[3]	5.0	5.1	4.4	4.2	5.5	2.4	2.8	3.0	3.2	4.0
OPEC	12.0	12.5	11.5	11.9	11.1	12.8	13.8	13.8	12.6	10.9
Far and Middle East[3]	23.5	27.6	28.8	30.4	35.5	22.7	24.1	25.4	26.0	25.5
Index, in real terms (1990 = 100)	100	101	106	105	119	100	106	111	108	119
Index of average value (1990 = 100)	100	100	99	95	94	100	97	95	91	89

Note: Due to Austria's integration in the EU, a new collection method for obtaining data on merchandise trade within EU has been introduced. At the moment of printing data for 1995 were not available.

1. Including Finland.
2. Excluding ex-Yugoslavia.
3. Including countries belonging to OPEC.

Source: OECD, *Monthly Statistics Of Foreign Trade, Series A.*

Table 1. **Labour-market indicators**

	Preceding 1987		1989	1990	1991	1992	1993	1994	1995
	Peak	Trough							
A. EVOLUTION									
Unemployment rate (surveys)									
Total	1983 = 4.1	1973 = 1.1	3.1	3.2	3.5	3.6	4.2	3.7	3.8
Male	1984 = 3.9	1973 = 0.7	2.8	3.0	3.4	3.5	4.0	3.3	3.2
Women	1983 = 5.1	1973 = 1.7	3.6	3.6	3.7	3.8	4.5	4.0	4.3
Unemployment rate (registered)									
Total	1987 = 5.6	1974 = 1.5	5.0	5.4	5.8	6.0	6.8	6.5	6.6
Male	1987 = 5.5	1973 = 0.6	4.6	4.9	5.3	5.7	6.7	6.4	6.4
Women	1987 = 5.7	1980 = 2.3	5.5	6.0	6.5	6.2	6.9	6.7	6.8
Youth			2.4	2.6	2.6	2.5	2.9	2.8	2.9
Share of long-term unemployment			16.7	15.8	19.2	20.9	20.6	22.8	20.9
Productivity index, 1991 = 100			97.0	99.1	100.0	100.6	101.3	104.2	106.5
Monthly hours of work in industry (wage earners) billions of hours			140	139	138	138	138	140	139
B. STRUCTURAL OR INSTITUTIONAL CHARACTERISTICS									
Participation rates[1]									
Global			66.3	67.2	68.0	68.3	68.0	67.8	67.5
Male			77.8	78.6	79.0	78.5	77.9	77.4	77.1
Women			54.7	55.7	56.9	57.8	57.9	57.9	57.7
Employment/population between 16 and 64 years[1]			65.0	65.5	66.0	66.9	66.3	69.1	68.7
Employment by sector									
Agriculture – per cent of total			7.9	7.9	7.4	7.1	6.9	7.2	7.5
– per cent change			-1.6	1.2	-4.3	-2.4	-1.9	7.7	4.7
Industry – per cent of total			37.0	36.8	36.9	35.6	35.0	32.3	32.2
– per cent change			-0.2	1.6	2.1	-1.7	-0.8	-4.3	0.5
Services – per cent of total			55.1	55.3	55.7	57.4	58.1	60.5	60.3
– per cent change			2.3	2.5	2.4	5.1	1.9	8.1	0.4
Voluntary part-time work			9.7	9.9	9.8	10.0	10.1	12.1	13.9
Non-filled vacancies, per cent of employment			1.5	1.8	1.6	1.4	1.0	0.9	0.8
Social insurance as a per cent of compensation			18.4	18.3	18.2	18.4	18.8	18.7	18.9

1. Including the self-employed.
Source: Statistical Yearbook; WIFO; OECD estimates; OECD, *Labour Force Statistics.*

Table J. **Public sector**

	1970	1980	1990	1994	1995
	BUDGET INDICATORS: GENERAL GOVERNMENT ACCOUNTS (% GDP)				
Current receipts	39.7	46.4	46.5	47.4	46.7
Non-interest expenditure	37.4	45.6	44.6	47.7	48.2
Primary budget balance	2.3	0.8	1.9	−0.3	−1.5
Gross interest	1.1	2.5	4.1	4.1	4.3
General government budget balance	1.2	−1.7	−2.2	−4.4	−5.9
of which: Federal government	0.2	−2.6	−3.1	−4.5	−5.3
	THE STRUCTURE OF EXPENDITURE (% GDP)				
Government expenditure					
Transfers	4.0	5.9	5.6	7.1	7.1
Subsidies	1.7	3.0	2.7	2.5	2.6
General expenditure	14.7	18.0	17.8	18.8	18.8
Education	2.9	3.9	4.0	..	..
Health	3.2	4.4	4.6	..	..
Social security and welfare	2.6	3.3	3.2	..	..

	TAX RATES	
	Prior to Tax Reform of 1989	Under the Tax Reform of 1989
Personal income tax		
Top rate	62	50
Lower rate	21	10
Average tax rate	12.7	11.5
Social security tax rate[1]		
Blue-collar workers	38.6	38.6
White-collar workers	34.5	34.5
Basic VAT rate	20	20
Corporation tax rate		
Top rate	55	30
Lower rate	30	30

1. The sum of employees' and employers' contributions to health, accident, pension and unemployment insurance.
Source: OECD, *National Accounts;* Ministry of Finance.

Table K. **Production structure and performance indicators**

A. Production structure (1990 prices)

	GDP share (per cent of total)					Employment share (per cent of total)				
	1980	1990	1992	1993	1994	1980	1990	1992	1993	1994
Tradeables										
Agriculture	4.2	3.8	3.3	3.2	3.2	1.7	1.3	1.2	1.2	1.2
Mining and quarrying	0.6	0.4	0.4	0.4	0.4	0.6	0.4	0.3	0.2	0.2
Manufacturing	31.4	31.1	30.4	29.3	29.6	40.5	35.9	34.2	33.1	32.1
Non-tradeables										
Electricity	3.4	3.3	3.4	3.5	3.3	1.7	1.7	1.6	1.6	1.6
Construction	10.5	8.3	8.8	9.3	9.5	11.2	10.0	10.4	10.6	10.9
Wholesale and retail trade, restaurants and hotels	19.4	20.1	20.0	19.7	19.5	21.4	24.2	24.9	25.2	25.4
Transport, storage and communication	6.8	7.5	8.0	8.1	8.3	9.6	10.2	10.4	10.5	10.5
Finance, insurance, real estate and business services	19.2	20.4	20.8	21.3	21.0	8.4	10.1	10.5	10.7	10.9
Community, social and personal services	4.4	4.9	5.0	5.1	5.1	5.1	6.3	6.6	6.9	7.1

B. Industrial sector performance

	Productivity growth (sector GDP/sector employment)					Investment share, current prices (per cent of total)				
	1980	1990	1992	1993	1994	1980	1990	1992	1993	1994
Tradeables										
Agriculture	8.7	4.2	-3.1	-0.2	6.8	6.4	4.8	3.9	..	..
Mining and quarrying	2.5	-1.3	-7.4	15.0	21.8	0.4	0.2	..	..	..
Manufacturing	2.1	4.0	3.1	1.2	7.2	20.5	19.4	..	..	..
Non-tradeables										
Electricity	5.9	4.3	3.9	3.4	2.2	6.9	4.9	..	..	..
Construction	0.0	-0.4	2.8	4.5	3.0	2.8	2.2	..	..	..
Wholesale and retail trade, restaurants and hotels	0.0	3.0	0.1	-0.9	1.2	..	..	..	..	..
Transport, storage and communication	4.8	3.7	3.1	1.8	4.8	..	..	..	..	..
Finance, insurance, real estate and business services	3.2	-0.6	1.5	1.9	-0.1	..	..	..	..	..
Community, social and personal services	1.4	2.7	-1.6	1.2	-2.0	..	..	..	..	..

Table K. **Production structure and performance indicators** (cont.)

	Numbers of enterprises (Per cent of total)					Numbers of employees (Per cent of total)				
	1971	1980	1989	1990	1991	1971	1980	1989	1990	1991
C. Other indicators										
Enterprises ranged by size of employees										
1 to 4	..	18.3	40.4	38.4	37.7	..	0.3	0.7	0.7	0.7
5 to 49	57.9	49.0	37.7	38.6	38.8	11.2	11.2	12.4	12.2	12.4
50 to 499	38.3	29.6	20.0	20.9	21.5	48.6	46.6	48.9	49.8	51.6
More than 500	3.9	3.1	2.0	2.1	2.0	40.2	41.9	38.0	37.3	35.4

	1986	1987	1988	1989	1990	1991	1992	1993	1994	1995
R&D as percentage of manufacturing output	4.72	4.97	4.99	5.20	5.52	6.09	6.35	6.96	7.22	4.72

Source: OECD, *National Accounts*; Österreichisches Statistisches Handbuch.

197

BASIC STATISTICS

BASIC STATISTICS:

INTERNATIONAL COMPARISONS

	Units	Reference period [1]	Australia	Austria
Population				
Total	Thousands	1994	17 840	8 031
Inhabitants per sq. km	Number	1994	2	96
Net average annual increase over previous 10 years	%	1994	1.4	0.6
Employment				
Total civilian employment (TCE)[2]	Thousands	1994	7 680 (93)	3 737
of which: Agriculture	% of TCE	1994	5.3 (93)	7.2
Industry	% of TCE	1994	23.7 (93)	33.2
Services	% of TCE	1994	71 (93)	59.6
Gross domestic product (GDP)				
At current prices and current exchange rates	Bill. US$	1994	331.6	198.1
Per capita	US$	1994	18 588	24 670
At current prices using current PPP's[3]	Bill. US$	1994	327.9	162.3
Per capita	US$	1994	18 382	20 210
Average annual volume growth over previous 5 years	%	1994	2.2	2.5
Gross fixed capital formation (GFCF)	% of GDP	1994	21.4	24.8
of which: Machinery and equipment	% of GDP	1993	9.8	8.7
Residential construction	% of GDP	1993	5.2	6.3
Average annual volume growth over previous 5 years	%	1994	0.8	3.7
Gross saving ratio[4]	% of GDP	1994	16.8	25.3
General government				
Current expenditure on goods and services	% of GDP	1994	17.5	
Current disbursements[5]	% of GDP	1993	36.9	48.4
Current receipts	% of GDP	1993	33.5	48.6
Net official development assistance	% of GNP	1993	0.34	0.31
Indicators of living standards				
Private consumption per capita using current PPP's[3]	US$	1993	10 803	10 546
Passenger cars, per 1 000 inhabitants	Number	1990	430	382
Telephones, per 1 000 inhabitants	Number	1991	464	432
Television sets, per 1 000 inhabitants	Number	1991	480	478
Doctors, per 1 000 inhabitants	Number	1993	2.2 (91)	2.3
Infant mortality per 1 000 live births	Number		6.1	6.5
Wages and prices (average annual increase over previous 5 years)				
Wages (earnings or rates according to availability)	%	1994	3	5.5
Consumer prices	%	1994	3	3.4
Foreign trade				
Exports of goods, fob*	Mill. US$	1994	47 363	44 881
As % of GDP	%	1994	14.3	22.7
Average annual increase over previous 5 years	%	1994	5	6.7
Imports of goods, cif*	Mill. US$	1994	49 731	55 071
As % of GDP	%	1994	15	27.8
Average annual increase over previous 5 years	%	1994	4	7.2
Total official reserves[6]	Mill. SDRs	1994	7 730	11 523
As ratio of average monthly imports of goods	Ratio	1994	1.9	2.5

* At current prices and exchange rates.
1. Unless otherwise stated.
2. According to the definitions used in OECD *Labour Force Statistics*.
3. PPPs = Purchasing Power Parities.
4. Gross saving = Gross national disposable income minus private and government consumption.
5. Current disbursements = Current expenditure on goods and services plus current transfers and payments of property income.
6. Gold included in reserves is valued at 35 SDRs per ounce. End of year.

BASIC STATISTICS: INTERNATIONAL COMPARISONS

	Belgium	Canada	Denmark	Finland	France	Germany	Greece	Iceland	Ireland	Italy	Japan	Luxembourg	Mexico	Netherlands	New Zealand	Norway	Portugal	Spain	Sweden	Switzerland	Turkey	United Kingdom	United States
	10 124	29 251	5 206	5 088	57 960	81 407	10 430	267	3 571	57 190	124 960	398	93 010	15 382	3 526	4 337	9 900	39 150	8 781	6 994	60 573	58 375	260 651
	332	3	121	15	106	228	79	3	51	190	331	153	47	377	13	13	107	78	20	169	78	238	28
	0.3	1.6	0.2	0.4	0.5	0.5	0.5	1.1	0.1	0	0.4	0.8	2	0.6	0.8	0.5	-0.1	0.2	0.5	0.7	2.1	0.3	1
	3 724 (92)	13 292	2 508	2 015	21 781 (93)	35 894	3 790	138	1 168 (93)	20 152 (93)	64 530	162 (91)	32 439	6 631	1 560	1 970 (93)	4 372	11 760	3 926	3 772	19 664	25 044 (93)	123 060
	2.6 (92)	4.1	5.1	8.3	5.1 (93)	3.3	20.8	9.4	12.7 (93)	7.5 (93)	5.8	3.7 (91)	25.8	4	10.4	5.6 (93)	11.5	9.8	3.4	4	44.8	2.2 (93)	2.9
	27.7 (92)	22.6	26.8	26.8	27.7 (93)	37.6	23.6	26.1	27.7 (93)	33 (93)	34	31.5 (91)	22.2	23	25	23.1 (93)	32.8	30.1	25	28.8	22.2	26.2 (93)	24
	69.7 (92)	73.3	68.1	64.9	67.2 (93)	59.1	55.5	65.2	59.7 (93)	59.6 (93)	60.2	64.8 (91)	52.1	73	64.6	71.3 (93)	55.7	60.2	71.6	67.2	33	71.6 (93)	73.1
	227.9	544	146.7	97.2	1 328.5	1 832.3 [8]	73.1 (93)	6.2	52	1 017.8	4 590	10.6 (92)	371.2	334.3	51.2	103.4 (93)	87	482.4	196.6	257.3	130.7	1 019.5	6 649.8
	22 515	18 598	28 181	19 106	22 944	27 826 [8]	7 051 (93)	23 199	14 550	17 796	36 732	27 073 (92)	3 991	21 733	14 513	23 984 (93)	8 792	12 321	22 389	36 790	2 157	17 468	25 512
	204.2	596.7	107	82.5	1 111.8	1 601.7 [8]	118	5.1	54.3	1 068.4	2 593.7	11.7	673.3	285.9	57.3	95.3	122	531.7	153	167.4	319.3	1 030.2	6 649.8
	20 166	20 401	20 546	16 208	19 201	24 325 [8]	1 450	19 271	15 212	18 681	20 756	29 454	7 239	18 589	16 248	21 968	12 335	13 581	17 422	23 942	5 271	17 650	25 512
	1.6	1.1	1.9	-1.6	1.1	2.6 [8]	1.4 (93)	0.6	4.7	1	2.1	4.1 (92)	3	2.3	2.5	2.1 (93)	1.4	1.5	-0.3	0.5	3.6	0.8	2.1
	17.4	18.7	14.8	14.3	18.1	18.5	17.4 (93)	15.2	15.1	16.4	28.6	20.4 (93)	20.7	19.3	20	22 (93)	17.2	19.8	13.7	22.8	24.5	15	17.2
	7.8	6.2	7.2	5.90	8.10	7.5	7.8	3.9	6.3	7.4	11.5	..	9.4	8.6	9.3	..	7.5	5.7	5.7	7.5	4	7.3	7.7
	4.6	6.1	2.9	3.7	4.9	6.5	3.6	4.4	4.1	5.3	5.4	..	4.9	5.1	4.9	..	..	4.1	..	14.9 [10]	9.1	3.1	4
	0.4	-0.1	-2.8	-12.9	-1	0.8	2.7 (93)	-4	1	-2.3	1.4	6.5 (92)	7.7	0.4	5.8	-3.93	2.7	-1.2	-7.6	-0.4	5.1	-2.1	4.6
	22	16	17	16.6	19	21	15.5 (93)	16.9	19.5	18.8	31.2	60.2 (92)	15.1	24.4	20.7	21.9 (93)	24.2	18.8	13.7	29.3	22.5	13.5	16.2
	15	20.2	25.3	22.4	19.6	17.7	19.1 (93)	20.6	16	17.1	9.8	17.1 (92)	11.8 [9]	14.2	14.7	22.1 (93)	17.2	16.9	27.3	14.1	11.7	21.6	16.4
	55.3	49	61.1	58.9	51.5	45.6	51.2	34.9	..	53.2	26.9	..	..	55.4	..	..	..	43.7	67.3	36.7	..	42.7	35.8
	50.1	43	58.3	52.5	46.8	45.7	40.2	35.9	..	47.1	32.9	..	..	54.5	..	..	..	40.1	59	36	..	36.8	31.7
	0.41	0.46	1.03	0.76	0.66	0.44	..	..	0.15	0.42	0.27	0.34 (92)	..	0.88	0.22	1.23	0.36	0.32	1.33	0.49	..	0.34	0.19
	12 090	11 863	10 042	8 814	11 395	10 733	6 367	11 546	7 750	11 029	11 791	15 545	4 853	10 726	9 266	9 826	7 780	8 412	9 240	13 730	3 617	10 942	16 444
	387	469	311	386	413	480 [8]	169	464	228	478	282	470	85	356	440	378	260	307	418	441	29	361	568
	410	586	577	544	511	420 [8]	413	527	300	400	454	511	70	477	436	515	273	340	687	603	143	445	553
	451	639	536	501	407	556 [8]	197	319	276	421	613	267	148	485	443	423	187	400	468	406	175	434	814
	3.7	2.2	2.8 (92)	2.6 (92)	2.8	3.2 (92)	3.8 (92)	3	1.7 (92)	1.7 (91)	2.1 (92)	2.1 (92)	1	2.5 (90)	2	3.2 (92)	2.9	4.1	3	3	0.9	1.5 (92)	2.3 (92)
	8	6.8	5.4	4.4	6.5	5.8	8.5	4.8	5.9	7.3	4.5 (92)	8.5 (92)	18	6.3	7.3	5	8.7	7.6	4.8	5.6	52.6	6.6	8.5 (92)
	3.7	3.3	3.5	4.8	3.5	5.2	14.6	..	4.6	5.9	2.4	..	5.3	3.2	2.1	4	..	7.2	5.4	..	..	6.7	2.8
	2.8	2.8	2.1	3.3	2.5	3.3	16.2	6.3	2.7	5.2	2	3.1	16.1	2.8	2.5	2.7	9	5.6	5.7	3.9	73	4.6	3.6
	137 259 [7]	165 358	41 850	29 514	235 337	422 243	8 958	1 628	34 125	189 802	396 149	..	60 882	155 084	12 169	34 645	17 072	73 129	61 122	70 467	18 456	205 170	512 627
	60.2	30.4	28.5	30.4	17.7	23	11.5 (93)	26.3	65.7	18.6	8.6	..	16.4	46.4	23.8	30.9 (93)	19.6	15.2	31.1	27.4	14.1	20.1	7.7
	6.5	7.1	8.3	4.9	5.6	4.4	3.4	2.7	10.5	6.2	7.6	..	21.7	7.6	6.5	5	6.1	10.5	3.4	6.4	9.5	6.1	7.1
	126 006 [7]	148 297	35 932	23 091	220 508	376 566	21 111	1 464	25 812	167 690	274 916	..	79 346	139 800	11 859	27 345	25 967	92 182	51 730	68 126	22 976	227 026	663 256
	55.3	27.3	24.5	23.8	16.6	20.6	30.1 (93)	23.6	49.7	16.5	6	..	21.4	41.8	23.2	23.3 (93)	41.8	23.3 (93)	29.9	26.5	17.6	22.3	10
	5	5.4	6.1	-1.3	3.5	6.9	5.4	0.7	8.1	1.9	5.5	..	25.5	6.1	6.1	2.9	6.1	2.9	6.6	3.2	37.9	2.8	7
	19 505 [7]	8 416	6 203	7 304	17 986	52 994	9 924	201	4 189	22 102	86 214	..	4 301	23 655	2 540	13 033	10 627	28 475	15 929	23 790	4 911	28 094	43 350
	0.9	0.7	2.1	3.8	1	1.7	5.6	1.6	1.9	1.6	3.8	..	0.7	2	2.6	5.7	4.9	3.7	3.7	4.2	2.6	1.5	0.8

November 1995

7. Data refer to the Belgo-Luxembourg Economic Union.
8. Data refer to western Germany.
9. Refers to the public sector including public enterprises.
10. Including non-residential construction.

Sources: Population and Employment: OECD, *Labour Force Statistics*. GDP, GFCF, and General Government: OECD, *National Accounts*, Vol. I and *OECD Economic Outlook*, Historical Statistics. Indicators of living standards: Miscellaneous national publications.
Wages and Prices: OECD, *Main Economic Indicators*. Foreign trade: OECD, *Monthly Foreign Trade Statistics*, series A. Total official reserves: IMF, *International Financial Statistics*.

EMPLOYMENT OPPORTUNITIES

Economics Department, OECD

The Economics Department of the OECD offers challenging and rewarding opportunities to economists interested in applied policy analysis in an international environment. The Department's concerns extend across the entire field of economic policy analysis, both macro-economic and microeconomic. Its main task is to provide, for discussion by committees of senior officials from Member countries, documents and papers dealing with current policy concerns. Within this programme of work, three major responsibilities are:

- to prepare regular surveys of the economies of individual Member countries;
- to issue full twice-yearly reviews of the economic situation and prospects of the OECD countries in the context of world economic trends;
- to analyse specific policy issues in a medium-term context for the OECD as a whole, and to a lesser extent for the non-OECD countries.

The documents prepared for these purposes, together with much of the Department's other economic work, appear in published form in the *OECD Economic Outlook, OECD Economic Surveys, OECD Economic Studies* and the Department's *Working Papers* series.

The Department maintains a world econometric model, INTERLINK, which plays an important role in the preparation of the policy analyses and twice-yearly projections. The availability of extensive cross-country data bases and good computer resources facilitates comparative empirical analysis, much of which is incorporated into the model.

The Department is made up of about 80 professional economists from a variety of backgrounds and Member countries. Most projects are carried out by small teams and last from four to eighteen months. Within the Department, ideas and points of view are widely discussed; there is a lively professional interchange, and all professional staff have the opportunity to contribute actively to the programme of work.

Skills the Economics Department is looking for:

a) Solid competence in using the tools of both microeconomic and macroeconomic theory to answer policy questions. Experience indicates that this normally requires the equivalent of a Ph.D. in economics or substantial relevant professional experience to compensate for a lower degree.

b) Solid knowledge of economic statistics and quantitative methods; this includes how to identify data, estimate structural relationships, apply basic techniques of time series analysis, and test hypotheses. It is essential to be able to interpret results sensibly in an economic policy context.

c) A keen interest in and extensive knowledge of policy issues, economic developments and their political/social contexts.

d) Interest and experience in analysing questions posed by policy-makers and presenting the results to them effectively and judiciously. Thus, work experience in government agencies or policy research institutions is an advantage.

e) The ability to write clearly, effectively, and to the point. The OECD is a bilingual organisation with French and English as the official languages. Candidates must have excellent knowledge of one of these languages, and some knowledge of the other. Knowledge of other languages might also be an advantage for certain posts.

f) For some posts, expertise in a particular area may be important, but a successful candidate is expected to be able to work on a broader range of topics relevant to the work of the Department. Thus, except in rare cases, the Department does not recruit narrow specialists.

g) The Department works on a tight time schedule with strict deadlines. Moreover, much of the work in the Department is carried out in small groups. Thus, the ability to work with other economists from a variety of cultural and professional backgrounds, to supervise junior staff, and to produce work on time is important.

General information

The salary for recruits depends on educational and professional background. Positions carry a basic salary from FF 305 700 or FF 377 208 for Administrators (economists) and from FF 438 348 for Principal Administrators (senior economists). This may be supplemented by expatriation and/or family allowances, depending on nationality, residence and family situation. Initial appointments are for a fixed term of two to three years.

Vacancies are open to candidates from OECD Member countries. The Organisation seeks to maintain an appropriate balance between female and male staff and among nationals from Member countries.

For further information on employment opportunities in the Economics Department, contact:

Administrative Unit
Economics Department
OECD
2, rue André-Pascal
75775 PARIS CEDEX 16
FRANCE

E-Mail: compte.esadmin@oecd.org

Applications citing ''ECSUR'', together with a detailed *curriculum vitae* in English or French, should be sent to the Head of Personnel at the above address.

MAIN SALES OUTLETS OF OECD PUBLICATIONS
PRINCIPAUX POINTS DE VENTE DES PUBLICATIONS DE L'OCDE

AUSTRALIA – AUSTRALIE
D.A. Information Services
648 Whitehorse Road, P.O.B 163
Mitcham, Victoria 3132   Tel. (03) 9210.7777
Fax: (03) 9210.7788

AUSTRIA – AUTRICHE
Gerold & Co.
Graben 31
Wien I   Tel. (0222) 533.50.14
Fax: (0222) 512.47.31.29

BELGIUM – BELGIQUE
Jean De Lannoy
Avenue du Roi, Koningslaan 202
B-1060 Bruxelles Tel. (02) 538.51.69/538.08.41
Fax: (02) 538.08.41

CANADA
Renouf Publishing Company Ltd.
5369 Canotek Road
Unit 1
Ottawa, Ont. K1J 9J3   Tel. (613) 745.2665
Fax: (613) 745.7660

Stores:
71 1/2 Sparks Street
Ottawa, Ont. K1P 5R1   Tel. (613) 238.8985
Fax: (613) 238.6041

12 Adelaide Street West
Toronto, QN M5H 1L6   Tel. (416) 363.3171
Fax: (416) 363.5963

Les Éditions La Liberté Inc.
3020 Chemin Sainte-Foy
Sainte-Foy, PQ G1X 3V6 Tel. (418) 658.3763
Fax: (418) 658.3763

Federal Publications Inc.
165 University Avenue, Suite 701
Toronto, ON M5H 3B8   Tel. (416) 860.1611
Fax: (416) 860.1608

Les Publications Fédérales
1185 Université
Montréal, QC H3B 3A7   Tel. (514) 954.1633
Fax: (514) 954.1635

CHINA – CHINE
Book Dept., China Natinal Publiations
Import and Export Corporation (CNPIEC)
16 Gongti E. Road, Chaoyang District
Beijing 100020   Tel. (10) 6506-6688 Ext. 8402
(10) 6506-3101

CHINESE TAIPEI – TAIPEI CHINOIS
Good Faith Worldwide Int'l. Co. Ltd.
9th Floor, No. 118, Sec. 2
Chung Hsiao E. Road
Taipei   Tel. (02) 391.7396/391.7397
Fax: (02) 394.9176

CZECH REPUBLIC –
RÉPUBLIQUE TCHÈQUE
National Information Centre
NIS – prodejna
Konviktská 5
Praha 1 – 113 57   Tel. (02) 24.23.09.07
Fax: (02) 24.22.94.33
E-mail: nkposp@dec.niz.cz
Internet: http://www.nis.cz

DENMARK – DANEMARK
Munksgaard Book and Subscription Service
35, Nørre Søgade, P.O. Box 2148
DK-1016 København K   Tel. (33) 12.85.70
Fax: (33) 12.93.87

J. H. Schultz Information A/S,
Herstedvang 12,
DK – 2620 Albertslung   Tel. 43 63 23 00
Fax: 43 63 19 69
Internet: s-info@inet.uni-c.dk

EGYPT – ÉGYPTE
The Middle East Observer
41 Sherif Street
Cairo   Tel. (2) 392.6919
Fax: (2) 360.6804

FINLAND – FINLANDE
Akateeminen Kirjakauppa
Keskuskatu 1, P.O. Box 128
00100 Helsinki

Subscription Services/Agence d'abonnements :
P.O. Box 23
00100 Helsinki   Tel. (358) 9.121.4403
Fax: (358) 9.121.4450

***FRANCE**
OECD/OCDE
Mail Orders/Commandes par correspondance :
2, rue André-Pascal
75775 Paris Cedex 16 Tel. 33 (0)1.45.24.82.00
Fax: 33 (0)1.49.10.42.76
Telex: 640048 OCDE
Internet: Compte.PUBSINQ@oecd.org

Orders via Minitel, France only/
Commandes par Minitel, France
exclusivement : 36 15 OCDE

OECD Bookshop/Librairie de l'OCDE :
33, rue Octave-Feuillet
75016 Paris   Tel. 33 (0)1.45.24.81.81
33 (0)1.45.24.81.67

Dawson
B.P. 40
91121 Palaiseau Cedex   Tel. 01.89.10.47.00
Fax: 01.64.54.83.26

Documentation Française
29, quai Voltaire
75007 Paris   Tel. 01.40.15.70.00

Economica
49, rue Héricart
75015 Paris   Tel. 01.45.78.12.92
Fax: 01.45.75.05.67

Gibert Jeune (Droit-Économie)
6, place Saint-Michel
75006 Paris   Tel. 01.43.25.91.19

Librairie du Commerce International
10, avenue d'Iéna
75016 Paris   Tel. 01.40.73.34.60

Librairie Dunod
Université Paris-Dauphine
Place du Maréchal-de-Lattre-de-Tassigny
75016 Paris   Tel. 01.44.05.40.13

Librairie Lavoisier
11, rue Lavoisier
75008 Paris   Tel. 01.42.65.39.95

Librairie des Sciences Politiques
30, rue Saint-Guillaume
75007 Paris   Tel. 01.45.48.36.02

P.U.F.
49, boulevard Saint-Michel
75005 Paris   Tel. 01.43.25.83.40

Librairie de l'Université
12a, rue Nazareth
13100 Aix-en-Provence   Tel. 04.42.26.18.08

Documentation Française
165, rue Garibaldi
69003 Lyon   Tel. 04.78.63.32.23

Librairie Decitre
29, place Bellecour
69002 Lyon   Tel. 04.72.40.54.54

Librairie Sauramps
Le Triangle
34967 Montpellier Cedex 2 Tel. 04.67.58.85.15
Fax: 04.67.58.27.36

A la Sorbonne Actual
23, rue de l'Hôtel-des-Postes
06000 Nice   Tel. 04.93.13.77.75
Fax: 04.93.80.75.69

GERMANY – ALLEMAGNE
OECD Bonn Centre
August-Bebel-Allee 6
D-53175 Bonn   Tel. (0228) 959.120
Fax: (0228) 959.12.17

GREECE – GRÈCE
Librairie Kauffmann
Stadiou 28
10564 Athens   Tel. (01) 32.55.321
Fax: (01) 32.30.320

HONG-KONG
Swindon Book Co. Ltd.
Astoria Bldg. 3F
34 Ashley Road, Tsimshatsui
Kowloon, Hong Kong   Tel. 2376.2062
Fax: 2376.0685

HUNGARY – HONGRIE
Euro Info Service
Margitsziget, Európa Ház
1138 Budapest   Tel. (1) 111.60.61
Fax: (1) 302.50.35
E-mail: euroinfo@mail.matav.hu
Internet: http://www.euroinfo.hu//index.html

ICELAND – ISLANDE
Mál og Menning
Laugavegi 18, Pósthólf 392
121 Reykjavik   Tel. (1) 552.4240
Fax: (1) 562.3523

INDIA – INDE
Oxford Book and Stationery Co.
Scindia House
New Delhi 110001   Tel. (11) 331.5896/5308
Fax: (11) 332.2639
E-mail: oxford.publ@axcess.net.in

17 Park Street
Calcutta 700016   Tel. 240832

INDONESIA – INDONÉSIE
Pdii-Lipi
P.O. Box 4298
Jakarta 12042   Tel. (21) 573.34.67
Fax: (21) 573.34.67

IRELAND – IRLANDE
Government Supplies Agency
Publications Section
4/5 Harcourt Road
Dublin 2   Tel. 661.31.11
Fax: 475.27.60

ISRAEL – ISRAËL
Praedicta
5 Shatner Street
P.O. Box 34030
Jerusalem 91430   Tel. (2) 652.84.90/1/2
Fax: (2) 652.84.93

R.O.Y. International
P.O. Box 13056
Tel Aviv 61130   Tel. (3) 546 1423
Fax: (3) 546 1442
E-mail: royil@netvision.net.il

Palestinian Authority/Middle East:
INDEX Information Services
P.O.B. 19502
Jerusalem   Tel. (2) 627.16.34
Fax: (2) 627.12.19

ITALY – ITALIE
Libreria Commissionaria Sansoni
Via Duca di Calabria, 1/1
50125 Firenze   Tel. (055) 64.54.15
Fax: (055) 64.12.57
E-mail: licosa@ftbcc.it

Via Bartolini 29
20155 Milano   Tel. (02) 36.50.83

Editrice e Libreria Herder
Piazza Montecitorio 120
00186 Roma   Tel. 679.46.28
Fax: 678.47.51